Cram101 Textbook Outlines to accompany:

The Struggle for Democracy

Edward S. Greenberg, Benjamin I. Page, Melvin E. Page, 8th Edition

A Cram101 Inc. publication (c) 2011.

PRACTICE EXAMS.

Get all of the self-teaching practice exams for each chapter of this textbook at
www.Cram101.com and ace the tests. Here is an example:

Chapter 1

The Struggle for Democracy
Edward S. Greenberg, Benjamin I. Page, Melvin E. Page, 8th Edition,
All Material Written and Prepared by Cram101

1 A _____ (some of which are titled instead as a "Commission" larger deliberative assembly--which when
organized so that action on _____ requires a vote by all its entitled members, is called the _____ of the
Whole". _____ s often serve several different functions:

• Governance: in organizations considered too large for all the members to participate in decisions affecting the
organization as a whole, a _____ (such as a Board of Directors or "Executive _____) is given the
power to make decisions, spend money the Board of directors can frequently enter into binding contracts and
make decisions which once taken or made, can"t be taken back or undone under the law.

• Coordination: individuals from different parts of an organization (for example, all senior vice presidents) might
meet regularly to discuss developments in their areas, review projects that cut across organizational
boundaries, talk about future options, etc. Where there is a large _____ it is common to have smaller
_____ s with more specialized functions - for example, Boards of Directors of large corporations typically
have an (ongoing) audit _____ finance _____ compensation _____ etc. Large academic
conferences are usually organized by a co-ordinating _____ drawn from the relevant professional body.

◯ Committee	◯ Cabinet collective responsibility
◯ Cabotage	◯ CAEI

2 A _____ is the legal or moral entitlement to do or refrain from doing something thing or recognition in civil society.
_____ s serve as rules of interaction between people, and, as such, they place constraints and obligations upon
the actions of individuals or groups (for example, if one has a _____ to life, this means that others do not have

With Cram101.com online, you also have access to extensive reference material.

You will nail those essays and papers. Here is an example from a Cram101 Biology text:

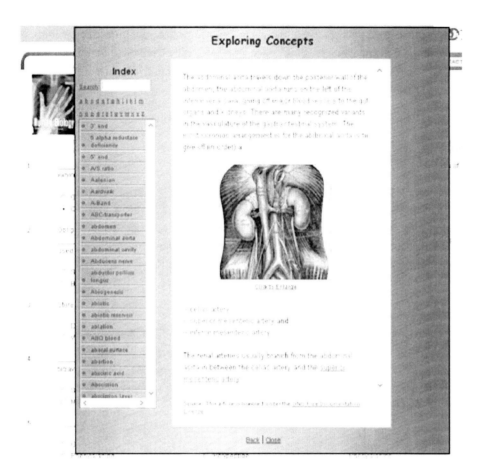

Visit **www.Cram101.com**, click Sign Up at the top of the screen, and enter DK73DW6724 in the promo code box on the registration screen. Access to www.Cram101.com is normally $9.95 per month, but because you have purchased this book, your access fee is only $4.95 per month, cancel at any time. Sign up and stop highlighting textbooks forever.

Learning System

Cram101 Textbook Outlines is a learning system. The notes in this book are the highlights of your textbook, you will never have to highlight a book again.

How to use this book. Take this book to class, it is your notebook for the lecture. The notes and highlights on the left hand side of the pages follow the outline and order of the textbook. All you have to do is follow along while your instructor presents the lecture. Circle the items emphasized in class and add other important information on the right side. With Cram101 Textbook Outlines you'll spend less time writing and more time listening. Learning becomes more efficient.

Cram101.com Online

Increase your studying efficiency by using Cram101.com's practice tests and online reference material. It is the perfect complement to Cram101 Textbook Outlines. Use self-teaching matching tests or simulate in-class testing with comprehensive multiple choice tests, or simply use Cram's true and false tests for quick review. Cram101.com even allows you to enter your in-class notes for an integrated studying format combining the textbook notes with your class notes.

Visit **www.Cram101.com**, click Sign Up at the top of the screen, and enter **DK73DW6724** in the promo code box on the registration screen. Access to www.Cram101.com is normally $9.95 per month, but because you have purchased this book, your access fee is only $4.95 per month. Sign up and stop highlighting textbooks forever.

The Struggle for Democracy
Edward S. Greenberg, Benjamin I. Page, Melvin E. Page, 8th

CONTENTS

Committee	A Committee (some of which are titled instead as a "Commission" larger deliberative assembly--which when organized so that action on Committee requires a vote by all its entitled members, is called the Committee of the Whole". Committee s often serve several different functions:

- Governance: in organizations considered too large for all the members to participate in decisions affecting the organization as a whole, a Committee (such as a Board of Directors or "Executive Committee) is given the power to make decisions, spend money the Board of directors can frequently enter into binding contracts and make decisions which once taken or made, can"t be taken back or undone under the law.

- Coordination: individuals from different parts of an organization (for example, all senior vice presidents) might meet regularly to discuss developments in their areas, review projects that cut across organizational boundaries, talk about future options, etc. Where there is a large Committee it is common to have smaller Committee s with more specialized functions - for example, Boards of Directors of large corporations typically have an (ongoing) audit Committee finance Committee compensation Committee etc. Large academic conferences are usually organized by a co-ordinating Committee drawn from the relevant professional body.

Right	A right is the legal or moral entitlement to do or refrain from doing something thing or recognition in civil society. Rights serve as rules of interaction between people, and, as such, they place constraints and obligations upon the actions of individuals or groups (for example, if one has a right to life, this means that others do not have the liberty to kill him.)
	Most modern conceptions of rights are universalist and egalitarian -- in other words, equal rights are granted to all people.
Ancient Greece	The term ancient Greece refers to the period of Greek history lasting from the Greek Dark Ages ca. 1100 BC and the Dorian invasion, to 146 BC and the Roman conquest of Greece after the Battle of Corinth. It is generally considered to be the seminal culture which provided the foundation of Western civilization and shaped cultures throughout Southwest Asia and North Africa.
Iran	Iran , officially the Islamic Republic of Iran and formerly known internationally as Persia until 1935, is a country in Central Eurasia, located on the northeastern shore of the Persian Gulf, northwestern shore of the Gulf of Oman, and the southern shore of the Caspian Sea. Both "Persia" and "Iran" are used interchangeably in cultural context; however, Iran is the name used officially in political context. The name Iran is a cognate of Aryan, and means "Land of the Aryans".

Politics	Politics are an integral part of the Unification Church"s concerns and activities, although the church itself largely remains aloof from Politics The degree of involvement of the movement, as well as some of its specific stances, have also been part of the reason for the movement"s controversial status over the years. The belief in the establishment of a literal Kingdom of Heaven on earth and Rev. Moon"s teaching that religion alone is not enough to bring this provides a motivation for political involvement.
Republic	The Republic is a left-of-centre political party in the Faroe Islands committed to Faroese Independence. It was founded in 1948 as a reaction to independence not being proclaimed after a public vote on the matter showed a marginal majority for it in 1946. In 1998 Høgni Hoydal succeeded Heini O. Heinesen as party leader.
Axis of evil	"Axis of evil" is a term coined by United States President George W. Bush in his State of the Union Address on January 29, 2002 in order to describe governments that he accused of helping terrorism and seeking weapons of mass destruction. President Bush named Iran, Iraq and North Korea in his speech. President Bush"s presidency was marked by this notion as a justification for the War on Terror.
Power	Power in international relations is defined in several different ways. Political scientists, historians, and practitioners of international relations (diplomats) have used the following concepts of political Power: • Power as a goal of states or leaders; • Power as a measure of influence or control over outcomes, events, actors and issues; • Power as reflecting victory in conflict and the attainment of security; and, • Power as control over resources and capabilities. Modern discourse generally speaks in terms of state Power, indicating both economic and military Power. Those states that have significant amounts of Power within the international system are referred to as middle powers, regional powers, great powers, superpowers, or hyperpowers, although there is no commonly accepted standard for what defines a powerful state. Entities other than states can also acquire and wield Power in international relations.
Ancient Rome	Ancient Rome was a civilization that grew out of a small agricultural community founded on the Italian Peninsula as early as the 10th century BC. Located along the Mediterranean Sea, it became one of the largest empires in the ancient world. In its centuries of existence, Roman civilization shifted from a monarchy to an oligarchic republic to an increasingly autocratic empire. It came to dominate South-Western Europe, South-Eastern Europe/Balkans and the Mediterranean region through conquest and assimilation.

Direct democracy	Direct democracy, classically termed pure democracy, comprises a form of democracy and theory of civics wherein sovereignty is lodged in the assembly of all citizens who choose to participate. Depending on the particular system, this assembly might pass executive motions, make laws, elect and dismiss officials and conduct trials. Direct democracy stands in contrast to representative democracy, where sovereignty is exercised by a subset of the people, usually on the basis of election.
India	India, officially the Republic of India , is a country in South Asia. It is the seventh-largest country by geographical area, the second-most populous country, and the most populous democracy in the world. Bounded by the Indian Ocean on the south, the Arabian Sea on the west, and the Bay of Bengal on the east, India has a coastline of 7,517 kilometres .
Iraq	Iraq , officially the Republic of Iraq JumhÅ«rÄ«yat Al-Ê¿IrÄ q, Kurdish: ÙƒÛ†Ù…Ø§Ø±Û’ Ø¹ÛŽØ±Ø§Ù‚ê, Komara Iraqê), is a country in Western Asia spanning most of the northwestern end of the Zagros mountain range, the eastern part of the Syrian Desert and the northern part of the Arabian Desert. Iraq shares borders with Jordan to the west, Syria to the northwest, Turkey to the north, Iran to the east, and Kuwait and Saudi Arabia to the south. Iraq has a narrow section of coastline measuring 58 km between Umm Qasr and Al Faw on the Persian Gulf.
Israel	Israel officially the State of Israel , Medinat Yisra"el; Arabic: Ø¯ ÙŽÙˆÙÙ„ÙŽØ©Ù Ø¥Ù Ø³Ù'Ø±ÙŽØ§Ø¦Ù ÙŠÙ„ÙŽâ€Ž, Dawlat IsrÄ "Ä«l), is a country in Western Asia located on the eastern shore of the Mediterranean Sea. It borders Lebanon in the north, Syria in the northeast, Jordan in the east, and Egypt on the southwest, and contains geographically diverse features within its relatively small area. Also adjacent are the West Bank to the east and Gaza Strip to the southwest.
Kibbutz	A Kibbutz is a collective community in Israel that was traditionally based on agriculture. Today, farming has been partly supplanted by other economic branches, including industrial plants and high-tech enterprises. Kibbutz im began as utopian communities, a combination of socialism and Zionism.
Public Service of Canada	The Public Service of Canada is the staff of the federal government of Canada. Its function is to support the Canadian monarch, and to handle the hiring of employees for the federal government ministries. It is represented by the Governor General, and the appointed [[list of Canadian ministries|ministry].
Popular sovereignty	Popular sovereignty or the sovereignty of the people is the belief that the legitimacy of the state is created by the will or consent of its people, who are the source of all political power. It is closely associated with the social contract philosophers, among whom are Thomas Hobbes, John Locke, and Jean-Jacques Rousseau. Popular sovereignty expresses a concept and does not necessarily reflect or describe a political reality.
Representative Democracy	Representative democracy is a form of government founded on the principle of elected individuals representing the people, as opposed to either autocracy or direct democracy.

The representatives form more than what it used to be when it was an independent ruling body (for an election period) charged with the responsibility of acting in the people"s interest, but not as their proxy representatives; that is, not necessarily always according to their wishes, but with enough authority to exercise swift and resolute initiative in the face of changing circumstances. It is often contrasted with direct democracy, where representatives are absent or are limited in power as proxy representatives.

Constitution

A Constitution is set of rules for government -- often codified as a written document -- that establishes principles of an autonomous political entity. In the case of countries, this term refers specifically to a national Constitution defining the fundamental political principles, and establishing the structure, procedures, powers and duties, of a government. By limiting the government"s own reach, most Constitution s guarantee certain rights to the people.

Presidential election

A presidential election was held in Chile on 4 September 1970. A narrow plurality (36.6 percent of the total vote) was secured by Salvador Allende, the candidate of the Popular Unity coalition of leftist parties. Because he did not obtain an absolute majority, his election required a further vote by the National Congress of Chile which resulted in Allende assuming the presidency in accordance with the Chilean Constitution of 1925.

Natural justice

Natural justice or procedural fairness is a legal philosophy used in some jurisdictions in the determination of just processes in legal proceedings. The concept is very closely related to the principle of natural law which has been applied as a philosophical and practical principle in the law in several common law jurisdictions, particularly the UK and Australia.

In common law legal systems the term Natural justice refers to two specific legal principles.

Citizenship

Citizenship is an act of being a citizen of one community.

Citizenship status, under social contract theory, carries with it both rights and responsibilities. "Active Citizenship" is the philosophy that citizens should work towards the betterment of their community through economic participation, public service, volunteer work, and other such efforts to improve life for all citizens.

Anti-Americanism

Dictionaries tend to define Anti-Americanism, often anti-American sentiment, as a widespread opposition or hostility to the people, government or policies of the United States. In practice, a broad range of attitudes and actions critical of or opposed to the United States have been labeled Anti-Americanism. Thus, the nature and applicability of the term is often disputed.

Bill of Rights

A Bill of rights is a list or summary of rights that are considered important and essential by a nation. The purpose of these bills is to protect those rights against infringement by the government. The term "Bill of rights" originates from Britain, where it referred to a bill that was passed by Parliament in 1689.

Civil liberties	Civil liberties are freedoms that protect an individual from the government of the nation in which they reside. Civil liberties set limits for government so that it cannot abuse its power and interfere unduly with the lives of its citizens.
	Common Civil liberties include the rights of people, freedom of religion, and freedom of speech, and additionally, the right to due process, to a fair trial, to own property, and to privacy.
First Amendment	The First Amendment to the United States Constitution is the part of the United States Bill of Rights that expressly prohibits the United States Congress from making laws "respecting an establishment of religion" or that prohibit the free exercise of religion, infringe the freedom of speech, infringe the freedom of the press, limit the right to peaceably assemble, or limit the right to petition the government for a redress of grievances.
	Although the First Amendment only explicitly applies to the Congress, the Supreme Court has interpreted it as applying to the executive and judicial branches. Additionally, in the 20th century, the Supreme Court held that the Due Process Clause of the Fourteenth Amendment applies the limitations of the First Amendment to each state, including any local government within a state.
Contract	Agreement is said to be reached when an offer capable of immediate acceptance is met with a "mirror image" acceptance (ie, an unqualified acceptance.) The parties must have the necessary capacity to Contract and the Contract must not be either trifling, indeterminate, impossible or illegal. Contract law is based on the principle expressed in the Latin phrase pacta sunt servanda .
News media	The News media refers to the section of the mass media that focuses on presenting current news to the public. These include print media (newspapers, magazines); broadcast media (radio stations, television stations, television networks), and increasingly Internet-based media (World Wide Web pages, weblogs.)
	The term news trade refers to the concept of the News media as a business separate from, but integrally connected to, the profession of journalism.
Joseph	Joseph or Josephus Scottus (died between 791 and 804), called the Deacon, was an Irish scholar, diplomat, poet, and ecclesiastic, a minor figure in the Carolingian Renaissance. He has been cited as an early example of "the scholar in public life".
	His early life is obscure, but he studied first under Colcu, probably at Clonmacnoise, and then under Alcuin at York, probably in the 770s.

Judicial activism	Judicial activism is a critical term used to describe judicial rulings that are viewed as imposing a personal biased interpretation by a given court of what a law means as opposed to what a neutral, unbiased observer would naturally interpret a law to be. The term has most often been used to describe left-wing judges, however; the Supreme Court"s activity since the confirmation of justices Alito and Roberts under George W. Bush, and the ensuing perception that the conservative court was expanding the rights of corporations at the cost of the rights of citizens, has since led to conservative judges being labeled activists. The term "Judicial activism" is frequently used in political debate without definition, which has created some confusion over its precise meaning or meanings.
Civil rights movement	The Civil rights movement was a worldwide political movement for equality before the law occurring between approximately 1950 and 1980. It was accompanied by much civil unrest and popular rebellion. The process was long and tenuous in many countries, and most of these movements did not achieve or fully achieve their objectives.
Ethnicity	Ethnicity plays a prominent role in pornography. Distinct genres of pornography focus on performers of specific ethnic groups, or on the depiction of interracial sexual activity. Ethnic pornography typically employs ethnic and racial stereotypes in its depiction of performers.
Civil service	The term Civil service has two distinct meanings: • Branch of governmental service in which individuals are hired on the basis of merit which is proven by the use of competitive examinations. • Body of employees in any government agency, except the military. A civil servant or public servant is a civilian public sector employee working for a government department or agency. The term explicitly excludes the armed services, although civilian officials will work at "Defence Ministry" headquarters. The term always includes the (sovereign) state"s employees; whether regional, or sub-state, or even municipal employees are called "civil servants" varies from country to country. In the United Kingdom, for instance, only Crown employees are civil servants, county or city employees are not.
Minority	Minority, and the related concept of "becoming-minor," is a philosophical concept developed by Gilles Deleuze and Félix Guattari in their books Kafka: Towards a Minor Literature (1975), A Thousand Plateaus (1980), and elsewhere. In these texts, they criticize the concept of "majority" as being based on a form of domination that works by naturalizing a purely numerical conception. They argue that the concept of a "dominant Minority" is an oxymoron, because the term "majority" always refers to those who are in a position of dominance.
Vietnam	Vietnam " href="/wiki/Battle_of_B%E1%BA%A1ch_%C4%90%E1%BA%B1ng_River_(938)">battle of Bá°¡ch Ä á°±ng River. Successive dynasties flourished along with geographic and political expansion deeper into Southeast Asia, until it was colonized by the French in the mid-19th century. Efforts to resist the French eventually led to their expulsion from the country in the mid-20th century, leaving a nation divided politically into two countries.

Vietnam War

The Vietnam War was a military conflict that occurred in Vietnam, Laos and Cambodia from 1959 to 30 April 1975. The war was fought between the communist North Vietnam, supported by its communist allies, and the government of South Vietnam, supported by the United States and other member nations of the Southeast Asia Treaty Organization (SEATO.)

The following outline is provided as an overview of and topical guide to the Vietnam War:

Listed by starting date:

- Operation 34A - (1964)
- Operation Starlite - August 18-24 1965
- Operation Hump- November 5 1965
- Operation Crimp - January 7, 1966
- Operation Birmingham - April 1966
- Operation Hastings - Late May 1966
- Operation Prairie - August 1966
- Operation Deckhouse Five - January 6, 1967
- Operation Cedar Falls - January 8, 1967
- Operation Junction City - February 21, 1967
- Operation Francis Marion - April 6 - April 30, 1967
- Operation Union - April 21-May 16, 1967
- Operations Malheur I and Malheur II - 11 May - July 1, 1967
- Operation Baker - May 11, 1967
- Operation Scotland - See Battle of Khe Sanh
- Operation Pegasus - August 8, 1968
- Operation Dewey Canyon - January 22, 1969
- Operation Twinkletoes - 1969
- Operation Apache Snow - May 10 - May 20, 1969
- Operation Chicago Peak - April 1970
- Operation Texas Star - April - September, 1970
- Operation Ivory Coast - November 21, 1970
- Operation Jefferson Glenn - 1970-1971
- Operation Lam Son 719 - February 8, 1971
- Ho Chi Minh Campaign January 24 - April 30, 1975
- Operation Frequent Wind - April, 1975

- Battle of Ap Bac - January 2, 1963
- Battle of Kien Long - April 11 - April 15, 1964
- Battle of Thanh Hóa - July 31, 1964
- Battle of Binh Gia - December 28, 1964 - January 1, 1965
- Battle of Dong Xoai - June 10, 1965
- Battle near Minh Thanh - October 25 - October 27, 1965
- Battle of Ia Drang - November 14 - November 16, 1965
- Battle of Cu Nghi - January 28 - January 31, 1966
- Battle of Kim Son Valley - February 16 - February 28, 1966
- Battle of A Shau - March 9 - March 10, 1966
- Battle of Xa Cam My - April 11 - April 12, 1966
- First Battle of Dong Ha - Late May - June, 1966
- Battle on Minh Thanh Road - July 9, 1966
- Battle of Ä á»©c CÆ¡ - August 9, 1966
- Battle of Long Tá°§n - August 18- August 19, 1966
- Viet Cong attack on Tan Son Nhut airbase - December 4, 1966
- Battle of LZ Bird - December 27, 1966

- Battle of Tra Binh Dong - February 14 - February 15, 1967
- Battle of Hills 881 and 861 - April 24-May 9, 1967
- Nine Days in May - May 18 - May 28, 1967
- Battle of Vinh Huy - May 30 - June 2, 1967
- Battle of Con Thien - July 2 - July 3, 1967
- Battle of Dong Son - September 4, 1967
- Battle of Ong Thang - October 17, 1967
- First Battle of Loc Ninh - October 29 - November, 1967
- Battle of Dak To - November 3-November 22, 1967
- Battle in the Mekong Delta - December 4, 1967
- Battle of Tam Quan - December 6 - December 20, 1967
- Battle of Thom Tham Khe - December 27 - December 28, 1967
- Phoenix Program - 1967 - 1972
- Battle of Khe Sanh - January 21 - April 8, 1968
- Tet Offensive - January 30 - February 25, 1968
- Battle of Bien Hoa - January 31 - July 1, 1968
- Battle of Kham Duc - May 10 - May 12, 1968
- First Battle of Saigon - January 31, - February 3, 1968
- Battle of Hue - January 31, - February 25, 1968
- Tet 1969 - February 1969
- Battle of Hamburger Hill - May 10 - May 20, 1969
- Firebase Ripcord - March 12 - July 23, 1970
- Cambodian Incursion - April 29 - July 22, 1970
- Battle of Snoul - January 5 - May 30, 1971
- Easter Offensive - March 30 - October 22, 1972
- First Battle of Quang Tri - March 30 - May 1, 1972
- Battle of Loc Ninh - April 4 - April 7, 1972
- Battle of An Loc - April 20 - July 20, 1972
- Second Battle of Quang Tri - June 28 - September 16, 1972
- Battle of Phuoc Long - December 13, 1974 - January 6, 1975
- Battle of Buon Me Thuot - March 10 - March 12, 1975
- Battle of Xuan Loc - April 9 - April 20, 1975

- Operation Farm Gate
- Operation Chopper (1962)
- Operation Ranch Hand (1962-1971)
- Operation Pierce Arrow (1964)
- Operation Barrell Roll (1964-1972)
- Operation Pony Express (1965-1970)
- Operation Flaming Dart (1965)
- Operation Rolling Thunder (1965-1968)
- Operation Steel Tiger (1965-1968)
- Operation Arc Light (1965-1973)
- Operation Tiger Hound (1965-1968)
- Operation Shed Light (1966-1972)
- Operation Carolina Moon (1966)
- Operation Wahiawa (1966)
- Operation Bolo (1967)
- Operation Popeye (1967-1972
- Operation Niagara (1968)
- Operation Igloo White (1968-1973

- Operation Giant Lance (1969)
- Operation Commando Hunt (1968-1972)
- Operation Menu (1969-1970)
- Operation Patio (1970)
- Operation Freedom Deal (1970-1973)
- Operation Linebacker (1972)
- Operation Enhance Plus (1972)
- Operation Linebacker II (1972)
- Operation Homecoming (1973)
- Operation Baby Lift (1975)
- Operation Eagle Pull (1975)
- Operation Frequent Wind (1975)

- National Order of Vietnam
- Vietnam Military Merit Medal
- Vietnam Distinguished Service Order
- Vietnam Meritorious Service Medal
- Vietnam Special Service Medal
- Vietnam Gallantry Cross
- Vietnam Air Gallantry Cross
- Vietnam Navy Gallantry Cross
- Vietnam Armed Forces Honor Medal
- Vietnam Civil Actions Medal
- Vietnam Staff Service Medal
- Vietnam Technical Service Medal
- Vietnam Wound Medal
- Vietnam Campaign Medal
- Presidential Unit Citation (Vietnam)
- Vietnam Gallantry Cross Unit Citation
- Vietnam Civil Actions Unit Citation

- Golden Star Medal
- Ho Chi Minh Order
- Defeat American Aggression Badge
- Vietnam Liberation Order
- Resolution for Victory Order

- Medal of Honor rare
- Distinguished Service Cross rare
- Navy Cross uncommon
- Air Force Cross uncommon
- Silver Star uncommon
- Purple Heart frequent
- Bronze Star frequent
- Presidential Unit Citation rare
- Vietnam Service Medal very common
- National Defense Service Medal very common
- Commendation Medal common

- "Fatigue Press" at Fort Hood,
- "Last Harass" at Fort Gordon, Georgia
- "Pawn"s Pawn" at Fort Leonard Wood, Missouri

- "Ultimate Weapon" at Fort Dix, New Jersey
- "Attitude Check" at Camp Pendleton, California
- "Green Machine" at Fort Greely, Alaska
- "Napalm" at Fort Campbell, Tennessee
- "Arctic Arsenal" at Fort Greely, Alaska
- "Black Voice" at Fort McClellan, Alabama
- "Fragging Action" at Fort Dix
- "Fort Polk Puke" at Fort Polk, Louisiana
- "Custer"s Last Stand" at Fort Riley, Kansas
- "Whack!" from the Women"s Army Corps School
- "Where Are We?" at Fort Huachuca, Arizona
- "Voice of the Lumpen" (affiliated with the Black Panther Party) in Frankfurt
- "Can You Bear McNair?" at McNair Barracks, Berlin
- "Seasick" at Subic Bay
- "The Man Can"t Win If You Grin" in Okinawa
- "Korea Free Press"
- "Semper Fi" in Japan
- "Stars and Bars" in England
- "Separated From Life" in England
- "Duck Power" in San Diego
- "Harass the Brass" at Canute Air Force Base, Illinois
- "All Hands Abandon Ship", Newport, Rhode Island
- "Now Hear This", Long Beach
- "Potemkin" on the USS Forestall
- "Star Spangled Bummer" at Wright-Patterson Air Force Base in Ohio
- "Fat Albert"s Death Ship" in Charlestown
- "Pig Boat Blues", USS Agerholm
- "Special Weapons", Kirtland AFB, New Mexico
- "I Will Fear No Evil", Kirtland AFB, New Mexico
- "Blows Against the Empire", Kirtland AFB, New Mexico

source: "The American War" - see references below

- Bao Dai
- Duong Van Minh
- Madame Ngo Dinh Nhu
- Ngo Dinh Diem
- Ngo Dinh Nhu
- Nguyen Cao Ky
- Nguyen Khanh
- Nguyen Van Thieu

- Creighton W. Abrams
- Dean Acheson
- Spiro Agnew
- Ellsworth Bunker
- McGeorge Bundy
- William Bundy
- William Calley
- Clark Clifford
- William Colby
- A. Peter Dewey
- John Foster Dulles
- Dwight D. Eisenhower
- Daniel Ellsberg
- J. William Fulbright
- Barry Goldwater
- David Hackworth
- Alexander Haig
- Paul D. Harkins
- Seymour Hersh
- Hubert Humphrey
- Lyndon Johnson
- John F. Kennedy
- John Kerry
- Henry Kissinger
- Melvin Laird
- Edward Lansdale
- Henry Cabot Lodge, Jr.
- Mike Mansfield
- Graham Martin
- Robert McNamara
- George McGovern
- Richard Nixon
- Pete Peterson
- Charika Pugh
- Dean Rusk

- Maxwell D. Taylor
- Hugh C. Thompson, Jr
- John Paul Vann
- Gary Varsel
- William Westmoreland

- Ho Chi Minh
- Le Duan
- Tran Van Tra
- Le Duc Tho
- Pham Van Dong
- General Giap
- Poewll Ward

- Lon Nol
- Pol Pot
- Norodom Sihanouk
- Sirik Matak
- Sosthene Fernandez

- David H. Hackworth. 1989 About Face
- A.J. Langguth. 2000. Our Vietnam: the War 1954-1975.
- Mann, Robert. 2002. Grand Delusion, A: America"s Descent Into Vietnam.
- Windrow, Martin. 2005. The Last Valley: Dien Bien Phu and the French Defeat in Vietnam.
- Bernard Fall. 1967. Hell in a Very Small Place: the Siege of Dien Bien Phu.
- Harvey Pekar. 2003. American Splendor: Unsung Hero
- Prados, John. 2000. The Blood Road: The Ho Chi Minh Trail and the Vietnam War.
- Prados, John. 1999. Valley of Decision: The Siege of Khe Sanh.
- Shultz, Robert H. Jr. 2000. The Secret War Against Hanoi: The Untold Story of Spies, Saboteurs, and Covert Warriors in North Vietnam.
- Plaster, John L. 1998. SOG: The Secret Wars of America"s Commandos in Vietnam.
- Murphy, Edward F. 1995. Dak To: America"s Sky Soldiers in South Vietnam"s Central Highlands.
- Nolan, Keith W. 1996. The Battle for Saigon: Tet 1968.
- Nolan, Keith W. 1996. Sappers in the Wire: The Life and Death of Firebase Mary Ann.
- Nolan, Keith W. 1992. Operation Buffalo: USMC Fight for the DMZ.
- Nolan, Keith W. 2003. Ripcord : Screaming Eagles Under Siege, Vietnam 1970.
- Robert S. McNamara. 1996. In Retrospect: The Tragedy and Lessons of Vietnam.
- Larry Berman. 2002. No Peace, No Honor: Nixon, Kissinger, and Betrayal in Vietnam.
- Bergerud, Eric M. 1994. Red Thunder, Tropic Lightning: The World of a Combat Division in Vietnam.
- Bernard Edelman. 2002. Dear America: Letters Home from Vietnam.
- Darrel D. Whitcomb. 1999. The Rescue of Bat 21.
- Oberdorfer, Don. 1971. Tet: the Story of a Battle and its Historic Aftermath.
- LTG Harold G. Moore and Joseph L. Galloway. 1992. We Were Soldiers Once ... And Young.
- Duiker, William J. 2002. Ho Chi Minh: A Life.
- John Laurence. 2002. The Cat from Hue: A Vietnam War Story.
- Emerson, Gloria. 1976. Winners and Losers: Battles, Retreats, Gains, Losses and Ruins from a Long War.
- Philip Caputo. 1977. A Rumor of War.

- Al Santoli. 1981. Everything We Had: an Oral History of the Vietnam War by 33 American Soldiers Who Fought It.
- Robert C. Mason. 1983. Chickenhawk.
- Michael Herr. 1977. Dispatches.
- Joseph T. Ward. 1991. Dear Mom: a Sniper"s Vietnam.
- Hemphill, Robert. 1998. Platoon: Bravo Company.
- Noam Chomsky. 1967. The Responsibility of Intellectuals.
- Moore, Robin. 1965 The Green Berets (ISBN 0-312-98492-8)

- Robert Olen Butler. 1992.

Articles of Confederation	The Articles of Confederation and Perpetual Union, commonly referred to as the Articles of Confederation, was the first constitution of the thirteen United States of America. The Second Continental Congress appointed a committee to draft the "Articles" in June 1776 and proposed the draft to the States for ratification in November 1777. The ratification process was completed in March 1781, legally federating the sovereign and independent states, allied under the Articles of Association, into a new federation styled the "United States of America".
Foreign policy	A country"s Foreign policy is a set of goals outlining how the country will interact with other countries economically, politically, socially and militarily, and to a lesser extent, how the country will interact with non-state actors. The aforementioned interaction is evaluated and monitored in attempts to maximize benefits of multilateral international cooperation. Foreign policies are designed to help protect a country"s national interests, national security, ideological goals, and economic prosperity.
Anti-Americanism	Dictionaries tend to define Anti-Americanism, often anti-American sentiment, as a widespread opposition or hostility to the people, government or policies of the United States. In practice, a broad range of attitudes and actions critical of or opposed to the United States have been labeled Anti-Americanism. Thus, the nature and applicability of the term is often disputed.
Declaration of Independence	A Declaration of independence is an assertion of the independence of an aspiring state or states. Such places are usually declared from part or all of the territory of another nation or failed nation, or are breakaway territories from within the larger state. Not all declarations of independence were successful and resulted in independence for these regions.
Second Continental Congress	The Second Continental Congress was a convention of delegates from the Thirteen Colonies that met beginning in May 10, 1775, in Philadelphia, Pennsylvania, soon after shooting in the American Revolutionary War had begun. It succeeded the First Continental Congress, which met briefly during 1774, also in Philadelphia. The second Congress managed the colonial war effort, and moved slowly towards independence, adopting the United States Declaration of Independence on July 4, 1776.
Penalty	In the Latter Day Saint movement, a Penalty is an oath made by participants of the original Nauvoo Endowment instituted by Joseph Smith, Jr. in 1843 and further developed by Brigham Young after Smith"s death. Mormon antagonists refer to the Penalty as a blood oath, because it required the participant to swear never to reveal certain key symbols of the Endowment ceremony, including the Penalty itself, while symbolically enacting ways in which a person may be executed.
Constitution	A Constitution is set of rules for government -- often codified as a written document -- that establishes principles of an autonomous political entity. In the case of countries, this term refers specifically to a national Constitution defining the fundamental political principles, and establishing the structure, procedures, powers and duties, of a government. By limiting the government"s own reach, most Constitution s guarantee certain rights to the people.
Constitutions	Bahrain has had two constitutions in its modern history. The first one was promulgated in 1973, and the second one in 2002.

Chapter 2. The Constitution

Contract	Agreement is said to be reached when an offer capable of immediate acceptance is met with a "mirror image" acceptance (ie, an unqualified acceptance.) The parties must have the necessary capacity to Contract and the Contract must not be either trifling, indeterminate, impossible or illegal. Contract law is based on the principle expressed in the Latin phrase pacta sunt servanda .
Constitutional Convention	A Constitutional convention is an informal and uncodified procedural agreement that is followed by the institutions of a state. In some states, notably those Commonwealth of Nations states which follow the Westminster system and whose political systems are derived from British constitutional law, most of the functions of government are guided by Constitutional convention rather than by a formal written constitution. In these states, the actual distribution of power may be markedly different from those which are described in the formal constitutional documents.
Republicanism	Republicanism is the ideology of governing a nation as a republic, where the head of state is appointed by other means than hereditary, often elections. The exact meaning of Republicanism varies depending on the cultural and historical context. The sometimes contrary definitions are all covered in Radicalism emerged in European states in the 19th century.
Public Service of Canada	The Public Service of Canada is the staff of the federal government of Canada. Its function is to support the Canadian monarch, and to handle the hiring of employees for the federal government ministries. It is represented by the Governor General, and the appointed [[list of Canadian ministries | ministry].
Property right	A Property right is the exclusive authority to determine how a resource is used, whether that resource is owned by government or by individuals. All economic goods have a property rights attribute. This attribute has three broad components 1. The right to use the good 2. The right to earn income from the good 3. The right to transfer the good to others The concept of property rights as used by economists and legal scholars are related but distinct. The distinction is largely seen in the economists" focus on the ability of an individual or collective to control the use of the good.
Popular democracy	Popular democracy is a notion of direct democracy based on referendums and other devices of empowerment and concretization of popular will. The concept evolved out of the political philosophy of Populism, as a fully democratic version of this popular empowerment ideology, but since it has become independent of it, and some even discuss if they are antagonistic or unrelated now Though the expression has been used since the 19th century and may be applied to English Civil War politics, at least the notion is deemed recent and only recently got fully developed.

Chapter 2. The Constitution

Centralized government	A Centralized government is the form of government in which power is concentrated in a central authority to which local governments are subject. Centralization occurs both geographically and politically.
	A Centralized government is characterized in which the local governments are designated by the central Government of the country, like the local administrative authorities.
Bicameralism	In government, Bicameralism is the practice of having two legislative or parliamentary chambers. Thus, a bicameral parliament or bicameral legislature is a legislature which consists of two chambers or houses. Bicameralism is an essential and defining feature of the classical notion of mixed government.
Committee	A Committee (some of which are titled instead as a "Commission" larger deliberative assembly-- which when organized so that action on Committee requires a vote by all its entitled members, is called the Committee of the Whole". Committee s often serve several different functions:

- Governance: in organizations considered too large for all the members to participate in decisions affecting the organization as a whole, a Committee (such as a Board of Directors or "Executive Committee) is given the power to make decisions, spend money the Board of directors can frequently enter into binding contracts and make decisions which once taken or made, can"t be taken back or undone under the law.

- Coordination: individuals from different parts of an organization (for example, all senior vice presidents) might meet regularly to discuss developments in their areas, review projects that cut across organizational boundaries, talk about future options, etc. Where there is a large Committee it is common to have smaller Committee s with more specialized functions - for example, Boards of Directors of large corporations typically have an (ongoing) audit Committee finance Committee compensation Committee etc. Large academic conferences are usually organized by a co-ordinating Committee drawn from the relevant professional body.

Presidential election	A presidential election was held in Chile on 4 September 1970. A narrow plurality (36.6 percent of the total vote) was secured by Salvador Allende, the candidate of the Popular Unity coalition of leftist parties. Because he did not obtain an absolute majority, his election required a further vote by the National Congress of Chile which resulted in Allende assuming the presidency in accordance with the Chilean Constitution of 1925.
Federalism	Federalism is a political philosophy in which a group of members are bound together ">covenant) with a governing representative head. The term Federalism is also used to describe a system of the government in which sovereignty is constitutionally divided between a central governing authority and constituent political units (like states or provinces.) Federalism is a system in which the power to govern is shared between national and central(state) governments, creating what is often called a federation.

Chapter 2. The Constitution

Bill of Rights	A Bill of rights is a list or summary of rights that are considered important and essential by a nation. The purpose of these bills is to protect those rights against infringement by the government. The term "Bill of rights" originates from Britain, where it referred to a bill that was passed by Parliament in 1689.
Civil liberties	Civil liberties are freedoms that protect an individual from the government of the nation in which they reside. Civil liberties set limits for government so that it cannot abuse its power and interfere unduly with the lives of its citizens. Common Civil liberties include the rights of people, freedom of religion, and freedom of speech, and additionally, the right to due process, to a fair trial, to own property, and to privacy.
Limited government	Limited government is a government where any more than minimal governmental intervention in personal liberties and the economy is not usually allowed by law, usually in a written Constitution. It is closely related to libertarianism, classical liberalism, and some tendencies of liberalism and conservatism in the United States. Limited government is a common practice through Western culture.
Right	A right is the legal or moral entitlement to do or refrain from doing something thing or recognition in civil society. Rights serve as rules of interaction between people, and, as such, they place constraints and obligations upon the actions of individuals or groups (for example, if one has a right to life, this means that others do not have the liberty to kill him.) Most modern conceptions of rights are universalist and egalitarian -- in other words, equal rights are granted to all people.
Suffrage	Suffrage is the civil right to vote, or the exercise of that right. In that context, it is also called political franchise or simply the franchise. Suffrage is very valuable to the extent that there are opportunities to vote .
Separation of powers	The Separation of powers is a model for the governance of democratic states. The model was first developed in ancient Greece and came into widespread use by the Roman Republic as part of the uncodified Constitution of the Roman Republic. Under this model, the state is divided into branches or estates, each with separate and independent powers and areas of responsibility.
Balance	Balance is sometimes used in reference to political content in the mass media. This usage began in Britain in the early part of the 20th century when the conservative Tories were unpopular and receiving little coverage through the BBC. In order to provide an intellectual rationalization for an increased level of Conservative content, Lord John Reith, the BBC"s founding General Manager and later Chairman, promoted a concept called Balance.

In practise Balance means ensuring that statements by those challenging the establishment are balanced with statements of those whom they are criticising, though not necessarily the other way round.

Power

Power in international relations is defined in several different ways. Political scientists, historians, and practitioners of international relations (diplomats) have used the following concepts of political Power:

- Power as a goal of states or leaders;
- Power as a measure of influence or control over outcomes, events, actors and issues;
- Power as reflecting victory in conflict and the attainment of security; and,
- Power as control over resources and capabilities.

Modern discourse generally speaks in terms of state Power, indicating both economic and military Power. Those states that have significant amounts of Power within the international system are referred to as middle powers, regional powers, great powers, superpowers, or hyperpowers, although there is no commonly accepted standard for what defines a powerful state.

Entities other than states can also acquire and wield Power in international relations.

Globalization

Globalization or (globalisation) is the process by which the people of the world are unified into a single society and function together. Globalization is often used to refer to economic Globalization: the integration of national economies into the international economy through trade, foreign direct investment, capital flows, migration, and the spread of technology. This process is usually recognized as being driven by a combination of economic, technological, sociocultural, political and biological factors.

New Deal

The New Deal is a programme of active labour market policies introduced in the United Kingdom by the Labour government in 1998, initially funded by a one off Â£5bn windfall tax on privatised utility companies. The stated purpose is to reduce unemployment by providing training, subsidised employment and voluntary work to the unemployed. Spending on the New Deal was Â£1.3 billion in 2001.

Judicial review

Judicial review is the doctrine in democratic theory under which legislative and executive action is subject to invalidation by the judiciary. Specific courts with Judicial review power must annul the acts of the state when it finds them incompatible with a higher authority, such as the terms of a written constitution. Judicial review is an example of the functioning of separation of powers in a modern governmental system (where the judiciary is one of three branches of government .)

Finland

Finland , officially the Republic of Finland), is a Nordic country situated in the Fennoscandian region of northern Europe. It borders Sweden on the west, Russia on the east, and Norway on the north, while Estonia lies to its south across the Gulf of Finland. The capital city is Helsinki.

Germany	Germany), officially the Federal Republic of Germany), is a country in Central Europe. It is bordered to the north by the North Sea, Denmark, and the Baltic Sea; to the east by Poland and the Czech Republic; to the south by Austria and Switzerland; and to the west by France, Luxembourg, Belgium, and the Netherlands. The territory of Germany covers 357,021 square kilometers and is influenced by a temperate seasonal climate.
Parliamentary system	A Parliamentary system is a system of government wherein the ministers of the executive branch are drawn from the legislature, and are accountable to that body, such that the executive and legislative branches are intertwined. In such a system, the head of government is both de facto chief executive and chief legislator.
	Parliamentary system s are characterized by no clear-cut separation of powers between the executive and legislative branches, leading to a different set of checks and balances compared to those found in presidential systems.
Republic	The Republic is a left-of-centre political party in the Faroe Islands committed to Faroese Independence. It was founded in 1948 as a reaction to independence not being proclaimed after a public vote on the matter showed a marginal majority for it in 1946.
	In 1998 Høgni Hoydal succeeded Heini O. Heinesen as party leader.

National Guard	The National Guard was the name given at the time of the French Revolution to the militias formed in each city, in imitation of the National Guard created in Paris. It was a military force separate from the regular army. Initially under the command of the Marquis de la Fayette, then briefly under the Marquis de Mandat, it was strongly identified until the summer of 1792 with the middle class and its support for constitutional monarchy.
New Deal	The New Deal is a programme of active labour market policies introduced in the United Kingdom by the Labour government in 1998, initially funded by a one off Â£5bn windfall tax on privatised utility companies. The stated purpose is to reduce unemployment by providing training, subsidised employment and voluntary work to the unemployed. Spending on the New Deal was Â£1.3 billion in 2001.
Confederation	A Confederation in modern political terms, is a permanent union of sovereign states for common action in relation to other states. Usually created by treaty but often later adopting a common constitution, Confederation s tend to be established for dealing with critical issues such as defense, foreign affairs, or a common currency, with the central government being required to provide support for all members. The nature of the relationship among the states constituting a Confederation varies considerably.
European Union	The European Union is an economic and political union of 27 member states, located primarily in Europe. Committed to regional integration, the European Union was established by the Treaty of Maastricht on 1 November 1993 upon the foundations of the pre-existing European Economic Community. Encompassing a population of 500 million the European Union generates an estimated 30% share (US$18.4 trillion in 2008) of the nominal gross world product.
Nation	A nation are regional corporations of students at university, once widespread across central and northern Europe in medieval times, they are now largely restricted to the two ancient universities of Sweden. The students, who were all born within the same region, usually spoke the same language, and expected to be ruled by their own familiar law. The most similar comparison in the Anglo-world to the nation system is in the collegiate system of older British universities or fraternities at American universities; however, both of these comparisons are imperfect.
Union of Utrecht	The Union of Utrecht was a treaty signed on 23 January 1579 in Utrecht, the Netherlands, unifying the northern provinces of the Netherlands, until then under the control of Spain. The Union of Utrecht is regarded as the foundation of the Republic of the Seven United Netherlands, which was not recognized by the Spanish Empire until the Twelve Years" Truce in 1609. The treaty was signed on 23 January by Holland, Zeeland, Utrecht (but not all of Utrecht) and the province (but not the city) of Groningen.

Chapter 3. Federalism: States and Nation

| United Nations | The United Nations is an international organization whose stated aims are facilitating cooperation in international law, international security, economic development, social progress, human rights, and the achieving of world peace. The United Nations was founded in 1945 after World War II to replace the League of Nations, to stop wars between countries, and to provide a platform for dialogue. It contains multiple subsidiary organizations to carry out its missions. |

Led by Lorrin A. Thurston and Sanford B. Dole, the Provisional Government ruled over HawaiÊ»i until the formal establishment of a republic. Pictured above is the cabinet, (Left to Right) James A. King, Sanford B. Dole, William O. Smith and Peter C. Jones.

Capital	Flag

Capital	Honolulu
Language(s)	Hawaiian, English
Government	Not specified
Provisional Government	
- 1893-1894	Committee of Safety
Historical era	New Imperialism
- Monarchy overthrown	January 17, 1893
- Republic declared	July 4, 1894
Currency	U.S. dollar, Hawaiian dollar

The Provisional Government of HawaiÊ»i was proclaimed on January 17, 1893 by the 13 member Committee of Safety under the leadership of Lorrin A. Thurston and Sanford B. Dole. It governed the Kingdom of HawaiÊ»i after the overthrow of Queen LiliÊ»uokalani until the Republic of HawaiÊ»i was established on July 4, 1894.

| Capital punishment | Capital punishment, the death penalty or execution, is the killing of a person by judicial process for retribution, general deterrence, and incapacitation. Crimes that can result in a death penalty are known as capital crimes or capital offences. The term capital originates from Latin capitalis, literally "regarding the head" . |

| Canada | Canada has been a member of the North Atlantic Treaty Organization (NATO) since its inception in 1949. |
| | Canada was not only a member but one of the principal initiators of the alliance. This was a marked break with Canada"s pre-war isolationism, and was the first peacetime alliance Canada had ever joined. |

| Constitution | A Constitution is set of rules for government -- often codified as a written document -- that establishes principles of an autonomous political entity. In the case of countries, this term refers specifically to a national Constitution defining the fundamental political principles, and establishing the structure, procedures, powers and duties, of a government. By limiting the government"s own reach, most Constitution s guarantee certain rights to the people. |

Ethnicity	Ethnicity plays a prominent role in pornography. Distinct genres of pornography focus on performers of specific ethnic groups, or on the depiction of interracial sexual activity. Ethnic pornography typically employs ethnic and racial stereotypes in its depiction of performers.
Germany	Germany), officially the Federal Republic of Germany), is a country in Central Europe. It is bordered to the north by the North Sea, Denmark, and the Baltic Sea; to the east by Poland and the Czech Republic; to the south by Austria and Switzerland; and to the west by France, Luxembourg, Belgium, and the Netherlands. The territory of Germany covers 357,021 square kilometers and is influenced by a temperate seasonal climate.
Iraq	Iraq , officially the Republic of Iraq JumhÅ«rÄ«yat Al-Ê¿IrÄ q, Kurdish: ÙƒÛ†Ù…Ø§Ø±ÛŒ Ø¹ÛŽØ±Ø§Ù‚â€Ž, Komara Iraqê), is a country in Western Asia spanning most of the northwestern end of the Zagros mountain range, the eastern part of the Syrian Desert and the northern part of the Arabian Desert. Iraq shares borders with Jordan to the west, Syria to the northwest, Turkey to the north, Iran to the east, and Kuwait and Saudi Arabia to the south. Iraq has a narrow section of coastline measuring 58 km between Umm Qasr and Al Faw on the Persian Gulf.
Anti-Americanism	Dictionaries tend to define Anti-Americanism, often anti-American sentiment, as a widespread opposition or hostility to the people, government or policies of the United States. In practice, a broad range of attitudes and actions critical of or opposed to the United States have been labeled Anti-Americanism. Thus, the nature and applicability of the term is often disputed.
Federalism	Federalism is a political philosophy in which a group of members are bound together ">covenant) with a governing representative head. The term Federalism is also used to describe a system of the government in which sovereignty is constitutionally divided between a central governing authority and constituent political units (like states or provinces.) Federalism is a system in which the power to govern is shared between national and central(state) governments, creating what is often called a federation.
Power	Power in international relations is defined in several different ways. Political scientists, historians, and practitioners of international relations (diplomats) have used the following concepts of political Power: • Power as a goal of states or leaders; • Power as a measure of influence or control over outcomes, events, actors and issues; • Power as reflecting victory in conflict and the attainment of security; and, • Power as control over resources and capabilities. Modern discourse generally speaks in terms of state Power, indicating both economic and military Power. Those states that have significant amounts of Power within the international system are referred to as middle powers, regional powers, great powers, superpowers, or hyperpowers, although there is no commonly accepted standard for what defines a powerful state.

Entities other than states can also acquire and wield Power in international relations.

Bill of Rights

A Bill of rights is a list or summary of rights that are considered important and essential by a nation. The purpose of these bills is to protect those rights against infringement by the government. The term "Bill of rights" originates from Britain, where it referred to a bill that was passed by Parliament in 1689.

Right

A right is the legal or moral entitlement to do or refrain from doing something thing or recognition in civil society. Rights serve as rules of interaction between people, and, as such, they place constraints and obligations upon the actions of individuals or groups (for example, if one has a right to life, this means that others do not have the liberty to kill him.)

Most modern conceptions of rights are universalist and egalitarian -- in other words, equal rights are granted to all people.

Federal government

A federal government is the common government of a federation.

The structure of federal government s vary from institution to institution based on a broad definition of a basic federal political system, there are two or more levels of government that exist within an established territory and govern through common institutions with overlapping or shared powers as prescribed by a constitution.

- Government of Australia
- Government of Belgium
- Government of Brazil
- Government of Canada
- Government of Germany
- Government of India
- Government of Malaysia
- Government of Mexico
- Government of Russia
- Government of Switzerland
- Government of the United States

The United States is considered the first modern federation. After declaring independence from Britain, the U.S. adopted its first constitution, the Articles of Confederation in 1781.

Globalization

Globalization or (globalisation) is the process by which the people of the world are unified into a single society and function together. Globalization is often used to refer to economic Globalization: the integration of national economies into the international economy through trade, foreign direct investment, capital flows, migration, and the spread of technology. This process is usually recognized as being driven by a combination of economic, technological, sociocultural, political and biological factors.

Constitutional Convention	A Constitutional convention is an informal and uncodified procedural agreement that is followed by the institutions of a state. In some states, notably those Commonwealth of Nations states which follow the Westminster system and whose political systems are derived from British constitutional law, most of the functions of government are guided by Constitutional convention rather than by a formal written constitution. In these states, the actual distribution of power may be markedly different from those which are described in the formal constitutional documents.
Declaration of Independence	A Declaration of independence is an assertion of the independence of an aspiring state or states. Such places are usually declared from part or all of the territory of another nation or failed nation, or are breakaway territories from within the larger state. Not all declarations of independence were successful and resulted in independence for these regions.
Judicial review	Judicial review is the doctrine in democratic theory under which legislative and executive action is subject to invalidation by the judiciary. Specific courts with Judicial review power must annul the acts of the state when it finds them incompatible with a higher authority, such as the terms of a written constitution. Judicial review is an example of the functioning of separation of powers in a modern governmental system (where the judiciary is one of three branches of government .)
Federal Trade Commission	The Federal Trade Commission is an independent agency of the United States government, established in 1914 by the Federal Trade Commission Act. Its principal mission is the promotion of "consumer protection" and the elimination and prevention of what regulators perceive to be harmfully "anti-competitive" business practices, such as coercive monopoly. The Federal Trade Commission Act was one of President Wilson"s major acts against trusts.
Freedom	Freedom is the right to act according to ones will without being held up by the power of others. From a philosophical point of view, it can be defined as the capacity to determine your own choices. It can be defined negatively as an absence of subordination, servitude and constraint.
Social Security	Social Security, in Australia, refers to a system of social welfare payments provided by Commonwealth Government of Australia. These payments are administered by a Government body named Centrelink. In Australia, most benefits are subject to a means test.
Democratic party	Democratic Party was a political party in Gambia. The party was founded during the pre-independence period in the colony of Bathurst (currently the national capital Banjul.) Ahead of the 1962 election, the Democratic Party merged with the Muslim Congress Party to form the Democratic Congress Alliance.
Leadership	Leadership has been described as the "process of social influence in which one person can enlist the aid and support of others in the accomplishment of a common task". A definition more inclusive of followers comes from Alan Keith of Genentech who said "Leadership is ultimately about creating a way for people to contribute to making something extraordinary happen." Leadership is one of the most salient aspects of the organizational context. However, defining Leadership has been challenging.

Chapter 3. Federalism: States and Nation

Mandate	In international law, a Mandate is a binding obligation issued from an inter-governmental organization like the United Nations to a country which is bound to follow the instructions of the organization. Before the creation of the United Nations, all mandates were issued from the League of Nations. An example of such a Mandate would be Australian New Guinea, which is officially the Territory of Papua.
Region	Region is most commonly a geographical term that is used in various ways among the different branches of geography. In general, a Region is a medium-scale area of land or water, smaller than the whole areas of interest (which could be, for example, the world, a nation, a river basin, mountain range, and so on), and larger than a specific site. A Region may be seen as a collection of smaller units (as in "the New England states") or as one part of a larger whole (as in "the New England Region of the United States".)
Devolution	Devolution is the statutory granting of powers from the central government of a state to government at a subnational level, such as a regional, local, or state level. It differs from federalism in that the powers devolved may be temporary and ultimately reside in central government, thus the state remains, de jure, unitary. Any devolved parliaments or assemblies can be repealed by central government in the same way an ordinary statute can be.
Medicare	Medicare is a social insurance program administered by the United States government, providing health insurance coverage to people who are aged 65 and over, or who meet other special criteria. Medicare operates as a single-payer health care system. The Social Security Act of 1965 was passed by Congress in late-spring of 1965 and signed into law on July 30, 1965, by President Lyndon B. Johnson as amendments to Social Security legislation.
Prescription	In law, Prescription is the method of sovereignty transfer of a territory through international law analogous to the common law doctrine of adverse possession for private real-estate. Prescription involves the open encroachment by the new sovereign upon the territory in question for a prolonged period of time, acting as the sovereign, without protest or other contest by the original sovereign. This doctrine legalizes de jure the de facto transfer of sovereignty caused in part by the original sovereign"s extended negligence and/or neglect of the area in question.
Cooperative federalism	Cooperative federalism is a concept of federalism in which national, state, and local governments interact cooperatively and collectively to solve common problems, rather than making policies separately but more or less equally (such as the nineteenth century"s dual federalism) or clashing over a policy in a system dominated by the national government. The EU and Germany are special cases of federalism. Competences are shared to a very high degree by both federal and state level, states are directly involved at a very high degree in federal decision making, state governments are represented directly in the upper houses.

Welfare state	There are two main interpretations of the idea of a Welfare state

      • A model in which the state assumes primary responsibility for the welfare of its citizens. This responsibility in theory ought to be comprehensive, because all aspects of welfare are considered and universally applied to citizens as a "right". Welfare state can also mean the creation of a "social safety net" of minimum standards of varying forms of welfare. Here is found some confusion between a Welfare state and a "welfare society" in common debate about the definition of the term.

      • The provision of welfare in society. In many " Welfare state s", especially in continental Europe, welfare is not actually provided by the state, but by a combination of independent, voluntary, mutualist and government services. The functional provider of benefits and services may be a central or state government, a state-sponsored company or agency, a private corporation, a charity or another form of non-profit organization. However, this phenomenon has been more appropriately termed a "welfare society," and the term "welfare system" has been used to describe the range of Welfare state and welfare society mixes that are found.

The English term Welfare state is believed by Asa Briggs to have been coined by Archbishop William Temple during the Second World War, contrasting wartime Britain with the "warfare state" of Nazi Germany. Friedrich Hayek contends that the term derived from the older German word Wohlfahrtsstaat, which itself was used by nineteenth century historians to describe a variant of the ideal of Polizeistaat . It was fully developed by the German academic Sozialpolitiker--"socialists of the chair"--from 1870 and first implemented through Bismarck"s "state socialism". Bismarck"s policies have also been seen as the creation of a Welfare state

New Federalism	New Federalism is a political philosophy of devolution, or of transfer of certain powers from the United States federal government to the U.S. states. The primary objective of New Federalism, unlike that of the eighteenth-century political philosophy of Federalism, is the restoration to the states of some of the autonomy and power which they lost to the federal government as a consequence of President Franklin Roosevelt"s New Deal and federal civil rights laws of the 1960s.

It relies upon a Federalist tradition dating back to the founding of the country, as well as the Tenth Amendment.

Contract	Agreement is said to be reached when an offer capable of immediate acceptance is met with a "mirror image" acceptance (ie, an unqualified acceptance.) The parties must have the necessary capacity to Contract and the Contract must not be either trifling, indeterminate, impossible or illegal. Contract law is based on the principle expressed in the Latin phrase pacta sunt servanda .

Presidential election	A presidential election was held in Chile on 4 September 1970. A narrow plurality (36.6 percent of the total vote) was secured by Salvador Allende, the candidate of the Popular Unity coalition of leftist parties. Because he did not obtain an absolute majority, his election required a further vote by the National Congress of Chile which resulted in Allende assuming the presidency in accordance with the Chilean Constitution of 1925.
Public Service of Canada	The Public Service of Canada is the staff of the federal government of Canada. Its function is to support the Canadian monarch, and to handle the hiring of employees for the federal government ministries. It is represented by the Governor General, and the appointed [[list of Canadian ministries | ministry].
Civil liberties	Civil liberties are freedoms that protect an individual from the government of the nation in which they reside. Civil liberties set limits for government so that it cannot abuse its power and interfere unduly with the lives of its citizens. Common Civil liberties include the rights of people, freedom of religion, and freedom of speech, and additionally, the right to due process, to a fair trial, to own property, and to privacy.

Chapter 4. The Structural Foundations of American Government and Politics

Ethnicity	Ethnicity plays a prominent role in pornography. Distinct genres of pornography focus on performers of specific ethnic groups, or on the depiction of interracial sexual activity. Ethnic pornography typically employs ethnic and racial stereotypes in its depiction of performers.
Anti-Americanism	Dictionaries tend to define Anti-Americanism, often anti-American sentiment, as a widespread opposition or hostility to the people, government or policies of the United States. In practice, a broad range of attitudes and actions critical of or opposed to the United States have been labeled Anti-Americanism. Thus, the nature and applicability of the term is often disputed.
Federalism	Federalism is a political philosophy in which a group of members are bound together ">covenant) with a governing representative head. The term Federalism is also used to describe a system of the government in which sovereignty is constitutionally divided between a central governing authority and constituent political units (like states or provinces.) Federalism is a system in which the power to govern is shared between national and central(state) governments, creating what is often called a federation.
Page	A Page or Page boy is a traditionally young male servant. In medieval times, a Page was an attendant to a knight; an apprentice squire. A young boy served as a Page for seven years, serving, cleaning, and even learning the basic of combat.
Power	Power in international relations is defined in several different ways. Political scientists, historians, and practitioners of international relations (diplomats) have used the following concepts of political Power: • Power as a goal of states or leaders; • Power as a measure of influence or control over outcomes, events, actors and issues; • Power as reflecting victory in conflict and the attainment of security; and, • Power as control over resources and capabilities. Modern discourse generally speaks in terms of state Power, indicating both economic and military Power. Those states that have significant amounts of Power within the international system are referred to as middle powers, regional powers, great powers, superpowers, or hyperpowers, although there is no commonly accepted standard for what defines a powerful state. Entities other than states can also acquire and wield Power in international relations.
Public opinion	Public opinion is the aggregate of individual attitudes or beliefs held by the adult population. Public opinion can also be defined as the complex collection of opinions of many different people and the sum of all their views. The principle approaches to the study of Public opinion may be divided into 4 categories:

a) quantitative measurement of opinion distributions;

b) investigation of the internal relationships among the individual opinions that make up Public opinion on an issue;

c) description or analysis of the public role of Public opinion;

d) study both of the communication media that disseminate the ideas on which opinions are based and of the uses that propagandists and other manipulators make of these media.

Public opinion as a concept gained credence with the rise of "public" in the eighteenth century.

Right	A right is the legal or moral entitlement to do or refrain from doing something thing or recognition in civil society. Rights serve as rules of interaction between people, and, as such, they place constraints and obligations upon the actions of individuals or groups (for example, if one has a right to life, this means that others do not have the liberty to kill him.) Most modern conceptions of rights are universalist and egalitarian -- in other words, equal rights are granted to all people.
Medicare	Medicare is a social insurance program administered by the United States government, providing health insurance coverage to people who are aged 65 and over, or who meet other special criteria. Medicare operates as a single-payer health care system. The Social Security Act of 1965 was passed by Congress in late-spring of 1965 and signed into law on July 30, 1965, by President Lyndon B. Johnson as amendments to Social Security legislation.
Presidential election	A presidential election was held in Chile on 4 September 1970. A narrow plurality (36.6 percent of the total vote) was secured by Salvador Allende, the candidate of the Popular Unity coalition of leftist parties. Because he did not obtain an absolute majority, his election required a further vote by the National Congress of Chile which resulted in Allende assuming the presidency in accordance with the Chilean Constitution of 1925.
Social Security	Social Security, in Australia, refers to a system of social welfare payments provided by Commonwealth Government of Australia. These payments are administered by a Government body named Centrelink. In Australia, most benefits are subject to a means test.
Civil rights movement	The Civil rights movement was a worldwide political movement for equality before the law occurring between approximately 1950 and 1980. It was accompanied by much civil unrest and popular rebellion. The process was long and tenuous in many countries, and most of these movements did not achieve or fully achieve their objectives.
Civil service	The term Civil service has two distinct meanings: • Branch of governmental service in which individuals are hired on the basis of merit which is proven by the use of competitive examinations. • Body of employees in any government agency, except the military.

A civil servant or public servant is a civilian public sector employee working for a government department or agency. The term explicitly excludes the armed services, although civilian officials will work at "Defence Ministry" headquarters. The term always includes the (sovereign) state"s employees; whether regional, or sub-state, or even municipal employees are called "civil servants" varies from country to country. In the United Kingdom, for instance, only Crown employees are civil servants, county or city employees are not.

Minority

Minority, and the related concept of "becoming-minor," is a philosophical concept developed by Gilles Deleuze and Félix Guattari in their books Kafka: Towards a Minor Literature (1975), A Thousand Plateaus (1980), and elsewhere. In these texts, they criticize the concept of "majority" as being based on a form of domination that works by naturalizing a purely numerical conception. They argue that the concept of a "dominant Minority" is an oxymoron, because the term "majority" always refers to those who are in a position of dominance.

Capitalism

Capitalism has been critiqued from many perspectives during its history. Criticisms range from people who disagree with the principles of Capitalism in its entirety, to those who disagree with particular outcomes of Capitalism. Among those wishing to replace Capitalism with a different method of distributing goods, a distinction can be made between those believing that Capitalism can only be overcome with revolution (e.g. communist revolution) and those believing that change can come slowly through reformism (e.g. classic social democracy.)

Globalization

Globalization or (globalisation) is the process by which the people of the world are unified into a single society and function together. Globalization is often used to refer to economic Globalization: the integration of national economies into the international economy through trade, foreign direct investment, capital flows, migration, and the spread of technology. This process is usually recognized as being driven by a combination of economic, technological, sociocultural, political and biological factors.

Boosterism

Boosterism is the act of "boosting," or promoting, one"s town, city with the goal of improving public perception of it. Boosting can be as simple as "talking up" the entity at a party or as elaborate as establishing a visitors" bureau. It is somewhat associated with American small towns.

Public Service of Canada

The Public Service of Canada is the staff of the federal government of Canada. Its function is to support the Canadian monarch, and to handle the hiring of employees for the federal government ministries. It is represented by the Governor General, and the appointed [[list of Canadian ministries | ministry].

Gini coefficient

The Gini coefficient is a measure of statistical dispersion developed by the Italian statistician Corrado Gini and published in his 1912 paper "Variability and Mutability" (Italian: Variabilità e mutabilità.) It is commonly used as a measure of inequality of income or wealth. It has, however, also found application in the study of inequalities in disciplines as diverse as health science, ecology, and chemistry.

Luxembourg	Luxembourg , officially the Grand Duchy of Luxembourg , is a small, landlocked country in western Europe, bordered by Belgium, France, and Germany. Luxembourg has a population of under half a million people in an area of approximately 2,586 square kilometres .
	Luxembourg is a parliamentary representative democracy with a constitutional monarch; it is ruled by a Grand Duke.
East Timor	East Timor is a small country in Southeast Asia. It comprises the eastern half of the island of Timor, the nearby islands of Atauro and Jaco. The first people"s are thought to be descendant of Australoid and Melanesian peoples.
Superpower	A Superpower is a state with a leading position in the international system and the ability to influence events and its own interests and project power on a worldwide scale to protect those interests; it is traditionally considered to be one step higher than a great power. Alice Lyman Miller (Professor of National Security Affairs at the Naval Postgraduate School), defines a Superpower as "a country that has the capacity to project dominating power and influence anywhere in the world, and sometimes, in more than one region of the globe at a time, and so may plausibly attain the status of global hegemon." It was a term first applied in 1944 to the United States, the Soviet Union, and the British Empire. Following World War II, as the British Empire transformed itself into the Commonwealth and its territories became independent, the Soviet Union and the United States generally came to be regarded as the only two Superpower s, and confronted each other in the Cold War.
European Union	The European Union is an economic and political union of 27 member states, located primarily in Europe. Committed to regional integration, the European Union was established by the Treaty of Maastricht on 1 November 1993 upon the foundations of the pre-existing European Economic Community. Encompassing a population of 500 million the European Union generates an estimated 30% share (US$18.4 trillion in 2008) of the nominal gross world product.
France	France , officially the French Republic , is a country located in Western Europe, with several overseas islands and territories located on other continents. Metropolitan France extends from the Mediterranean Sea to the English Channel and the North Sea, and from the Rhine to the Atlantic Ocean. It is often referred to as L"Hexagone ("The Hexagon") because of the geometric shape of its territory.
Germany	Germany), officially the Federal Republic of Germany), is a country in Central Europe. It is bordered to the north by the North Sea, Denmark, and the Baltic Sea; to the east by Poland and the Czech Republic; to the south by Austria and Switzerland; and to the west by France, Luxembourg, Belgium, and the Netherlands. The territory of Germany covers 357,021 square kilometers and is influenced by a temperate seasonal climate.

Iraq	Iraq , officially the Republic of Iraq JumhÅ«rÄ«yat Al-Ê¿IrÄ q, Kurdish: ÙƒÛ†Ù…Ø§Ø±ÛŒ Ø¹ÛŽØ±Ø§Ù‚â€Ž, Komara Iraqê), is a country in Western Asia spanning most of the northwestern end of the Zagros mountain range, the eastern part of the Syrian Desert and the northern part of the Arabian Desert. Iraq shares borders with Jordan to the west, Syria to the northwest, Turkey to the north, Iran to the east, and Kuwait and Saudi Arabia to the south. Iraq has a narrow section of coastline measuring 58 km between Umm Qasr and Al Faw on the Persian Gulf.
Soviet	A Soviet originally was a workers" local council in late Imperial Russia. According to the official historiography of the Soviet Union, the first Soviet was organized during the 1905 Russian Revolution in Ivanovo (Ivanovo region) in May 1905. However in his memoirs Volin claims that he witnessed the creation of the St Petersburg Soviet in Saint Petersburg in January 1905.
Union of Soviet Socialist Republics	The Union of Soviet Socialist Republics, occasionally called the United Soviet Socialist Republic, was a constitutionally socialist state that existed in Eurasia from 1922 to 1991. The name is a translation of the Russian: Â·), tr. Soyuz Sovetskikh Sotsialisticheskikh Respublik, abbreviated Ð¡Ð¡Ð¡Ð , SSSR. The common short name is Soviet Union, from Ð¡Ð¾Ð²ÐµÑ‚ ÐºÐ¸Ð¹ Ð¡Ð¾ÑŽÐ·, Sovetskiy Soyuz.

Countries

This is a list of articles on the constitutions of contemporary countries, states and dependencies.

- Constitution of Abkhazia - Republic of Abkhazia
- Constitution of Afghanistan - Islamic Republic of Afghanistan
- Constitution of Akrotiri - Sovereign Base Area of Akrotiri (UK overseas territory)
- Constitution of Åland - Åland (Autonomous province of Finland)
- Constitution of Albania - Republic of Albania
- Constitution of Algeria - People"s Democratic Republic of Algeria
- Constitution of American Samoa - Territory of American Samoa (US overseas territory)
- Constitution of Andorra - Principality of Andorra
- Constitution of Angola - Republic of Angola
- Constitution of Anguilla - Anguilla (UK overseas territory)
- Constitution of Antigua and Barbuda - Antigua and Barbuda
- Constitution of Argentina - Argentine Republic
- Constitution of Armenia - Republic of Armenia
- Constitution of Aruba - Aruba (Self-governing country in the Kingdom of the Netherlands)
- Constitution of Ascension Island - Ascension Island (Dependency of the UK overseas territory of Saint Helena)
- Constitution of Australia - Commonwealth of Australia
- Constitution of Austria - Republic of Austria
- Constitution of Azerbaijan - Republic of Azerbaijan

- Constitution of The Bahamas - Commonwealth of The Bahamas
- Constitution of Bahrain - Kingdom of Bahrain
- Constitution of Bangladesh - People"s Republic of Bangladesh
- Constitution of Barbados - Barbados
- Constitution of Belarus - Republic of Belarus
- Constitution of Belgium - Kingdom of Belgium
- Constitution of Belize - Belize
- Constitution of Benin - Republic of Benin
- Constitution of Bermuda - Bermuda (UK overseas territory)
- Constitution of Bhutan - Kingdom of Bhutan
- Constitution of Bolivia - Plurinational State of Bolivia
- Constitution of Bosnia and Herzegovina - Bosnia and Herzegovina
- Constitution of Botswana - Republic of Botswana
- Constitution of Brazil - Federative Republic of Brazil
- Constitution of Brunei - Negara Brunei Darussalam
- Constitution of Bulgaria - Republic of Bulgaria
- Constitution of Burkina Faso - Burkina Faso
- Constitution of Burma - Burma (Union of Myanmar)
- Constitution of Burundi - Republic of Burundi

- Constitution of Cambodia - Kingdom of Cambodia
- Constitution of Cameroon - Republic of Cameroon
- Constitution of Canada - Canada
- Constitution of Cape Verde - Republic of Cape Verde
- Constitution of the Cayman Islands - Cayman Islands (UK overseas territory)

- Constitution of the Central African Republic - Central African Republic
- Constitution of Chad - Republic of Chad
- Constitution of Chile - Republic of Chile
- Constitution of the People"s Republic of China - People"s Republic of China
- Constitution of the Republic of China - Republic of China
- Constitution of Christmas Island - Territory of Christmas Island (Australian overseas territory)
- Constitution of the Cocos (Keeling) Islands - Territory of Cocos (Keeling) Islands (Australian overseas territory)
- Constitution of Colombia - Republic of Colombia
- Constitution of Comoros - Union of the Comoros
- Constitution of the Democratic Republic of the Congo - Democratic Republic of the Congo
- Constitution of the Republic of the Congo - Republic of the Congo
- Constitution of the Cook Islands - Cook Islands (Associated state of New Zealand)
- Constitution of Costa Rica - Republic of Costa Rica
- Constitution of Côte d"Ivoire - Republic of Côte d"Ivoire
- Constitution of Croatia - Republic of Croatia
- Constitution of Cuba - Republic of Cuba
- Constitution of Cyprus - Republic of Cyprus
- Constitution of the Czech Republic - Czech Republic

- Constitution of Denmark - Kingdom of Denmark
- Constitution of Dhekelia - Sovereign Base Areas of Dhekelia (UK overseas territory)
- Constitution of Djibouti - Republic of Djibouti
- Constitution of Dominica - Commonwealth of Dominica
- Constitution of the Dominican Republic - Dominican Republic

- Constitution of East Timor (Timor-Leste) - Democratic Republic of Timor-Leste
- Constitution of Ecuador - Republic of Ecuador
- Constitution of Egypt - Arab Republic of Egypt
- Constitution of El Salvador - Republic of El Salvador
- Constitution of Equatorial Guinea - Republic of Equatorial Guinea
- Constitution of Eritrea - State of Eritrea
- Constitution of Estonia - Republic of Estonia
- Constitution of Ethiopia - Federal Democratic Republic of Ethiopia

- Constitution of the Falkland Islands - Falkland Islands (UK overseas territory)
- Constitution of the Faroe Islands - Faroe Islands (Self-governing country in the Kingdom of Denmark)
- Constitution of Fiji - Republic of the Fiji Islands
- Constitution of Finland - Republic of Finland
- Constitution of France - French Republic
- Constitution of French Polynesia - French Polynesia

- Constitution of Gabon - Gabonese Republic
- Constitution of Gambia - Republic of The Gambia
- Constitution of Georgia - Georgia
- Constitution of Germany - Federal Republic of Germany
- Constitution of Ghana - Republic of Ghana
- Constitution of Gibraltar - Gibraltar
- Constitution of Greece - Hellenic Republic
- Constitution of Greenland - Greenland (Self-governing country in the Kingdom of Denmark)

- Constitution of Grenada - Grenada
- Constitution of Guam - Territory of Guam (US overseas territory)
- Constitution of Guatemala - Republic of Guatemala
- Constitution of Guernsey - Bailiwick of Guernsey (British Crown dependency)
- Constitution of Guinea - Republic of Guinea
- Constitution of Guinea-Bissau - Republic of Guinea-Bissau
- Constitution of Guyana - Co-operative Republic of Guyana

- Constitution of Iceland - Republic of Iceland
- Constitution of India - Republic of India
- Constitution of Indonesia - Republic of Indonesia
- Constitution of Iran - Islamic Republic of Iran
- Constitution of Iraq - Republic of Iraq
- Constitution of Ireland - Ireland
  - ○ .

Chapter 4. The Structural Foundations of American Government and Politics

Axis of evil	"Axis of evil" is a term coined by United States President George W. Bush in his State of the Union Address on January 29, 2002 in order to describe governments that he accused of helping terrorism and seeking weapons of mass destruction. President Bush named Iran, Iraq and North Korea in his speech. President Bush"s presidency was marked by this notion as a justification for the War on Terror.
Foreign policy	A country"s Foreign policy is a set of goals outlining how the country will interact with other countries economically, politically, socially and militarily, and to a lesser extent, how the country will interact with non-state actors. The aforementioned interaction is evaluated and monitored in attempts to maximize benefits of multilateral international cooperation. Foreign policies are designed to help protect a country"s national interests, national security, ideological goals, and economic prosperity.
Political culture	Political culture can be defined as "The orientation of the citizens of a nation toward politics, and their perceptions of political legitimacy and the traditions of political practice," and the feelings expressed by individuals in the position of the elected offices that allow for the nurture of a political society. • Dennis Kavanagh defines Political culture as "A shorthand expression to denote the set of values within which the political system operates". • Lucian Pye describes it as "the sum of the fundamental values, sentiments and knowledge that give form and substance to political process". Political culture is how we think government should be carried out. It is different from ideology because people can disagree on ideology, but still have a common Political culture.
Declaration of Independence	A Declaration of independence is an assertion of the independence of an aspiring state or states. Such places are usually declared from part or all of the territory of another nation or failed nation, or are breakaway territories from within the larger state. Not all declarations of independence were successful and resulted in independence for these regions.
Individualism	Individualism is the moral stance, political philosophy, ideology, or social outlook that stresses independence and self-reliance. Individualists promote the exercise of one"s goals and desires, while opposing most external interference upon one"s choices, whether by society, or any other group or institution. Individualism is opposed to collectivism, which stress that communal, community, group, societal, or national goals should take priority over individual goals.
Nation	A nation are regional corporations of students at university, once widespread across central and northern Europe in medieval times, they are now largely restricted to the two ancient universities of Sweden. The students, who were all born within the same region, usually spoke the same language, and expected to be ruled by their own familiar law. The most similar comparison in the Anglo-world to the nation system is in the collegiate system of older British universities or fraternities at American universities; however, both of these comparisons are imperfect.

Chapter 4. The Structural Foundations of American Government and Politics

Ownership	Ownership is the state or fact of exclusive rights and control over property, which may be an object, land/real estate or intellectual property. An Ownership right is also referred to as title. The concept of Ownership has existed for thousands of years and in all cultures.
Classical liberalism	Classical liberalism is a form of liberalism stressing individual freedom, free markets, and limited government. This includes the importance of human rationality, individual property rights, natural rights, the protection of civil liberties, individual freedom from restraint, equality under the law, constitutional limitation of government and free markets, as exemplified in the writings of John Locke, Adam Smith, David Hume,Thomas Jefferson, Voltaire, Bastiat, Montesquieu and others. As such, it is the fusion of economic liberalism with political liberalism of the late 18th and 19th centuries.
Constitution	A Constitution is set of rules for government -- often codified as a written document -- that establishes principles of an autonomous political entity. In the case of countries, this term refers specifically to a national Constitution defining the fundamental political principles, and establishing the structure, procedures, powers and duties, of a government. By limiting the government"s own reach, most Constitution s guarantee certain rights to the people.
Freedom	Freedom is the right to act according to ones will without being held up by the power of others. From a philosophical point of view, it can be defined as the capacity to determine your own choices. It can be defined negatively as an absence of subordination, servitude and constraint.
Populism	Populism is a discourse that aims to support and favor the general whole of the electorate rather than elite lobbyist influences. Populism may comprise an ideology urging social and political system changes and/or a rhetorical style deployed by members of political or social movements. Generally, Populism invokes an idea of democracy as being, above all, the expression of the people"s will.
Politics	Politics are an integral part of the Unification Church"s concerns and activities, although the church itself largely remains aloof from Politics The degree of involvement of the movement, as well as some of its specific stances, have also been part of the reason for the movement"s controversial status over the years. The belief in the establishment of a literal Kingdom of Heaven on earth and Rev. Moon"s teaching that religion alone is not enough to bring this provides a motivation for political involvement.
Civil liberties	Civil liberties are freedoms that protect an individual from the government of the nation in which they reside. Civil liberties set limits for government so that it cannot abuse its power and interfere unduly with the lives of its citizens. Common Civil liberties include the rights of people, freedom of religion, and freedom of speech, and additionally, the right to due process, to a fair trial, to own property, and to privacy.

Pentagon Papers	The Pentagon Papers, officially titled United States-Vietnam Relations, 1945-1967: A Study Prepared by the Department of Defense, were a top-secret United States Department of Defense history of the United States" political-military involvement in Vietnam from 1945 to 1967. Commissioned by United States Secretary of Defense Robert S. McNamara in 1967, the study was completed in 1968. The papers first surfaced on the front page on the New York Times in 1971.
Tonkin Gulf Resolution	The Tonkin Gulf Resolution was a joint resolution of the United States Congress passed on August 7, 1964 in response to two alleged minor naval skirmishes off the coast of North Vietnam between U.S. destroyers and Vietnamese torpedo ships from the North, known collectively as the Gulf of Tonkin Incident. The Tonkin Gulf Resolution is of historical significance because it gave U.S. President Lyndon B. Johnson authorization, without a formal declaration of war by Congress, for the use of military force in Southeast Asia. Specifically, the resolution authorized the President to do whatever necessary in order to assist "any member or protocol state of the Southeast Asia Collective Defense Treaty." This included involving armed forces.
Vietnam	Vietnam " href="/wiki/Battle_of_B%E1%BA%A1ch_%C4%90%E1%BA%B1ng_River_(938)">battle of Bá²¡ch Ä á²±ng River. Successive dynasties flourished along with geographic and political expansion deeper into Southeast Asia, until it was colonized by the French in the mid-19th century. Efforts to resist the French eventually led to their expulsion from the country in the mid-20th century, leaving a nation divided politically into two countries.
Vietnam War	The Vietnam War was a military conflict that occurred in Vietnam, Laos and Cambodia from 1959 to 30 April 1975. The war was fought between the communist North Vietnam, supported by its communist allies, and the government of South Vietnam, supported by the United States and other member nations of the Southeast Asia Treaty Organization (SEATO.) The following outline is provided as an overview of and topical guide to the Vietnam War:

Listed by starting date:

- Operation 34A - (1964)
- Operation Starlite - August 18-24 1965
- Operation Hump- November 5 1965
- Operation Crimp - January 7, 1966
- Operation Birmingham - April 1966
- Operation Hastings - Late May 1966
- Operation Prairie - August 1966
- Operation Deckhouse Five - January 6, 1967
- Operation Cedar Falls - January 8, 1967
- Operation Junction City - February 21, 1967
- Operation Francis Marion - April 6 - April 30, 1967
- Operation Union - April 21-May 16, 1967
- Operations Malheur I and Malheur II - 11 May - July 1, 1967
- Operation Baker - May 11, 1967
- Operation Scotland - See Battle of Khe Sanh
- Operation Pegasus - August 8, 1968
- Operation Dewey Canyon - January 22, 1969
- Operation Twinkletoes - 1969
- Operation Apache Snow - May 10 - May 20, 1969
- Operation Chicago Peak - April 1970
- Operation Texas Star - April - September, 1970
- Operation Ivory Coast - November 21, 1970
- Operation Jefferson Glenn - 1970-1971
- Operation Lam Son 719 - February 8, 1971
- Ho Chi Minh Campaign January 24 - April 30, 1975
- Operation Frequent Wind - April, 1975

- Battle of Ap Bac - January 2, 1963
- Battle of Kien Long - April 11 - April 15, 1964
- Battle of Thanh Hóa - July 31, 1964
- Battle of Binh Gia - December 28, 1964 - January 1, 1965
- Battle of Dong Xoai - June 10, 1965
- Battle near Minh Thanh - October 25 - October 27, 1965
- Battle of Ia Drang - November 14 - November 16, 1965
- Battle of Cu Nghi - January 28 - January 31, 1966
- Battle of Kim Son Valley - February 16 - February 28, 1966
- Battle of A Shau - March 9 - March 10, 1966
- Battle of Xa Cam My - April 11 - April 12, 1966
- First Battle of Dong Ha - Late May - June, 1966
- Battle on Minh Thanh Road - July 9, 1966
- Battle of Ä á»©c CÆ¡ - August 9, 1966
- Battle of Long Táº§n - August 18- August 19, 1966
- Viet Cong attack on Tan Son Nhut airbase - December 4, 1966
- Battle of LZ Bird - December 27, 1966

- Battle of Tra Binh Dong - February 14 - February 15, 1967
- Battle of Hills 881 and 861 - April 24-May 9, 1967
- Nine Days in May - May 18 - May 28, 1967
- Battle of Vinh Huy - May 30 - June 2, 1967
- Battle of Con Thien - July 2 - July 3, 1967
- Battle of Dong Son - September 4, 1967
- Battle of Ong Thang - October 17, 1967
- First Battle of Loc Ninh - October 29 - November, 1967
- Battle of Dak To - November 3-November 22, 1967
- Battle in the Mekong Delta - December 4, 1967
- Battle of Tam Quan - December 6 - December 20, 1967
- Battle of Thom Tham Khe - December 27 - December 28, 1967
- Phoenix Program - 1967 - 1972
- Battle of Khe Sanh - January 21 - April 8, 1968
- Tet Offensive - January 30 - February 25, 1968
- Battle of Bien Hoa - January 31 - July 1, 1968
- Battle of Kham Duc - May 10 - May 12, 1968
- First Battle of Saigon - January 31, - February 3, 1968
- Battle of Hue - January 31, - February 25, 1968
- Tet 1969 - February 1969
- Battle of Hamburger Hill - May 10 - May 20, 1969
- Firebase Ripcord - March 12 - July 23, 1970
- Cambodian Incursion - April 29 - July 22, 1970
- Battle of Snoul - January 5 - May 30, 1971
- Easter Offensive - March 30 - October 22, 1972
- First Battle of Quang Tri - March 30 - May 1, 1972
- Battle of Loc Ninh - April 4 - April 7, 1972
- Battle of An Loc - April 20 - July 20, 1972
- Second Battle of Quang Tri - June 28 - September 16, 1972
- Battle of Phuoc Long - December 13, 1974 - January 6, 1975
- Battle of Buon Me Thuot - March 10 - March 12, 1975
- Battle of Xuan Loc - April 9 - April 20, 1975

- Operation Farm Gate
- Operation Chopper (1962)
- Operation Ranch Hand (1962-1971)
- Operation Pierce Arrow (1964)
- Operation Barrell Roll (1964-1972)
- Operation Pony Express (1965-1970)
- Operation Flaming Dart (1965)
- Operation Rolling Thunder (1965-1968)
- Operation Steel Tiger (1965-1968)
- Operation Arc Light (1965-1973)
- Operation Tiger Hound (1965-1968)
- Operation Shed Light (1966-1972)
- Operation Carolina Moon (1966)
- Operation Wahiawa (1966)
- Operation Bolo (1967)
- Operation Popeye (1967-1972
- Operation Niagara (1968)
- Operation Igloo White (1968-1973

- Operation Giant Lance (1969)
- Operation Commando Hunt (1968-1972)
- Operation Menu (1969-1970)
- Operation Patio (1970)
- Operation Freedom Deal (1970-1973)
- Operation Linebacker (1972)
- Operation Enhance Plus (1972)
- Operation Linebacker II (1972)
- Operation Homecoming (1973)
- Operation Baby Lift (1975)
- Operation Eagle Pull (1975)
- Operation Frequent Wind (1975)

- National Order of Vietnam
- Vietnam Military Merit Medal
- Vietnam Distinguished Service Order
- Vietnam Meritorious Service Medal
- Vietnam Special Service Medal
- Vietnam Gallantry Cross
- Vietnam Air Gallantry Cross
- Vietnam Navy Gallantry Cross
- Vietnam Armed Forces Honor Medal
- Vietnam Civil Actions Medal
- Vietnam Staff Service Medal
- Vietnam Technical Service Medal
- Vietnam Wound Medal
- Vietnam Campaign Medal
- Presidential Unit Citation (Vietnam)
- Vietnam Gallantry Cross Unit Citation
- Vietnam Civil Actions Unit Citation

- Golden Star Medal
- Ho Chi Minh Order
- Defeat American Aggression Badge
- Vietnam Liberation Order
- Resolution for Victory Order

- Medal of Honor rare
- Distinguished Service Cross rare
- Navy Cross uncommon
- Air Force Cross uncommon
- Silver Star uncommon
- Purple Heart frequent
- Bronze Star frequent
- Presidential Unit Citation rare
- Vietnam Service Medal very common
- National Defense Service Medal very common
- Commendation Medal common

- "Fatigue Press" at Fort Hood,
- "Last Harass" at Fort Gordon, Georgia
- "Pawn"s Pawn" at Fort Leonard Wood, Missouri

- "Ultimate Weapon" at Fort Dix, New Jersey
- "Attitude Check" at Camp Pendleton, California
- "Green Machine" at Fort Greely, Alaska
- "Napalm" at Fort Campbell, Tennessee
- "Arctic Arsenal" at Fort Greely, Alaska
- "Black Voice" at Fort McClellan, Alabama
- "Fragging Action" at Fort Dix
- "Fort Polk Puke" at Fort Polk, Louisiana
- "Custer"s Last Stand" at Fort Riley, Kansas
- "Whack!" from the Women"s Army Corps School
- "Where Are We?" at Fort Huachuca, Arizona
- "Voice of the Lumpen" (affiliated with the Black Panther Party) in Frankfurt
- "Can You Bear McNair?" at McNair Barracks, Berlin
- "Seasick" at Subic Bay
- "The Man Can"t Win If You Grin" in Okinawa
- "Korea Free Press"
- "Semper Fi" in Japan
- "Stars and Bars" in England
- "Separated From Life" in England
- "Duck Power" in San Diego
- "Harass the Brass" at Canute Air Force Base, Illinois
- "All Hands Abandon Ship", Newport, Rhode Island
- "Now Hear This", Long Beach
- "Potemkin" on the USS Forestall
- "Star Spangled Bummer" at Wright-Patterson Air Force Base in Ohio
- "Fat Albert"s Death Ship" in Charlestown
- "Pig Boat Blues", USS Agerholm
- "Special Weapons", Kirtland AFB, New Mexico
- "I Will Fear No Evil", Kirtland AFB, New Mexico
- "Blows Against the Empire", Kirtland AFB, New Mexico

source: "The American War" - see references below

- Bao Dai
- Duong Van Minh
- Madame Ngo Dinh Nhu
- Ngo Dinh Diem
- Ngo Dinh Nhu
- Nguyen Cao Ky
- Nguyen Khanh
- Nguyen Van Thieu

- Creighton W. Abrams
- Dean Acheson
- Spiro Agnew
- Ellsworth Bunker
- McGeorge Bundy
- William Bundy
- William Calley
- Clark Clifford
- William Colby
- A. Peter Dewey
- John Foster Dulles
- Dwight D. Eisenhower
- Daniel Ellsberg
- J. William Fulbright
- Barry Goldwater
- David Hackworth
- Alexander Haig
- Paul D. Harkins
- Seymour Hersh
- Hubert Humphrey
- Lyndon Johnson
- John F. Kennedy
- John Kerry
- Henry Kissinger
- Melvin Laird
- Edward Lansdale
- Henry Cabot Lodge, Jr.
- Mike Mansfield
- Graham Martin
- Robert McNamara
- George McGovern
- Richard Nixon
- Pete Peterson
- Charika Pugh
- Dean Rusk

- Maxwell D. Taylor
- Hugh C. Thompson, Jr
- John Paul Vann
- Gary Varsel
- William Westmoreland

- Ho Chi Minh
- Le Duan
- Tran Van Tra
- Le Duc Tho
- Pham Van Dong
- General Giap
- Poewll Ward

- Lon Nol
- Pol Pot
- Norodom Sihanouk
- Sirik Matak
- Sosthene Fernandez

- David H. Hackworth. 1989 About Face
- A.J. Langguth. 2000. Our Vietnam: the War 1954-1975.
- Mann, Robert. 2002. Grand Delusion, A: America"s Descent Into Vietnam.
- Windrow, Martin. 2005. The Last Valley: Dien Bien Phu and the French Defeat in Vietnam.
- Bernard Fall. 1967. Hell in a Very Small Place: the Siege of Dien Bien Phu.
- Harvey Pekar. 2003. American Splendor: Unsung Hero
- Prados, John. 2000. The Blood Road: The Ho Chi Minh Trail and the Vietnam War.
- Prados, John. 1999. Valley of Decision: The Siege of Khe Sanh.
- Shultz, Robert H. Jr. 2000. The Secret War Against Hanoi: The Untold Story of Spies, Saboteurs, and Covert Warriors in North Vietnam.
- Plaster, John L. 1998. SOG: The Secret Wars of America"s Commandos in Vietnam.
- Murphy, Edward F. 1995. Dak To: America"s Sky Soldiers in South Vietnam"s Central Highlands.
- Nolan, Keith W. 1996. The Battle for Saigon: Tet 1968.
- Nolan, Keith W. 1996. Sappers in the Wire: The Life and Death of Firebase Mary Ann.
- Nolan, Keith W. 1992. Operation Buffalo: USMC Fight for the DMZ.
- Nolan, Keith W. 2003. Ripcord : Screaming Eagles Under Siege, Vietnam 1970.
- Robert S. McNamara. 1996. In Retrospect: The Tragedy and Lessons of Vietnam.
- Larry Berman. 2002. No Peace, No Honor: Nixon, Kissinger, and Betrayal in Vietnam.
- Bergerud, Eric M. 1994. Red Thunder, Tropic Lightning: The World of a Combat Division in Vietnam.
- Bernard Edelman. 2002. Dear America: Letters Home from Vietnam.
- Darrel D. Whitcomb. 1999. The Rescue of Bat 21.
- Oberdorfer, Don. 1971. Tet: the Story of a Battle and its Historic Aftermath.
- LTG Harold G. Moore and Joseph L. Galloway. 1992. We Were Soldiers Once ... And Young.
- Duiker, William J. 2002. Ho Chi Minh: A Life.
- John Laurence. 2002. The Cat from Hue: A Vietnam War Story.
- Emerson, Gloria. 1976. Winners and Losers: Battles, Retreats, Gains, Losses and Ruins from a Long War.
- Philip Caputo. 1977. A Rumor of War.

- Al Santoli. 1981. Everything We Had: an Oral History of the Vietnam War by 33 American Soldiers Who Fought It.
- Robert C. Mason. 1983. Chickenhawk.
- Michael Herr. 1977. Dispatches.
- Joseph T. Ward. 1991. Dear Mom: a Sniper"s Vietnam.
- Hemphill, Robert. 1998. Platoon: Bravo Company.
- Noam Chomsky. 1967. The Responsibility of Intellectuals.
- Moore, Robin. 1965 The Green Berets (ISBN 0-312-98492-8)

- Robert Olen Butler. 1992.

Chapter 5. Public Opinion

Public opinion	Public opinion is the aggregate of individual attitudes or beliefs held by the adult population. Public opinion can also be defined as the complex collection of opinions of many different people and the sum of all their views. The principle approaches to the study of Public opinion may be divided into 4 categories: a) quantitative measurement of opinion distributions; b) investigation of the internal relationships among the individual opinions that make up Public opinion on an issue; c) description or analysis of the public role of Public opinion; d) study both of the communication media that disseminate the ideas on which opinions are based and of the uses that propagandists and other manipulators make of these media. Public opinion as a concept gained credence with the rise of "public" in the eighteenth century.
Politics	Politics are an integral part of the Unification Church"s concerns and activities, although the church itself largely remains aloof from Politics The degree of involvement of the movement, as well as some of its specific stances, have also been part of the reason for the movement"s controversial status over the years. The belief in the establishment of a literal Kingdom of Heaven on earth and Rev. Moon"s teaching that religion alone is not enough to bring this provides a motivation for political involvement.
Public Service of Canada	The Public Service of Canada is the staff of the federal government of Canada. Its function is to support the Canadian monarch, and to handle the hiring of employees for the federal government ministries. It is represented by the Governor General, and the appointed [[list of Canadian ministries | ministry].
National party	The National Party of Belize was a political party established mainly to fight the anti-colonialist movement propagated by the People"s United Party (PUP.) It had only minimal success and was eventually deregistered. The Party was established on August 21, 1951 and dissolved on June 26, 1958.
Exit poll	An election Exit poll is a poll of voters taken immediately after they have exited the polling stations. Unlike an opinion poll, which asks whom the voter plans to vote for or some similar formulation, an Exit poll asks whom the voter actually voted for. A similar poll conducted before actual voters have voted is called an entrance poll.
Opinion poll	An Opinion poll is a survey of public opinion from a particular sample. Opinion poll s are usually designed to represent the opinions of a population by conducting a series of questions and then extrapolating generalities in ratio or within confidence intervals.

The first known example of an Opinion poll was a local straw poll conducted by The Harrisburg Pennsylvanian in 1824, showing Andrew Jackson leading John Quincy Adams by 335 votes to 169 in the contest for the United States Presidency.

Opinion polls

This article is a list of nation-wide public opinion polls that have been conducted relating to the United States presidential election, 2012, presumed to be between incumbent Democratic President Barack Obama and Republican and third party/independent challengers.

None of these candidates have, as of July 2009, formed an exploratory committee or formally showed interest in the presidency.

Among 9 polls conducted, Romney has won 4, Palin has won 2, Huckabee won 2 and Guiliani 1.

Presidential election

A presidential election was held in Chile on 4 September 1970. A narrow plurality (36.6 percent of the total vote) was secured by Salvador Allende, the candidate of the Popular Unity coalition of leftist parties. Because he did not obtain an absolute majority, his election required a further vote by the National Congress of Chile which resulted in Allende assuming the presidency in accordance with the Chilean Constitution of 1925.

Political socialization

Political socialization is a concept concerning the "study of the developmental processes by which children and adolescents acquire political cognition, attitudes and behaviors" (Davidson, 2009, p. 20.)

These Agents of Socialization all influence in one degree or another an individual"s political opinions: Family, Media, Friends, Teachers, Religion, Race, Gender, Age, Geography, etc.

Public policy

Public policy is the body of principles that underpin the operation of legal systems in each state. This addresses the social, moral and economic values that tie a society together: values that vary in different cultures and change over time. Law regulates behaviour either to reinforce existing social expectations or to encourage constructive change, and laws are most likely to be effective when they are consistent with the most generally accepted societal norms and reflect the collective morality of the society.

Popular culture

Popular culture is the totality of distinct memes, ideas, perspectives, and attitudes that are deemed preferred per an informal consensus within the mainstream of a given culture. Heavily influenced by mass media (at least from the early 20th century onward) and perpetuated by that culture"s vernacular language, this collection of ideas permeates the everyday lives of the society. Popular culture is often viewed as being trivial and "dumbed-down" in order to find consensual acceptance throughout the mainstream.

Democratic party	Democratic Party was a political party in Gambia. The party was founded during the pre-independence period in the colony of Bathurst (currently the national capital Banjul.) Ahead of the 1962 election, the Democratic Party merged with the Muslim Congress Party to form the Democratic Congress Alliance.
Ethnicity	Ethnicity plays a prominent role in pornography. Distinct genres of pornography focus on performers of specific ethnic groups, or on the depiction of interracial sexual activity. Ethnic pornography typically employs ethnic and racial stereotypes in its depiction of performers.
Federalism	Federalism is a political philosophy in which a group of members are bound together ">covenant) with a governing representative head. The term Federalism is also used to describe a system of the government in which sovereignty is constitutionally divided between a central governing authority and constituent political units (like states or provinces.) Federalism is a system in which the power to govern is shared between national and central(state) governments, creating what is often called a federation.
Social Security	Social Security, in Australia, refers to a system of social welfare payments provided by Commonwealth Government of Australia. These payments are administered by a Government body named Centrelink. In Australia, most benefits are subject to a means test.
Social class	The most basic class distinction is between the powerful and the powerless. People in Social class es with greater power attempt to cement their own positions in society and maintain their ranking above the lower Social class es in the social hierarchy. Social class es with a great deal of power are usually viewed as elites, at least within their own societies.
Party identification	Party identification is a political term to describe a voter"s underlying allegiance to a political party. The term was first used in the United States in the 1950s, but use of the term has decreased in usage as the process of party dealignment has accelerated. According to modern theories of political socialization, partisanship is typically formed between the ages of 18 and 24, and is generally stable after that.
Socioeconomic status	Socioeconomic status is an economic and sociological combined total measure of a person"s work experience and of an individual"s or family"s economic and social position relative to others, based on income, education, and occupation. When analyzing a family"s SES, the household income earners" education and occupation are examined, as well as combined income, versus with an individual, when their own attributes are assessed. Socioeconomic status is typically broken into three categories, high SES, middle SES, and low SES to describe the three areas a family or an individual may fall into.

Region	Region is most commonly a geographical term that is used in various ways among the different branches of geography. In general, a Region is a medium-scale area of land or water, smaller than the whole areas of interest (which could be, for example, the world, a nation, a river basin, mountain range, and so on), and larger than a specific site. A Region may be seen as a collection of smaller units (as in "the New England states") or as one part of a larger whole (as in "the New England Region of the United States".)
Right	A right is the legal or moral entitlement to do or refrain from doing something thing or recognition in civil society. Rights serve as rules of interaction between people, and, as such, they place constraints and obligations upon the actions of individuals or groups (for example, if one has a right to life, this means that others do not have the liberty to kill him.) Most modern conceptions of rights are universalist and egalitarian -- in other words, equal rights are granted to all people.
Iraq	Iraq , officially the Republic of Iraq JumhÅ«rÄ«yat Al-Ê¿IrÄ q, Kurdish: ÙƒÙˆÙ…Ø§Ø±ÛŒ Ø¹ÛŽØ±Ø§Ù‚â€Ž, Komara Iraqê), is a country in Western Asia spanning most of the northwestern end of the Zagros mountain range, the eastern part of the Syrian Desert and the northern part of the Arabian Desert. Iraq shares borders with Jordan to the west, Syria to the northwest, Turkey to the north, Iran to the east, and Kuwait and Saudi Arabia to the south. Iraq has a narrow section of coastline measuring 58 km between Umm Qasr and Al Faw on the Persian Gulf.
New Deal	The New Deal is a programme of active labour market policies introduced in the United Kingdom by the Labour government in 1998, initially funded by a one off Â£5bn windfall tax on privatised utility companies. The stated purpose is to reduce unemployment by providing training, subsidised employment and voluntary work to the unemployed. Spending on the New Deal was Â£1.3 billion in 2001.

Led by Lorrin A. Thurston and Sanford B. Dole, the Provisional Government ruled over HawaiÊ»i until the formal establishment of a republic. Pictured above is the cabinet, (Left to Right) James A. King, Sanford B. Dole, William O. Smith and Peter C. Jones.

Capital | Flag

Capital
Language(s)
Government
Provisional Government
- 1893-1894
Historical era
- Monarchy overthrown
- Republic declared
Currency

Honolulu
Hawaiian, English
Not specified

Committee of Safety
New Imperialism
January 17, 1893
July 4, 1894
U.S. dollar, Hawaiian dollar

The Provisional Government of HawaiÊ»i was proclaimed on January 17, 1893 by the 13 member Committee of Safety under the leadership of Lorrin A. Thurston and Sanford B. Dole. It governed the Kingdom of HawaiÊ»i after the overthrow of Queen LiliÊ»uokalani until the Republic of HawaiÊ»i was established on July 4, 1894.

Capital punishment	Capital punishment, the death penalty or execution, is the killing of a person by judicial process for retribution, general deterrence, and incapacitation. Crimes that can result in a death penalty are known as capital crimes or capital offences. The term capital originates from Latin capitalis, literally "regarding the head" .
Pro-life	Pro-life is a term representing a variety of perspectives and activist movements in medical ethics. It is most commonly used, especially in the media and popular discourse, to refer to opposition to abortion. More generally, the term describes a political and ethical view which maintains that human fetuses and embryos are persons and therefore have a right to live.
Penalty	In the Latter Day Saint movement, a Penalty is an oath made by participants of the original Nauvoo Endowment instituted by Joseph Smith, Jr. in 1843 and further developed by Brigham Young after Smith"s death. Mormon antagonists refer to the Penalty as a blood oath, because it required the participant to swear never to reveal certain key symbols of the Endowment ceremony, including the Penalty itself, while symbolically enacting ways in which a person may be executed.
KSA	A KSA Skills, and Abilities, is a series of narrative statements that are required when applying to Federal government job openings. KSA"s are used to determine, along with resumes, who the best applicants are when several candidates qualify for a job. The knowledge, skills and abilities (KSA"s) necessary for the successful performance of a position are contained on each job vacancy announcement.
Bill of Rights	A Bill of rights is a list or summary of rights that are considered important and essential by a nation. The purpose of these bills is to protect those rights against infringement by the government. The term "Bill of rights" originates from Britain, where it referred to a bill that was passed by Parliament in 1689.
Civil liberties	Civil liberties are freedoms that protect an individual from the government of the nation in which they reside. Civil liberties set limits for government so that it cannot abuse its power and interfere unduly with the lives of its citizens.
	Common Civil liberties include the rights of people, freedom of religion, and freedom of speech, and additionally, the right to due process, to a fair trial, to own property, and to privacy.

Taliban	The Taliban, also Taleban, is a Sunni Islamist, predominantly Pashtun fundamentalist religious and political movement that governed Afghanistan from 1996 until 2001, when its leaders were removed from power by Northern Alliance and NATO forces. It has regrouped and since 2004 revived as a strong insurgency movement fighting a guerrilla war against the current government of Afghanistan, Pakistan, allied NATO forces participating in Operation Enduring Freedom, and the NATO-led International Security Assistance Force (ISAF.) It operates in Afghanistan and the Frontier Tribal Areas of Pakistan.
Anti-Americanism	Dictionaries tend to define Anti-Americanism, often anti-American sentiment, as a widespread opposition or hostility to the people, government or policies of the United States. In practice, a broad range of attitudes and actions critical of or opposed to the United States have been labeled Anti-Americanism. Thus, the nature and applicability of the term is often disputed.
Iran	Iran , officially the Islamic Republic of Iran and formerly known internationally as Persia until 1935, is a country in Central Eurasia, located on the northeastern shore of the Persian Gulf, northwestern shore of the Gulf of Oman, and the southern shore of the Caspian Sea. Both "Persia" and "Iran" are used interchangeably in cultural context; however, Iran is the name used officially in political context. The name Iran is a cognate of Aryan, and means "Land of the Aryans".
Iranian hostage crisis	The Iranian hostage crisis was a diplomatic crisis between Iran and the United States where 53 Americans were held hostage for 444 days from November 4, 1979 to January 20, 1981, after a group of Islamist students and militants took over the American embassy in support of the Iranian Revolution.
	The episode reached a climax when, after failed attempts to negotiate a release, the United States military attempted a rescue operation, Operation Eagle Claw, on April 24, 1980, which resulted in a failed mission, the crash of two aircraft and the deaths of eight American servicemen and one Iranian civilian. It ended with the signing of the Algiers Accords in Algeria on January 19, 1981.
Axis of evil	"Axis of evil" is a term coined by United States President George W. Bush in his State of the Union Address on January 29, 2002 in order to describe governments that he accused of helping terrorism and seeking weapons of mass destruction. President Bush named Iran, Iraq and North Korea in his speech. President Bush"s presidency was marked by this notion as a justification for the War on Terror.
Government spending	Government spending or government expenditure is classified by economists into three main types. Government purchases of goods and services for current use are classed as government consumption. Government purchases of goods and services intended to create future benefits, such as infrastructure investment or research spending, are classed as government investment.

Chapter 5. Public Opinion

Conservatism	Conservatism is a political and social term from the Latin verb conservare meaning to save or preserve. As the name suggests it usually indicates support for tradition and traditional values though the meaning has changed in different countries and time periods. The modern political term conservative was used by French politician Chateaubriand in 1819.
Germany	Germany), officially the Federal Republic of Germany), is a country in Central Europe. It is bordered to the north by the North Sea, Denmark, and the Baltic Sea; to the east by Poland and the Czech Republic; to the south by Austria and Switzerland; and to the west by France, Luxembourg, Belgium, and the Netherlands. The territory of Germany covers 357,021 square kilometers and is influenced by a temperate seasonal climate.
Foreign policy	A country"s Foreign policy is a set of goals outlining how the country will interact with other countries economically, politically, socially and militarily, and to a lesser extent, how the country will interact with non-state actors. The aforementioned interaction is evaluated and monitored in attempts to maximize benefits of multilateral international cooperation. Foreign policies are designed to help protect a country"s national interests, national security, ideological goals, and economic prosperity.
North Atlantic Treaty	The North Atlantic Treaty is the treaty that brought North Atlantic Treaty O into existence, signed in Washington, DC on April 4, 1949. The original twelve nations that signed it and thus became the founding members of North Atlantic Treaty O were: Map of North Atlantic Treaty O countries chronological membership. Later the following nations joined: When Germany was reunified in 1990, the country as a whole became a member of North Atlantic Treaty O. During the April 2008 summit in Bucharest, Croatia and Albania were officially invited to join North Atlantic Treaty O. They both signed the treaty and officially joined North Atlantic Treaty O on April 1st, 2009
North Atlantic Treaty Organization	During the early years of the Cold War, the United States Air Force deployed thousands of personnel and hundreds of combat aircraft to France to counter the buildup of Soviet forces in Eastern Europe. The Cold War that developed in Europe during 1948 and escalated into the attempted seizure of West Berlin, convinced the western nations to form a common defense organization. Discussions led to a multinational defense agreement that evolved into the North Atlantic Treaty Organization .

Unilateralism	Unilateralism is any doctrine or agenda that supports one-sided action. Such action may be in disregard for other parties, or as an expression of a commitment toward a direction which other parties may find agreeable. Unilateralism is a neologism, (used in all countries) coined to be an antonym for multilateralism --the doctrine which asserts the benefits of participation from as many parties as possible.
Anti-war	The term Anti-war usually refers to the opposition to a particular nation"s decision to start or carry on an armed conflict, unconditional of a maybe-existing just cause. The term can also refer to pacifism, which is the opposition to all use of military force during conflicts. Many activists distinguish between Anti-war movements and peace movements.

Chapter 6. The News Media

CNN effect	The CNN effect is a theory in political science and media studies that postulates that the development of the popular 24-hour international television news channel known as Cable News Network had a major impact on the conduct of states" foreign policy in the late Cold War period and that CNN and its subsequent industry competitors have had a similar impact in the post-Cold War era. While the free press has, in its role as the "Fourth Estate", always had an influence on policy-making in representative democracies, proponents of the CNN effect argue that "the extent, depth, and speed of the new global media have created a new species of effects" qualitatively different from those which preceded them historically. The term"s coinage reflects the pioneering role played by the network CNN in the field, whose "saturation coverage" of events like the Tiananmen Square protests of 1989, the fall of Communism in eastern Europe, the first Gulf War, and the Battle of Mogadishu was viewed as being strongly influential in bringing images and issues to the immediate forefront of American political consciousness and beyond.
Iraq	Iraq , officially the Republic of Iraq JumhÅ«rÄ«yat Al-Ê¿IrÄ q, Kurdish: ÙƒÙˆÙ…Ø§Ø±ÛŒ Ø¹ÛŽØ±Ø§Ù‚â€Ž, Komara Iraqê), is a country in Western Asia spanning most of the northwestern end of the Zagros mountain range, the eastern part of the Syrian Desert and the northern part of the Arabian Desert. Iraq shares borders with Jordan to the west, Syria to the northwest, Turkey to the north, Iran to the east, and Kuwait and Saudi Arabia to the south. Iraq has a narrow section of coastline measuring 58 km between Umm Qasr and Al Faw on the Persian Gulf.
National Guard	The National Guard was the name given at the time of the French Revolution to the militias formed in each city, in imitation of the National Guard created in Paris. It was a military force separate from the regular army. Initially under the command of the Marquis de la Fayette, then briefly under the Marquis de Mandat, it was strongly identified until the summer of 1792 with the middle class and its support for constitutional monarchy.
News media	The News media refers to the section of the mass media that focuses on presenting current news to the public. These include print media (newspapers, magazines); broadcast media (radio stations, television stations, television networks), and increasingly Internet-based media (World Wide Web pages, weblogs.) The term news trade refers to the concept of the News media as a business separate from, but integrally connected to, the profession of journalism.
Bill of Rights	A Bill of rights is a list or summary of rights that are considered important and essential by a nation. The purpose of these bills is to protect those rights against infringement by the government. The term "Bill of rights" originates from Britain, where it referred to a bill that was passed by Parliament in 1689.
Civil liberties	Civil liberties are freedoms that protect an individual from the government of the nation in which they reside. Civil liberties set limits for government so that it cannot abuse its power and interfere unduly with the lives of its citizens.

Common Civil liberties include the rights of people, freedom of religion, and freedom of speech, and additionally, the right to due process, to a fair trial, to own property, and to privacy.

First Amendment	The First Amendment to the United States Constitution is the part of the United States Bill of Rights that expressly prohibits the United States Congress from making laws "respecting an establishment of religion" or that prohibit the free exercise of religion, infringe the freedom of speech, infringe the freedom of the press, limit the right to peaceably assemble, or limit the right to petition the government for a redress of grievances. Although the First Amendment only explicitly applies to the Congress, the Supreme Court has interpreted it as applying to the executive and judicial branches. Additionally, in the 20th century, the Supreme Court held that the Due Process Clause of the Fourteenth Amendment applies the limitations of the First Amendment to each state, including any local government within a state.
Right	A right is the legal or moral entitlement to do or refrain from doing something thing or recognition in civil society. Rights serve as rules of interaction between people, and, as such, they place constraints and obligations upon the actions of individuals or groups (for example, if one has a right to life, this means that others do not have the liberty to kill him.) Most modern conceptions of rights are universalist and egalitarian -- in other words, equal rights are granted to all people.
Anti-Americanism	Dictionaries tend to define Anti-Americanism, often anti-American sentiment, as a widespread opposition or hostility to the people, government or policies of the United States. In practice, a broad range of attitudes and actions critical of or opposed to the United States have been labeled Anti-Americanism. Thus, the nature and applicability of the term is often disputed.
Public Service of Canada	The Public Service of Canada is the staff of the federal government of Canada. Its function is to support the Canadian monarch, and to handle the hiring of employees for the federal government ministries. It is represented by the Governor General, and the appointed [[list of Canadian ministries | ministry].
Brazil	Brazil, officially the Federative Republic of Brazil (Portuguese: República Federativa do Brasil) Â·), is a country in South America. It is the fifth largest country by geographical area, occupying nearly half of South America, the fifth most populous country, and the fourth most populous democracy in the world. Bounded by the Atlantic Ocean on the east, Brazil has a coastline of over 7,491 kilometers (4,655 mi.)
Israel	Israel officially the State of Israel , Medinat Yisra"el; Arabic: Ø¯ ÙŽÙˆÙˆÙ,ÙŽØ¥Ùˆ Ø¥Ù Ø³Ù'رÙŽØ§Ø¡Ù ÙŠÙÙ,ÙŽâ€Ž, Dawlat IsrÄ "Ä«l), is a country in Western Asia located on the eastern shore of the Mediterranean Sea. It borders Lebanon in the north, Syria in the northeast, Jordan in the east, and Egypt on the southwest, and contains geographically diverse features within its relatively small area. Also adjacent are the West Bank to the east and Gaza Strip to the southwest.

Japan	Japan is an island nation in East Asia. Located in the Pacific Ocean, it lies to the east of the Sea of Japan, People"s Republic of China, North Korea, South Korea and Russia, stretching from the Sea of Okhotsk in the north to the East China Sea and Taiwan in the south. The characters which make up Japan"s name mean "sun-origin", which is why Japan is sometimes identified as the "Land of the Rising Sun".
Sweden	Sweden , officially the Kingdom of Sweden), is a Nordic country on the Scandinavian Peninsula in Northern Europe. Sweden has land borders with Norway to the west and Finland to the northeast, and it is connected to Denmark by the Öresund Bridge in the south. At 450,000 km^2 (173,746 sq mi), Sweden is the third largest country in the European Union in terms of area, and it has a total population of over 9.2 million.

Led by Lorrin A. Thurston and Sanford B. Dole, the Provisional Government ruled over HawaiÊ»i until the formal establishment of a republic. Pictured above is the cabinet, (Left to Right) James A. King, Sanford B. Dole, William O. Smith and Peter C. Jones.

Capital	Flag
Capital	Honolulu
Language(s)	Hawaiian, English
Government	Not specified
Provisional Government	
- 1893-1894	Committee of Safety
Historical era	New Imperialism
- Monarchy overthrown	January 17, 1893
- Republic declared	July 4, 1894
Currency	U.S. dollar, Hawaiian dollar

	The Provisional Government of HawaiÊ»i was proclaimed on January 17, 1893 by the 13 member Committee of Safety under the leadership of Lorrin A. Thurston and Sanford B. Dole. It governed the Kingdom of HawaiÊ»i after the overthrow of Queen LiliÊ»uokalani until the Republic of HawaiÊ»i was established on July 4, 1894.
Capital punishment	Capital punishment, the death penalty or execution, is the killing of a person by judicial process for retribution, general deterrence, and incapacitation. Crimes that can result in a death penalty are known as capital crimes or capital offences. The term capital originates from Latin capitalis, literally "regarding the head" .
Joseph	Joseph or Josephus Scottus (died between 791 and 804), called the Deacon, was an Irish scholar, diplomat, poet, and ecclesiastic, a minor figure in the Carolingian Renaissance. He has been cited as an early example of "the scholar in public life".

His early life is obscure, but he studied first under Colcu, probably at Clonmacnoise, and then under Alcuin at York, probably in the 770s.

Spain

Spain is a country located in southwestern Europe on the Iberian Peninsula. Its mainland is bordered to the south and east by the Mediterranean Sea except for a small land boundary with Gibraltar; to the north by France, Andorra, and the Bay of Biscay; and to the northwest and west by the Atlantic Ocean and Portugal. Spanish territory also includes the Balearic Islands in the Mediterranean, the Canary Islands in the Atlantic Ocean off the African coast, and two autonomous cities in North Africa, Ceuta and Melilla, that border Morocco.

Tribune

Tribune is a democratic socialist weekly, currently a magazine though in the past more often a newspaper, published in London. It considers itself "A thorn in the side of all governments, constructively to Labour, unforgiving to Conservatives."

Tribune was set up in early 1937 by two left-wing Labour Party Members of Parliament (MPs), Stafford Cripps and George Strauss, to back the Unity Campaign, an attempt to secure an anti-fascist and anti-appeasement United Front between the Labour Party and socialist parties to its left which involved Cripps"s (Labour-affiliated) Socialist League, the Independent Labour Party and the Communist Party of Great Britain (CP.)

The paper"s first editor was William Mellor, and its journalists included Michael Foot and Barbara Betts (later Barbara Castle.)

Air America

Air America was an American passenger and cargo airline established in 1946 and covertly owned and operated by the Central Intelligence Agency (CIA) from 1950 to 1976. It supplied and supported covert operations in Southeast Asia during the Vietnam War.

In 1951, the parent company of Air America"s forerunner, Civil Air Transport (CAT), was reorganized.

Foreign Policy

A country"s Foreign policy is a set of goals outlining how the country will interact with other countries economically, politically, socially and militarily, and to a lesser extent, how the country will interact with non-state actors. The aforementioned interaction is evaluated and monitored in attempts to maximize benefits of multilateral international cooperation. Foreign policies are designed to help protect a country"s national interests, national security, ideological goals, and economic prosperity.

Nation

A nation are regional corporations of students at university, once widespread across central and northern Europe in medieval times, they are now largely restricted to the two ancient universities of Sweden. The students, who were all born within the same region, usually spoke the same language, and expected to be ruled by their own familiar law. The most similar comparison in the Anglo-world to the nation system is in the collegiate system of older British universities or fraternities at American universities; however, both of these comparisons are imperfect.

Republic	The Republic is a left-of-centre political party in the Faroe Islands committed to Faroese Independence. It was founded in 1948 as a reaction to independence not being proclaimed after a public vote on the matter showed a marginal majority for it in 1946. In 1998 Høgni Hoydal succeeded Heini O. Heinesen as party leader.
Thing	A Thing or ting was the governing assembly in Germanic societies, made up of the free people of the community and presided by lawspeakers, meeting in a place called a thingstead. Today the term lives on in the official names of national legislatures and political and judicial institutions in the North-Germanic countries. The Old Norse, Old Frisian and Old English þing with the meaning "assembly" is identical in origin to the English word Thing, German Ding, Dutch ding, and modern Scandinavian ting when meaning "object".

Public opinion	Public opinion is the aggregate of individual attitudes or beliefs held by the adult population. Public opinion can also be defined as the complex collection of opinions of many different people and the sum of all their views. The principle approaches to the study of Public opinion may be divided into 4 categories:
	
	    a) quantitative measurement of opinion distributions;
	    b) investigation of the internal relationships among the individual opinions that make up Public opinion on an issue;
	    c) description or analysis of the public role of Public opinion;
	    d) study both of the communication media that disseminate the ideas on which opinions are based and of the uses that propagandists and other manipulators make of these media.
	
	Public opinion as a concept gained credence with the rise of "public" in the eighteenth century.

Individualism	Individualism is the moral stance, political philosophy, ideology, or social outlook that stresses independence and self-reliance. Individualists promote the exercise of one"s goals and desires, while opposing most external interference upon one"s choices, whether by society, or any other group or institution. Individualism is opposed to collectivism, which stress that communal, community, group, societal, or national goals should take priority over individual goals.
Boosterism	Boosterism is the act of "boosting," or promoting, one"s town, city with the goal of improving public perception of it. Boosting can be as simple as "talking up" the entity at a party or as elaborate as establishing a visitors" bureau. It is somewhat associated with American small towns.

95

Ownership	Ownership is the state or fact of exclusive rights and control over property, which may be an object, land/real estate or intellectual property. An Ownership right is also referred to as title. The concept of Ownership has existed for thousands of years and in all cultures.
Infotainment	Infotainment is "information-based media content or programming that also includes entertainment content in an effort to enhance popularity with audiences and consumers." It is a neologistic portmanteau of information and entertainment, referring to a type of media which provides a combination of information and entertainment. According to many dictionaries Infotainment is always television, and the term is "mainly disapproving." However, many self-described Infotainment websites exist which provide a variety of functions and services. The label "Infotainment" is emblematic of concern and criticism that journalism is devolving from a medium which conveys serious information about issues that affect the public interest, into a form of entertainment which happens to have fresh "facts" in the mix.
Politics	Politics are an integral part of the Unification Church"s concerns and activities, although the church itself largely remains aloof from Politics The degree of involvement of the movement, as well as some of its specific stances, have also been part of the reason for the movement"s controversial status over the years. The belief in the establishment of a literal Kingdom of Heaven on earth and Rev. Moon"s teaching that religion alone is not enough to bring this provides a motivation for political involvement.
Identity	Identity is an umbrella term used throughout the social sciences to describe an individual"s comprehension of him or herself as a discrete, separate entity. This term, though generic, can be further specified by the disciplines of psychology and sociology, including the two forms of social psychology. A psychological Identity relates to self-image (a person"s mental model of him or herself), self-esteem, and individuality.
Intelligence	Intelligence refers to discrete information with currency and relevance, and the abstraction, evaluation, and understanding of such information for its accuracy and value.
Taliban	The Taliban, also Taleban, is a Sunni Islamist, predominantly Pashtun fundamentalist religious and political movement that governed Afghanistan from 1996 until 2001, when its leaders were removed from power by Northern Alliance and NATO forces. It has regrouped and since 2004 revived as a strong insurgency movement fighting a guerrilla war against the current government of Afghanistan, Pakistan, allied NATO forces participating in Operation Enduring Freedom, and the NATO-led International Security Assistance Force (ISAF.) It operates in Afghanistan and the Frontier Tribal Areas of Pakistan.

Chapter 6. The News Media

Axis of evil	"Axis of evil" is a term coined by United States President George W. Bush in his State of the Union Address on January 29, 2002 in order to describe governments that he accused of helping terrorism and seeking weapons of mass destruction. President Bush named Iran, Iraq and North Korea in his speech. President Bush"s presidency was marked by this notion as a justification for the War on Terror.
Power	Power in international relations is defined in several different ways. Political scientists, historians, and practitioners of international relations (diplomats) have used the following concepts of political Power: • Power as a goal of states or leaders; • Power as a measure of influence or control over outcomes, events, actors and issues; • Power as reflecting victory in conflict and the attainment of security; and, • Power as control over resources and capabilities. Modern discourse generally speaks in terms of state Power, indicating both economic and military Power. Those states that have significant amounts of Power within the international system are referred to as middle powers, regional powers, great powers, superpowers, or hyperpowers, although there is no commonly accepted standard for what defines a powerful state. Entities other than states can also acquire and wield Power in international relations.
Germany	Germany), officially the Federal Republic of Germany), is a country in Central Europe. It is bordered to the north by the North Sea, Denmark, and the Baltic Sea; to the east by Poland and the Czech Republic; to the south by Austria and Switzerland; and to the west by France, Luxembourg, Belgium, and the Netherlands. The territory of Germany covers 357,021 square kilometers and is influenced by a temperate seasonal climate.
Homeland	A Homeland is the concept of the place (cultural geography) to which an ethnic group holds a long history and a deep cultural association with --the country in which a particular national identity began. As a common noun, it simply connotes the country of one"s origin.
Pakistan	Pakistan), officially the Islamic Republic of Pakistan, is a country located in South Asia. It has a 1,046 kilometre coastline along the Arabian Sea and Gulf of Oman in the south, and is bordered by Afghanistan and Iran in the west, the Republic of India in the east and the People"s Republic of China in the far northeast. Tajikistan also lies adjacent to Pakistan but is separated by the narrow Wakhan Corridor.

Orange Revolution	The Orange Revolution was a series of protests and political events that took place in Ukraine from late November 2004 to January 2005, in the immediate aftermath of the run-off vote of the 2004 Ukrainian presidential election which was claimed to be marred by massive corruption, voter intimidation and direct electoral fraud. Kiev, the Ukrainian capital, was the focal point of the movement with thousands of protesters demonstrating daily. Nationwide, the democratic revolution was highlighted by a series of acts of civil disobedience, sit-ins, and general strikes organized by the opposition movement.
East Timor	East Timor is a small country in Southeast Asia. It comprises the eastern half of the island of Timor, the nearby islands of Atauro and Jaco. The first people"s are thought to be descendant of Australoid and Melanesian peoples.
Indonesia	The Republic of Indonesia , is a country in Southeast Asia and Oceania. Indonesia comprises 17,508 islands, and with an estimated population of around 237 million people, it is the world"s fourth most populous country, and has the largest Muslim population in the world. Indonesia is a republic, with an elected legislature and president.
Iran	Iran , officially the Islamic Republic of Iran and formerly known internationally as Persia until 1935, is a country in Central Eurasia, located on the northeastern shore of the Persian Gulf, northwestern shore of the Gulf of Oman, and the southern shore of the Caspian Sea. Both "Persia" and "Iran" are used interchangeably in cultural context; however, Iran is the name used officially in political context. The name Iran is a cognate of Aryan, and means "Land of the Aryans".
Nationalism	Nationalism refers to an ideology, a sentiment, a form of culture, or a social movement that focuses on the nation. It is a type of collectivism emphasizing the collective of a specific nation. While there is significant debate over the historical origins of nations, nearly all specialists accept that Nationalism, at least as an ideology and social movement, is a modern phenomenon originating in Europe.
Nigeria	Nigeria , officially the Federal Republic of Nigeria, is a federal constitutional republic comprising thirty-six states and one Federal Capital Territory. The country is located in West Africa and shares land borders with the Republic of Benin in the west, Chad and Cameroon in the east, and Niger in the north. Its coast lies on the Gulf of Guinea, a part of the Atlantic Ocean, in the south.
Chile	Chile, officially the Republic of Chile , is a country in South America occupying a long and narrow coastal strip wedged between the Andes mountains and the Pacific Ocean. It borders Peru to the north, Bolivia to the northeast, Argentina to the east, and the Drake Passage at the country"s southernmost tip. It is one of only two countries in South America that does not have a border with Brazil.

Poland	Poland, officially the Republic of Poland (Rzeczpospolita Polska), is a country in Central Europe. Poland is bordered by Germany to the west; the Czech Republic and Slovakia to the south; Ukraine, Belarus and Lithuania to the east; and the Baltic Sea and Kaliningrad Oblast, a Russian exclave, to the north. The total area of Poland is 312,679 square kilometres , making it the 69th largest country in the world and the 9th largest in Europe.
Vietnam	Vietnam " href="/wiki/Battle_of_B%E1%BA%A1ch_%C4%90%E1%BA%B1ng_River_(938)">battle of Bá⁰¡ch Ä á⁰±ng River. Successive dynasties flourished along with geographic and political expansion deeper into Southeast Asia, until it was colonized by the French in the mid-19th century. Efforts to resist the French eventually led to their expulsion from the country in the mid-20th century, leaving a nation divided politically into two countries.
Vietnam War	The Vietnam War was a military conflict that occurred in Vietnam, Laos and Cambodia from 1959 to 30 April 1975. The war was fought between the communist North Vietnam, supported by its communist allies, and the government of South Vietnam, supported by the United States and other member nations of the Southeast Asia Treaty Organization (SEATO.)

The following outline is provided as an overview of and topical guide to the Vietnam War: |

Listed by starting date:

- Operation 34A - (1964)
- Operation Starlite - August 18-24 1965
- Operation Hump- November 5 1965
- Operation Crimp - January 7, 1966
- Operation Birmingham - April 1966
- Operation Hastings - Late May 1966
- Operation Prairie - August 1966
- Operation Deckhouse Five - January 6, 1967
- Operation Cedar Falls - January 8, 1967
- Operation Junction City - February 21, 1967
- Operation Francis Marion - April 6 - April 30, 1967
- Operation Union - April 21-May 16, 1967
- Operations Malheur I and Malheur II - 11 May - July 1, 1967
- Operation Baker - May 11, 1967
- Operation Scotland - See Battle of Khe Sanh
- Operation Pegasus - August 8, 1968
- Operation Dewey Canyon - January 22, 1969
- Operation Twinkletoes - 1969
- Operation Apache Snow - May 10 - May 20, 1969
- Operation Chicago Peak - April 1970
- Operation Texas Star - April - September, 1970
- Operation Ivory Coast - November 21, 1970
- Operation Jefferson Glenn - 1970-1971
- Operation Lam Son 719 - February 8, 1971
- Ho Chi Minh Campaign January 24 - April 30, 1975
- Operation Frequent Wind - April, 1975

- Battle of Ap Bac - January 2, 1963
- Battle of Kien Long - April 11 - April 15, 1964
- Battle of Thanh Hóa - July 31, 1964
- Battle of Binh Gia - December 28, 1964 - January 1, 1965
- Battle of Dong Xoai - June 10, 1965
- Battle near Minh Thanh - October 25 - October 27, 1965
- Battle of Ia Drang - November 14 - November 16, 1965
- Battle of Cu Nghi - January 28 - January 31, 1966
- Battle of Kim Son Valley - February 16 - February 28, 1966
- Battle of A Shau - March 9 - March 10, 1966
- Battle of Xa Cam My - April 11 - April 12, 1966
- First Battle of Dong Ha - Late May - June, 1966
- Battle on Minh Thanh Road - July 9, 1966
- Battle of Ä á»©c CÆ¡ - August 9, 1966
- Battle of Long Tá°§n - August 18- August 19, 1966
- Viet Cong attack on Tan Son Nhut airbase - December 4, 1966
- Battle of LZ Bird - December 27, 1966

- Battle of Tra Binh Dong - February 14 - February 15, 1967
- Battle of Hills 881 and 861 - April 24-May 9, 1967
- Nine Days in May - May 18 - May 28, 1967
- Battle of Vinh Huy - May 30 - June 2, 1967
- Battle of Con Thien - July 2 - July 3, 1967
- Battle of Dong Son - September 4, 1967
- Battle of Ong Thang - October 17, 1967
- First Battle of Loc Ninh - October 29 - November, 1967
- Battle of Dak To - November 3-November 22, 1967
- Battle in the Mekong Delta - December 4, 1967
- Battle of Tam Quan - December 6 - December 20, 1967
- Battle of Thom Tham Khe - December 27 - December 28, 1967
- Phoenix Program - 1967 - 1972
- Battle of Khe Sanh - January 21 - April 8, 1968
- Tet Offensive - January 30 - February 25, 1968
- Battle of Bien Hoa - January 31 - July 1, 1968
- Battle of Kham Duc - May 10 - May 12, 1968
- First Battle of Saigon - January 31, - February 3, 1968
- Battle of Hue - January 31, - February 25, 1968
- Tet 1969 - February 1969
- Battle of Hamburger Hill - May 10 - May 20, 1969
- Firebase Ripcord - March 12 - July 23, 1970
- Cambodian Incursion - April 29 - July 22, 1970
- Battle of Snoul - January 5 - May 30, 1971
- Easter Offensive - March 30 - October 22, 1972
- First Battle of Quang Tri - March 30 - May 1, 1972
- Battle of Loc Ninh - April 4 - April 7, 1972
- Battle of An Loc - April 20 - July 20, 1972
- Second Battle of Quang Tri - June 28 - September 16, 1972
- Battle of Phuoc Long - December 13, 1974 - January 6, 1975
- Battle of Buon Me Thuot - March 10 - March 12, 1975
- Battle of Xuan Loc - April 9 - April 20, 1975

- Operation Farm Gate
- Operation Chopper (1962)
- Operation Ranch Hand (1962-1971)
- Operation Pierce Arrow (1964)
- Operation Barrell Roll (1964-1972)
- Operation Pony Express (1965-1970)
- Operation Flaming Dart (1965)
- Operation Rolling Thunder (1965-1968)
- Operation Steel Tiger (1965-1968)
- Operation Arc Light (1965-1973)
- Operation Tiger Hound (1965-1968)
- Operation Shed Light (1966-1972)
- Operation Carolina Moon (1966)
- Operation Wahiawa (1966)
- Operation Bolo (1967)
- Operation Popeye (1967-1972
- Operation Niagara (1968)
- Operation Igloo White (1968-1973

- Operation Giant Lance (1969)
- Operation Commando Hunt (1968-1972)
- Operation Menu (1969-1970)
- Operation Patio (1970)
- Operation Freedom Deal (1970-1973)
- Operation Linebacker (1972)
- Operation Enhance Plus (1972)
- Operation Linebacker II (1972)
- Operation Homecoming (1973)
- Operation Baby Lift (1975)
- Operation Eagle Pull (1975)
- Operation Frequent Wind (1975)

- National Order of Vietnam
- Vietnam Military Merit Medal
- Vietnam Distinguished Service Order
- Vietnam Meritorious Service Medal
- Vietnam Special Service Medal
- Vietnam Gallantry Cross
- Vietnam Air Gallantry Cross
- Vietnam Navy Gallantry Cross
- Vietnam Armed Forces Honor Medal
- Vietnam Civil Actions Medal
- Vietnam Staff Service Medal
- Vietnam Technical Service Medal
- Vietnam Wound Medal
- Vietnam Campaign Medal
- Presidential Unit Citation (Vietnam)
- Vietnam Gallantry Cross Unit Citation
- Vietnam Civil Actions Unit Citation

- Golden Star Medal
- Ho Chi Minh Order
- Defeat American Aggression Badge
- Vietnam Liberation Order
- Resolution for Victory Order

- Medal of Honor rare
- Distinguished Service Cross rare
- Navy Cross uncommon
- Air Force Cross uncommon
- Silver Star uncommon
- Purple Heart frequent
- Bronze Star frequent
- Presidential Unit Citation rare
- Vietnam Service Medal very common
- National Defense Service Medal very common
- Commendation Medal common

- "Fatigue Press" at Fort Hood,
- "Last Harass" at Fort Gordon, Georgia
- "Pawn"s Pawn" at Fort Leonard Wood, Missouri

- "Ultimate Weapon" at Fort Dix, New Jersey
- "Attitude Check" at Camp Pendleton, California
- "Green Machine" at Fort Greely, Alaska
- "Napalm" at Fort Campbell, Tennessee
- "Arctic Arsenal" at Fort Greely, Alaska
- "Black Voice" at Fort McClellan, Alabama
- "Fragging Action" at Fort Dix
- "Fort Polk Puke" at Fort Polk, Louisiana
- "Custer"s Last Stand" at Fort Riley, Kansas
- "Whack!" from the Women"s Army Corps School
- "Where Are We?" at Fort Huachuca, Arizona
- "Voice of the Lumpen" (affiliated with the Black Panther Party) in Frankfurt
- "Can You Bear McNair?" at McNair Barracks, Berlin
- "Seasick" at Subic Bay
- "The Man Can"t Win If You Grin" in Okinawa
- "Korea Free Press"
- "Semper Fi" in Japan
- "Stars and Bars" in England
- "Separated From Life" in England
- "Duck Power" in San Diego
- "Harass the Brass" at Canute Air Force Base, Illinois
- "All Hands Abandon Ship", Newport, Rhode Island
- "Now Hear This", Long Beach
- "Potemkin" on the USS Forestall
- "Star Spangled Bummer" at Wright-Patterson Air Force Base in Ohio
- "Fat Albert"s Death Ship" in Charlestown
- "Pig Boat Blues", USS Agerholm
- "Special Weapons", Kirtland AFB, New Mexico
- "I Will Fear No Evil", Kirtland AFB, New Mexico
- "Blows Against the Empire", Kirtland AFB, New Mexico

source: "The American War" - see references below

- Bao Dai
- Duong Van Minh
- Madame Ngo Dinh Nhu
- Ngo Dinh Diem
- Ngo Dinh Nhu
- Nguyen Cao Ky
- Nguyen Khanh
- Nguyen Van Thieu

- Creighton W. Abrams
- Dean Acheson
- Spiro Agnew
- Ellsworth Bunker
- McGeorge Bundy
- William Bundy
- William Calley
- Clark Clifford
- William Colby
- A. Peter Dewey
- John Foster Dulles
- Dwight D. Eisenhower
- Daniel Ellsberg
- J. William Fulbright
- Barry Goldwater
- David Hackworth
- Alexander Haig
- Paul D. Harkins
- Seymour Hersh
- Hubert Humphrey
- Lyndon Johnson
- John F. Kennedy
- John Kerry
- Henry Kissinger
- Melvin Laird
- Edward Lansdale
- Henry Cabot Lodge, Jr.
- Mike Mansfield
- Graham Martin
- Robert McNamara
- George McGovern
- Richard Nixon
- Pete Peterson
- Charika Pugh
- Dean Rusk

- Maxwell D. Taylor
- Hugh C. Thompson, Jr
- John Paul Vann
- Gary Varsel
- William Westmoreland

- Ho Chi Minh
- Le Duan
- Tran Van Tra
- Le Duc Tho
- Pham Van Dong
- General Giap
- Poewll Ward

- Lon Nol
- Pol Pot
- Norodom Sihanouk
- Sirik Matak
- Sosthene Fernandez

- David H. Hackworth. 1989 About Face
- A.J. Langguth. 2000. Our Vietnam: the War 1954-1975.
- Mann, Robert. 2002. Grand Delusion, A: America"s Descent Into Vietnam.
- Windrow, Martin. 2005. The Last Valley: Dien Bien Phu and the French Defeat in Vietnam.
- Bernard Fall. 1967. Hell in a Very Small Place: the Siege of Dien Bien Phu.
- Harvey Pekar. 2003. American Splendor: Unsung Hero
- Prados, John. 2000. The Blood Road: The Ho Chi Minh Trail and the Vietnam War.
- Prados, John. 1999. Valley of Decision: The Siege of Khe Sanh.
- Shultz, Robert H. Jr. 2000. The Secret War Against Hanoi: The Untold Story of Spies, Saboteurs, and Covert Warriors in North Vietnam.
- Plaster, John L. 1998. SOG: The Secret Wars of America"s Commandos in Vietnam.
- Murphy, Edward F. 1995. Dak To: America"s Sky Soldiers in South Vietnam"s Central Highlands.
- Nolan, Keith W. 1996. The Battle for Saigon: Tet 1968.
- Nolan, Keith W. 1996. Sappers in the Wire: The Life and Death of Firebase Mary Ann.
- Nolan, Keith W. 1992. Operation Buffalo: USMC Fight for the DMZ.
- Nolan, Keith W. 2003. Ripcord : Screaming Eagles Under Siege, Vietnam 1970.
- Robert S. McNamara. 1996. In Retrospect: The Tragedy and Lessons of Vietnam.
- Larry Berman. 2002. No Peace, No Honor: Nixon, Kissinger, and Betrayal in Vietnam.
- Bergerud, Eric M. 1994. Red Thunder, Tropic Lightning: The World of a Combat Division in Vietnam.
- Bernard Edelman. 2002. Dear America: Letters Home from Vietnam.
- Darrel D. Whitcomb. 1999. The Rescue of Bat 21.
- Oberdorfer, Don. 1971. Tet: the Story of a Battle and its Historic Aftermath.
- LTG Harold G. Moore and Joseph L. Galloway. 1992. We Were Soldiers Once ... And Young.
- Duiker, William J. 2002. Ho Chi Minh: A Life.
- John Laurence. 2002. The Cat from Hue: A Vietnam War Story.
- Emerson, Gloria. 1976. Winners and Losers: Battles, Retreats, Gains, Losses and Ruins from a Long War.
- Philip Caputo. 1977. A Rumor of War.

- Al Santoli. 1981. Everything We Had: an Oral History of the Vietnam War by 33 American Soldiers Who Fought It.
- Robert C. Mason. 1983. Chickenhawk.
- Michael Herr. 1977. Dispatches.
- Joseph T. Ward. 1991. Dear Mom: a Sniper"s Vietnam.
- Hemphill, Robert. 1998. Platoon: Bravo Company.
- Noam Chomsky. 1967. The Responsibility of Intellectuals.
- Moore, Robin. 1965 The Green Berets (ISBN 0-312-98492-8)

- Robert Olen Butler. 1992.

American Spectator	The American Spectator is a conservative U.S. monthly magazine covering news and politics, edited by R. Emmett Tyrrell Jr. and published by the non-profit American Spectator Foundation. From its founding in 1967 until the late 1980s, the small-circulation magazine featured the writings of authors such as Thomas Sowell, Tom Wolfe, P.J. O"Rourke, George F. Will, Malcolm Gladwell, Patrick J. Buchanan, Alex Linder and Malcolm Muggeridge, although today the magazine is best known for its attacks in the 1990s on Bill Clinton and its "Arkansas Project" to discredit the president, funded by billionaire Richard Mellon Scaife and the Bradley Foundation.
Ethnic cleansing	Ethnic Cleansing is a controversial computer game developed by Resistance Records, an underground music label specializing in Neo-Nazi and white supremacist bands. In the game, the protagonist (the player can choose either a skinhead or a Klansman) runs through a ghetto killing black people and Latinos, before descending into a subway system to kill Jews. Finally he reaches the "Jewish Control Center", where Ariel Sharon, former Prime Minister of Israel, is directing plans for world domination.
Framing	A frame in social theory consists of a schema of interpretation--that is, a collection of stereotypes-- that individuals rely on to understand and respond to events. In psychology, Framing is influenced by the background of a context choice and the way in which the question is worded. To clarify: When one seeks to explain an event, the understanding often depends on the frame referred to.
Grenada	Grenada is an island nation and sovereign state consisting of the island of Grenada and six smaller islands at the southern end of the Grenadines in the southeastern Caribbean Sea. Grenada is located northwest of Trinidad and Tobago, northeast of Venezuela, and southwest of Saint Vincent and the Grenadines. Its size is 344 km^2 with an estimated population of 110,000.
New Deal	The New Deal is a programme of active labour market policies introduced in the United Kingdom by the Labour government in 1998, initially funded by a one off Â£5bn windfall tax on privatised utility companies. The stated purpose is to reduce unemployment by providing training, subsidised employment and voluntary work to the unemployed. Spending on the New Deal was Â£1.3 billion in 2001.
Panama	Panama, officially the Republic of Panama , is the southernmost country of both Central America and, in turn, North America. Situated on the isthmus connecting North and South America, it is bordered by Costa Rica to the northwest, Colombia to the southeast, the Caribbean Sea to the north and the Pacific Ocean to the south. The capital is Panama City.
Pentagon Papers	The Pentagon Papers, officially titled United States-Vietnam Relations, 1945-1967: A Study Prepared by the Department of Defense, were a top-secret United States Department of Defense history of the United States" political-military involvement in Vietnam from 1945 to 1967. Commissioned by United States Secretary of Defense Robert S. McNamara in 1967, the study was completed in 1968. The papers first surfaced on the front page on the New York Times in 1971.

Prior restraint	Prior restraint is a legal term referring to a government"s actions that prevent communications from reaching the public. Its main use is to keep materials from being published. Censorship that requires a person to seek governmental permission in the form of a license or imprimatur before publishing anything constitutes Prior restraint every time permission is denied.
Deregulation	Deregulation is the removal or simplification of government rules and regulations that constrain the operation of market forces. Deregulation does not mean elimination of laws against fraud, but eliminating or reducing government control of how business is done, thereby moving toward a more free market. The stated rationale for "Deregulation" is often that fewer and simpler regulations will lead to a raised level of competitiveness, therefore higher productivity, more efficiency and lower prices overall.
Cuban Missile Crisis	The Cuban Missile Crisis was a confrontation between the United States, the Soviet Union, and Cuba in October 1962, during the Cold War. In Russia, it is termed the "Caribbean Crisis" , while in Cuba it is called the "October Crisis." The Cuban and Soviet governments decided in September 1962 to place nuclear missiles on Cuba in order to protect it from United States harassment. When United States intelligence discovered the weapons its government decided to do all they could to ensure the removal of them.
Presidential election	A presidential election was held in Chile on 4 September 1970. A narrow plurality (36.6 percent of the total vote) was secured by Salvador Allende, the candidate of the Popular Unity coalition of leftist parties. Because he did not obtain an absolute majority, his election required a further vote by the National Congress of Chile which resulted in Allende assuming the presidency in accordance with the Chilean Constitution of 1925.

Social Security	Social Security, in Australia, refers to a system of social welfare payments provided by Commonwealth Government of Australia. These payments are administered by a Government body named Centrelink. In Australia, most benefits are subject to a means test.
Public policy	Public policy is the body of principles that underpin the operation of legal systems in each state. This addresses the social, moral and economic values that tie a society together: values that vary in different cultures and change over time. Law regulates behaviour either to reinforce existing social expectations or to encourage constructive change, and laws are most likely to be effective when they are consistent with the most generally accepted societal norms and reflect the collective morality of the society.
Power	Power in international relations is defined in several different ways. Political scientists, historians, and practitioners of international relations (diplomats) have used the following concepts of political Power: • Power as a goal of states or leaders; • Power as a measure of influence or control over outcomes, events, actors and issues; • Power as reflecting victory in conflict and the attainment of security; and, • Power as control over resources and capabilities. Modern discourse generally speaks in terms of state Power, indicating both economic and military Power. Those states that have significant amounts of Power within the international system are referred to as middle powers, regional powers, great powers, superpowers, or hyperpowers, although there is no commonly accepted standard for what defines a powerful state. Entities other than states can also acquire and wield Power in international relations.
Constitutional Convention	A Constitutional convention is an informal and uncodified procedural agreement that is followed by the institutions of a state. In some states, notably those Commonwealth of Nations states which follow the Westminster system and whose political systems are derived from British constitutional law, most of the functions of government are guided by Constitutional convention rather than by a formal written constitution. In these states, the actual distribution of power may be markedly different from those which are described in the formal constitutional documents.
Politics	Politics are an integral part of the Unification Church"s concerns and activities, although the church itself largely remains aloof from Politics The degree of involvement of the movement, as well as some of its specific stances, have also been part of the reason for the movement"s controversial status over the years. The belief in the establishment of a literal Kingdom of Heaven on earth and Rev. Moon"s teaching that religion alone is not enough to bring this provides a motivation for political involvement.

Public Service of Canada	The Public Service of Canada is the staff of the federal government of Canada. Its function is to support the Canadian monarch, and to handle the hiring of employees for the federal government ministries. It is represented by the Governor General, and the appointed [[list of Canadian ministries | ministry].
Iraq	Iraq , officially the Republic of Iraq JumhÅ«rÄ«yat Al-Ê¿IrÄ q, Kurdish: ÙƒÛ†Ù…Ø§Ø±ÛŒ Ø¹ÛŽØ±Ø§Ù‚ê€Ž, Komara Iraqê), is a country in Western Asia spanning most of the northwestern end of the Zagros mountain range, the eastern part of the Syrian Desert and the northern part of the Arabian Desert. Iraq shares borders with Jordan to the west, Syria to the northwest, Turkey to the north, Iran to the east, and Kuwait and Saudi Arabia to the south. Iraq has a narrow section of coastline measuring 58 km between Umm Qasr and Al Faw on the Persian Gulf.
Individualism	Individualism is the moral stance, political philosophy, ideology, or social outlook that stresses independence and self-reliance. Individualists promote the exercise of one"s goals and desires, while opposing most external interference upon one"s choices, whether by society, or any other group or institution. Individualism is opposed to collectivism, which stress that communal, community, group, societal, or national goals should take priority over individual goals.
Boosterism	Boosterism is the act of "boosting," or promoting, one"s town, city with the goal of improving public perception of it. Boosting can be as simple as "talking up" the entity at a party or as elaborate as establishing a visitors" bureau. It is somewhat associated with American small towns.
Homeland	A Homeland is the concept of the place (cultural geography) to which an ethnic group holds a long history and a deep cultural association with --the country in which a particular national identity began. As a common noun, it simply connotes the country of one"s origin.
Federation	A Federation is a type of sovereign state characterised by a union of partially self-governing states or regions united by a central government. In a Federation, the self-governing status of the component states is typically constitutionally entrenched and may not be altered by a unilateral decision of the central government. The form of government or constitutional structure found in a Federation is known as federalism
Leadership	Leadership has been described as the "process of social influence in which one person can enlist the aid and support of others in the accomplishment of a common task". A definition more inclusive of followers comes from Alan Keith of Genentech who said "Leadership is ultimately about creating a way for people to contribute to making something extraordinary happen." Leadership is one of the most salient aspects of the organizational context. However, defining Leadership has been challenging.

Medicare	Medicare is a social insurance program administered by the United States government, providing health insurance coverage to people who are aged 65 and over, or who meet other special criteria. Medicare operates as a single-payer health care system. The Social Security Act of 1965 was passed by Congress in late-spring of 1965 and signed into law on July 30, 1965, by President Lyndon B. Johnson as amendments to Social Security legislation.
National Taxpayers Union	National Taxpayers Union is a taxpayers advocacy organization in the United States, founded in 1969 by James Dale Davidson. National Taxpayers Union advertises that it is the largest and oldest grassroots taxpayer organization in the nation, with 362,000 members nationwide. It is closely affiliated with a non-profit foundation, the National Taxpayers Union Foundation (National Taxpayers Union F.)
Democratic party	Democratic Party was a political party in Gambia. The party was founded during the pre-independence period in the colony of Bathurst (currently the national capital Banjul.) Ahead of the 1962 election, the Democratic Party merged with the Muslim Congress Party to form the Democratic Congress Alliance.
American Civil Liberties Union	The American Civil Liberties Union consists of two separate non-profit organizations: the American Civil Liberties Union Foundation, a 501(c)(3) organization which focuses on litigation and communication efforts, and the American Civil Liberties Union, a 501(c)(4) organization which focuses on legislative lobbying. The American Civil Liberties Union"s stated mission is "to defend and preserve the individual rights and liberties guaranteed to every person in this country by the Constitution and laws of the United States." It works through litigation, legislation, and community education. Founded in 1920 by Crystal Eastman, Roger Baldwin and Walter Nelles, the American Civil Liberties Union was the successor organization to the earlier National Civil Liberties Bureau founded during World War I. The American Civil Liberties Union reported over 500,000 members at the end of 2005.
Civil Liberties	Civil liberties are freedoms that protect an individual from the government of the nation in which they reside. Civil liberties set limits for government so that it cannot abuse its power and interfere unduly with the lives of its citizens. Common Civil liberties include the rights of people, freedom of religion, and freedom of speech, and additionally, the right to due process, to a fair trial, to own property, and to privacy.
Coalition	A Coalition is an alliance among individuals or groups, during which they cooperate in joint action, each in his own self-interest, joining forces together for a common cause. This alliance may be temporary or a matter of convenience. A Coalition thus differs from a more formal covenant.

Committee	A Committee (some of which are titled instead as a "Commission" larger deliberative assembly--which when organized so that action on Committee requires a vote by all its entitled members, is called the Committee of the Whole". Committee s often serve several different functions:

<ul>
<li>Governance: in organizations considered too large for all the members to participate in decisions affecting the organization as a whole, a Committee (such as a Board of Directors or "Executive Committee) is given the power to make decisions, spend money the Board of directors can frequently enter into binding contracts and make decisions which once taken or made, can"t be taken back or undone under the law.</li>
<li>Coordination: individuals from different parts of an organization (for example, all senior vice presidents) might meet regularly to discuss developments in their areas, review projects that cut across organizational boundaries, talk about future options, etc. Where there is a large Committee it is common to have smaller Committee s with more specialized functions - for example, Boards of Directors of large corporations typically have an (ongoing) audit Committee finance Committee compensation Committee etc. Large academic conferences are usually organized by a co-ordinating Committee drawn from the relevant professional body.</li>
</ul>

Moral Majority	The Moral Majority was a political organization of the United States which had an agenda of evangelical Christian-oriented political lobbying. It was founded in 1979 and dissolved in the late 1980s.

Pre-Establishment

The origins of the Moral Majority can be traced to 1976 when Jerry Falwell embarked on a series of "I Love America" rallies across the country to raise awareness of social issues important to Falwell.

Red	Red is a political adjective which associates with communism, Soviet Union, or radical left politics. Depending on the context the adjective may be perceived to bear either a pejorative or positive connotation.

In its literal meaning, the word is used in the term Red flag and Red star, the object which are in fact of Red color, but which are the symbols of communism.

Appropriation	Appropriation is a non-violent process by which previously unowned natural resources, particularly land, become the property of a person or group of persons. The term is widely used in economics in this sense. In certain cases, it proceeds under very specifically defined forms, such as driving stakes or other such markers into the land claimed, which form gave rise to the term "staking a claim." "Squatter"s rights" are another form of Appropriation, but are usually asserted against land to which ownership rights of another party have been recognized.

Bribery	Bribery, a form of pecuniary corruption, is an act implying money or gift given that alters the behaviour of the recipient. Bribery constitutes a crime and is defined by Black"s Law Dictionary as the offering, giving, receiving, or soliciting of any item of value to influence the actions of an official or other person in discharge of a public or legal duty. The bribe is the gift bestowed to influence the recipient"s conduct.
Grassroots	A Grassroots movement (often referenced in the context of a political movement) is one driven by the politics of a community. The term implies that the creation of the movement and the group supporting it is natural and spontaneous, highlighting the differences between this and a movement that is orchestrated by traditional power structures. Often, Grassroots movements are at the local level, as many volunteers in the community give their time to support the local party, which can lead to helping the national party.
Judicial activism	Judicial activism is a critical term used to describe judicial rulings that are viewed as imposing a personal biased interpretation by a given court of what a law means as opposed to what a neutral, unbiased observer would naturally interpret a law to be. The term has most often been used to describe left-wing judges, however; the Supreme Court"s activity since the confirmation of justices Alito and Roberts under George W. Bush, and the ensuing perception that the conservative court was expanding the rights of corporations at the cost of the rights of citizens, has since led to conservative judges being labeled activists. The term "Judicial activism" is frequently used in political debate without definition, which has created some confusion over its precise meaning or meanings.
Free Trade	Free trade is a type of trade policy that allows traders to act and transact without interference from government. Thus, the policy permits trading partners mutual gains from trade, with goods and services produced according to the theory of comparative advantage. Under a Free trade policy, prices are a reflection of true supply and demand, and are the sole determinant of resource allocation.
Public opinion	Public opinion is the aggregate of individual attitudes or beliefs held by the adult population. Public opinion can also be defined as the complex collection of opinions of many different people and the sum of all their views. The principle approaches to the study of Public opinion may be divided into 4 categories: a) quantitative measurement of opinion distributions; b) investigation of the internal relationships among the individual opinions that make up Public opinion on an issue; c) description or analysis of the public role of Public opinion; d) study both of the communication media that disseminate the ideas on which opinions are based and of the uses that propagandists and other manipulators make of these media.

Public opinion as a concept gained credence with the rise of "public" in the eighteenth century.

Led by Lorrin A. Thurston and Sanford B. Dole, the Provisional Government ruled over HawaiÊ»i until the formal establishment of a republic. Pictured above is the cabinet, (Left to Right) James A. King, Sanford B. Dole, William O. Smith and Peter C. Jones.

Capital	Flag

Capital	Honolulu
Language(s)	Hawaiian, English
Government	Not specified
Provisional Government	
- 1893-1894	Committee of Safety
Historical era	New Imperialism
- Monarchy overthrown	January 17, 1893
- Republic declared	July 4, 1894
Currency	U.S. dollar, Hawaiian dollar

The Provisional Government of HawaiÊ»i was proclaimed on January 17, 1893 by the 13 member Committee of Safety under the leadership of Lorrin A. Thurston and Sanford B. Dole. It governed the Kingdom of HawaiÊ»i after the overthrow of Queen LiliÊ»uokalani until the Republic of HawaiÊ»i was established on July 4, 1894.

Constitution	A Constitution is set of rules for government -- often codified as a written document -- that establishes principles of an autonomous political entity. In the case of countries, this term refers specifically to a national Constitution defining the fundamental political principles, and establishing the structure, procedures, powers and duties, of a government. By limiting the government"s own reach, most Constitution s guarantee certain rights to the people.
Presidential election	A presidential election was held in Chile on 4 September 1970. A narrow plurality (36.6 percent of the total vote) was secured by Salvador Allende, the candidate of the Popular Unity coalition of leftist parties. Because he did not obtain an absolute majority, his election required a further vote by the National Congress of Chile which resulted in Allende assuming the presidency in accordance with the Chilean Constitution of 1925.
Prescription	In law, Prescription is the method of sovereignty transfer of a territory through international law analogous to the common law doctrine of adverse possession for private real-estate. Prescription involves the open encroachment by the new sovereign upon the territory in question for a prolonged period of time, acting as the sovereign, without protest or other contest by the original sovereign. This doctrine legalizes de jure the de facto transfer of sovereignty caused in part by the original sovereign"s extended negligence and/or neglect of the area in question.
Fiscal policy	In economics, Fiscal policy is the use of government spending and revenue collection to influence the economy.

Fiscal policy can be contrasted with the other main type of economic policy, monetary policy, which attempts to stabilize the economy by controlling interest rates and the supply of money. The two main instruments of Fiscal policy are government spending and taxation.

Iron triangle

In United States politics, the Iron triangle is a term used by political scientists to describe the policy-making relationship among the congressional committees, the bureaucracy (executive) (sometimes called "government agencies"), and interest groups.

In the Federal government of the United States, the congressional committees responsible for oversight along with the federal agencies (often independent agencies) responsible for regulation of those industries, and the industries and their trade associations.

Probably the earliest concept of the "Iron triangle" was on January 17, 1919 by Ralph Pulitzer.

Chapter 8. Social Movements

Suffrage	Suffrage is the civil right to vote, or the exercise of that right. In that context, it is also called political franchise or simply the franchise. Suffrage is very valuable to the extent that there are opportunities to vote .
Citizenship	Citizenship is an act of being a citizen of one community.
	Citizenship status, under social contract theory, carries with it both rights and responsibilities. "Active Citizenship" is the philosophy that citizens should work towards the betterment of their community through economic participation, public service, volunteer work, and other such efforts to improve life for all citizens.
Right	A right is the legal or moral entitlement to do or refrain from doing something thing or recognition in civil society. Rights serve as rules of interaction between people, and, as such, they place constraints and obligations upon the actions of individuals or groups (for example, if one has a right to life, this means that others do not have the liberty to kill him.)
	Most modern conceptions of rights are universalist and egalitarian -- in other words, equal rights are granted to all people.
Social movements	Social movements are a type of group action. They are large informal groupings of individuals and/or organizations focused on specific political or social issues, in other words, on carrying out, resisting or undoing a social change.
	Modern Western Social movements became possible through education (the wider dissemination of literature), and increased mobility of labour due to the industrialisation and urbanisation of 19th century societies.
Committee	A Committee (some of which are titled instead as a "Commission" larger deliberative assembly-- which when organized so that action on Committee requires a vote by all its entitled members, is called the Committee of the Whole". Committee s often serve several different functions:

- Governance: in organizations considered too large for all the members to participate in decisions affecting the organization as a whole, a Committee (such as a Board of Directors or "Executive Committee) is given the power to make decisions, spend money the Board of directors can frequently enter into binding contracts and make decisions which once taken or made, can"t be taken back or undone under the law.

- Coordination: individuals from different parts of an organization (for example, all senior vice presidents) might meet regularly to discuss developments in their areas, review projects that cut across organizational boundaries, talk about future options, etc. Where there is a large Committee it is common to have smaller Committee s with more specialized functions - for example, Boards of Directors of large corporations typically have an (ongoing) audit Committee finance Committee compensation Committee etc. Large academic conferences are usually organized by a co-ordinating Committee drawn from the relevant professional body.

Chapter 8. Social Movements

Grassroots	A Grassroots movement (often referenced in the context of a political movement) is one driven by the politics of a community. The term implies that the creation of the movement and the group supporting it is natural and spontaneous, highlighting the differences between this and a movement that is orchestrated by traditional power structures. Often, Grassroots movements are at the local level, as many volunteers in the community give their time to support the local party, which can lead to helping the national party.
Boosterism	Boosterism is the act of "boosting," or promoting, one"s town, city with the goal of improving public perception of it. Boosting can be as simple as "talking up" the entity at a party or as elaborate as establishing a visitors" bureau. It is somewhat associated with American small towns.
William Jennings Bryan	William Jennings Bryan was the Democratic Party nominee for President of the United States in 1896, 1900 and 1908, a lawyer, and the 41st United States Secretary of State under President Woodrow Wilson. One of the most popular speakers in American history, he was noted for a deep, commanding voice. Bryan was a devout Presbyterian, a supporter of popular democracy, a critic of banks and railroads, a leader of the silverite movement in the 1890s, a leading figure in the Democratic Party, a peace advocate, a prohibitionist, an opponent of Darwinism, and one of the most prominent leaders of populism in the late 19th - and early 20th century.
Democratic party	Democratic Party was a political party in Gambia. The party was founded during the pre-independence period in the colony of Bathurst (currently the national capital Banjul.) Ahead of the 1962 election, the Democratic Party merged with the Muslim Congress Party to form the Democratic Congress Alliance.
Anti-Americanism	Dictionaries tend to define Anti-Americanism, often anti-American sentiment, as a widespread opposition or hostility to the people, government or policies of the United States. In practice, a broad range of attitudes and actions critical of or opposed to the United States have been labeled Anti-Americanism. Thus, the nature and applicability of the term is often disputed.
Vietnam	Vietnam " href="/wiki/Battle_of_B%E1%BA%A1ch_%C4%90%E1%BA%B1ng_River_(938)">battle of Bá⁰¡ch Ä á⁰±ng River. Successive dynasties flourished along with geographic and political expansion deeper into Southeast Asia, until it was colonized by the French in the mid-19th century. Efforts to resist the French eventually led to their expulsion from the country in the mid-20th century, leaving a nation divided politically into two countries.
Vietnam War	The Vietnam War was a military conflict that occurred in Vietnam, Laos and Cambodia from 1959 to 30 April 1975. The war was fought between the communist North Vietnam, supported by its communist allies, and the government of South Vietnam, supported by the United States and other member nations of the Southeast Asia Treaty Organization (SEATO.) The following outline is provided as an overview of and topical guide to the Vietnam War:

Listed by starting date:

- Operation 34A - (1964)
- Operation Starlite - August 18-24 1965
- Operation Hump- November 5 1965
- Operation Crimp - January 7, 1966
- Operation Birmingham - April 1966
- Operation Hastings - Late May 1966
- Operation Prairie - August 1966
- Operation Deckhouse Five - January 6, 1967
- Operation Cedar Falls - January 8, 1967
- Operation Junction City - February 21, 1967
- Operation Francis Marion - April 6 - April 30, 1967
- Operation Union - April 21-May 16, 1967
- Operations Malheur I and Malheur II - 11 May - July 1, 1967
- Operation Baker - May 11, 1967
- Operation Scotland - See Battle of Khe Sanh
- Operation Pegasus - August 8, 1968
- Operation Dewey Canyon - January 22, 1969
- Operation Twinkletoes - 1969
- Operation Apache Snow - May 10 - May 20, 1969
- Operation Chicago Peak - April 1970
- Operation Texas Star - April - September, 1970
- Operation Ivory Coast - November 21, 1970
- Operation Jefferson Glenn - 1970-1971
- Operation Lam Son 719 - February 8, 1971
- Ho Chi Minh Campaign January 24 - April 30, 1975
- Operation Frequent Wind - April, 1975

- Battle of Ap Bac - January 2, 1963
- Battle of Kien Long - April 11 - April 15, 1964
- Battle of Thanh Hóa - July 31, 1964
- Battle of Binh Gia - December 28, 1964 - January 1, 1965
- Battle of Dong Xoai - June 10, 1965
- Battle near Minh Thanh - October 25 - October 27, 1965
- Battle of Ia Drang - November 14 - November 16, 1965
- Battle of Cu Nghi - January 28 - January 31, 1966
- Battle of Kim Son Valley - February 16 - February 28, 1966
- Battle of A Shau - March 9 - March 10, 1966
- Battle of Xa Cam My - April 11 - April 12, 1966
- First Battle of Dong Ha - Late May - June, 1966
- Battle on Minh Thanh Road - July 9, 1966
- Battle of Ä á»©c CÆ¡ - August 9, 1966
- Battle of Long Táº§n - August 18- August 19, 1966
- Viet Cong attack on Tan Son Nhut airbase - December 4, 1966
- Battle of LZ Bird - December 27, 1966

- Battle of Tra Binh Dong - February 14 - February 15, 1967
- Battle of Hills 881 and 861 - April 24-May 9, 1967
- Nine Days in May - May 18 - May 28, 1967
- Battle of Vinh Huy - May 30 - June 2, 1967
- Battle of Con Thien - July 2 - July 3, 1967
- Battle of Dong Son - September 4, 1967
- Battle of Ong Thang - October 17, 1967
- First Battle of Loc Ninh - October 29 - November, 1967
- Battle of Dak To - November 3-November 22, 1967
- Battle in the Mekong Delta - December 4, 1967
- Battle of Tam Quan - December 6 - December 20, 1967
- Battle of Thom Tham Khe - December 27 - December 28, 1967
- Phoenix Program - 1967 - 1972
- Battle of Khe Sanh - January 21 - April 8, 1968
- Tet Offensive - January 30 - February 25, 1968
- Battle of Bien Hoa - January 31 - July 1, 1968
- Battle of Kham Duc - May 10 - May 12, 1968
- First Battle of Saigon - January 31, - February 3, 1968
- Battle of Hue - January 31, - February 25, 1968
- Tet 1969 - February 1969
- Battle of Hamburger Hill - May 10 - May 20, 1969
- Firebase Ripcord - March 12 - July 23, 1970
- Cambodian Incursion - April 29 - July 22, 1970
- Battle of Snoul - January 5 - May 30, 1971
- Easter Offensive - March 30 - October 22, 1972
- First Battle of Quang Tri - March 30 - May 1, 1972
- Battle of Loc Ninh - April 4 - April 7, 1972
- Battle of An Loc - April 20 - July 20, 1972
- Second Battle of Quang Tri - June 28 - September 16, 1972
- Battle of Phuoc Long - December 13, 1974 - January 6, 1975
- Battle of Buon Me Thuot - March 10 - March 12, 1975
- Battle of Xuan Loc - April 9 - April 20, 1975

- Operation Farm Gate
- Operation Chopper (1962)
- Operation Ranch Hand (1962-1971)
- Operation Pierce Arrow (1964)
- Operation Barrell Roll (1964-1972)
- Operation Pony Express (1965-1970)
- Operation Flaming Dart (1965)
- Operation Rolling Thunder (1965-1968)
- Operation Steel Tiger (1965-1968)
- Operation Arc Light (1965-1973)
- Operation Tiger Hound (1965-1968)
- Operation Shed Light (1966-1972)
- Operation Carolina Moon (1966)
- Operation Wahiawa (1966)
- Operation Bolo (1967)
- Operation Popeye (1967-1972)
- Operation Niagara (1968)
- Operation Igloo White (1968-1973

- Operation Giant Lance (1969)
- Operation Commando Hunt (1968-1972)
- Operation Menu (1969-1970)
- Operation Patio (1970)
- Operation Freedom Deal (1970-1973)
- Operation Linebacker (1972)
- Operation Enhance Plus (1972)
- Operation Linebacker II (1972)
- Operation Homecoming (1973)
- Operation Baby Lift (1975)
- Operation Eagle Pull (1975)
- Operation Frequent Wind (1975)

- National Order of Vietnam
- Vietnam Military Merit Medal
- Vietnam Distinguished Service Order
- Vietnam Meritorious Service Medal
- Vietnam Special Service Medal
- Vietnam Gallantry Cross
- Vietnam Air Gallantry Cross
- Vietnam Navy Gallantry Cross
- Vietnam Armed Forces Honor Medal
- Vietnam Civil Actions Medal
- Vietnam Staff Service Medal
- Vietnam Technical Service Medal
- Vietnam Wound Medal
- Vietnam Campaign Medal
- Presidential Unit Citation (Vietnam)
- Vietnam Gallantry Cross Unit Citation
- Vietnam Civil Actions Unit Citation

- Golden Star Medal
- Ho Chi Minh Order
- Defeat American Aggression Badge
- Vietnam Liberation Order
- Resolution for Victory Order

- Medal of Honor rare
- Distinguished Service Cross rare
- Navy Cross uncommon
- Air Force Cross uncommon
- Silver Star uncommon
- Purple Heart frequent
- Bronze Star frequent
- Presidential Unit Citation rare
- Vietnam Service Medal very common
- National Defense Service Medal very common
- Commendation Medal common

- "Fatigue Press" at Fort Hood,
- "Last Harass" at Fort Gordon, Georgia
- "Pawn"s Pawn" at Fort Leonard Wood, Missouri

- "Ultimate Weapon" at Fort Dix, New Jersey
- "Attitude Check" at Camp Pendleton, California
- "Green Machine" at Fort Greely, Alaska
- "Napalm" at Fort Campbell, Tennessee
- "Arctic Arsenal" at Fort Greely, Alaska
- "Black Voice" at Fort McClellan, Alabama
- "Fragging Action" at Fort Dix
- "Fort Polk Puke" at Fort Polk, Louisiana
- "Custer"s Last Stand" at Fort Riley, Kansas
- "Whack!" from the Women"s Army Corps School
- "Where Are We?" at Fort Huachuca, Arizona
- "Voice of the Lumpen" (affiliated with the Black Panther Party) in Frankfurt
- "Can You Bear McNair?" at McNair Barracks, Berlin
- "Seasick" at Subic Bay
- "The Man Can"t Win If You Grin" in Okinawa
- "Korea Free Press"
- "Semper Fi" in Japan
- "Stars and Bars" in England
- "Separated From Life" in England
- "Duck Power" in San Diego
- "Harass the Brass" at Canute Air Force Base, Illinois
- "All Hands Abandon Ship", Newport, Rhode Island
- "Now Hear This", Long Beach
- "Potemkin" on the USS Forestall
- "Star Spangled Bummer" at Wright-Patterson Air Force Base in Ohio
- "Fat Albert"s Death Ship" in Charlestown
- "Pig Boat Blues", USS Agerholm
- "Special Weapons", Kirtland AFB, New Mexico
- "I Will Fear No Evil", Kirtland AFB, New Mexico
- "Blows Against the Empire", Kirtland AFB, New Mexico

source: "The American War" - see references below

- Bao Dai
- Duong Van Minh
- Madame Ngo Dinh Nhu
- Ngo Dinh Diem
- Ngo Dinh Nhu
- Nguyen Cao Ky
- Nguyen Khanh
- Nguyen Van Thieu

- Creighton W. Abrams
- Dean Acheson
- Spiro Agnew
- Ellsworth Bunker
- McGeorge Bundy
- William Bundy
- William Calley
- Clark Clifford
- William Colby
- A. Peter Dewey
- John Foster Dulles
- Dwight D. Eisenhower
- Daniel Ellsberg
- J. William Fulbright
- Barry Goldwater
- David Hackworth
- Alexander Haig
- Paul D. Harkins
- Seymour Hersh
- Hubert Humphrey
- Lyndon Johnson
- John F. Kennedy
- John Kerry
- Henry Kissinger
- Melvin Laird
- Edward Lansdale
- Henry Cabot Lodge, Jr.
- Mike Mansfield
- Graham Martin
- Robert McNamara
- George McGovern
- Richard Nixon
- Pete Peterson
- Charika Pugh
- Dean Rusk

- Maxwell D. Taylor
- Hugh C. Thompson, Jr
- John Paul Vann
- Gary Varsel
- William Westmoreland

- Ho Chi Minh
- Le Duan
- Tran Van Tra
- Le Duc Tho
- Pham Van Dong
- General Giap
- Poewll Ward

- Lon Nol
- Pol Pot
- Norodom Sihanouk
- Sirik Matak
- Sosthene Fernandez

- David H. Hackworth. 1989 About Face
- A.J. Langguth. 2000. Our Vietnam: the War 1954-1975.
- Mann, Robert. 2002. Grand Delusion, A: America"s Descent Into Vietnam.
- Windrow, Martin. 2005. The Last Valley: Dien Bien Phu and the French Defeat in Vietnam.
- Bernard Fall. 1967. Hell in a Very Small Place: the Siege of Dien Bien Phu.
- Harvey Pekar. 2003. American Splendor: Unsung Hero
- Prados, John. 2000. The Blood Road: The Ho Chi Minh Trail and the Vietnam War.
- Prados, John. 1999. Valley of Decision: The Siege of Khe Sanh.
- Shultz, Robert H. Jr. 2000. The Secret War Against Hanoi: The Untold Story of Spies, Saboteurs, and Covert Warriors in North Vietnam.
- Plaster, John L. 1998. SOG: The Secret Wars of America"s Commandos in Vietnam.
- Murphy, Edward F. 1995. Dak To: America"s Sky Soldiers in South Vietnam"s Central Highlands.
- Nolan, Keith W. 1996. The Battle for Saigon: Tet 1968.
- Nolan, Keith W. 1996. Sappers in the Wire: The Life and Death of Firebase Mary Ann.
- Nolan, Keith W. 1992. Operation Buffalo: USMC Fight for the DMZ.
- Nolan, Keith W. 2003. Ripcord : Screaming Eagles Under Siege, Vietnam 1970.
- Robert S. McNamara. 1996. In Retrospect: The Tragedy and Lessons of Vietnam.
- Larry Berman. 2002. No Peace, No Honor: Nixon, Kissinger, and Betrayal in Vietnam.
- Bergerud, Eric M. 1994. Red Thunder, Tropic Lightning: The World of a Combat Division in Vietnam.
- Bernard Edelman. 2002. Dear America: Letters Home from Vietnam.
- Darrel D. Whitcomb. 1999. The Rescue of Bat 21.
- Oberdorfer, Don. 1971. Tet: the Story of a Battle and its Historic Aftermath.
- LTG Harold G. Moore and Joseph L. Galloway. 1992. We Were Soldiers Once ... And Young.
- Duiker, William J. 2002. Ho Chi Minh: A Life.
- John Laurence. 2002. The Cat from Hue: A Vietnam War Story.
- Emerson, Gloria. 1976. Winners and Losers: Battles, Retreats, Gains, Losses and Ruins from a Long War.
- Philip Caputo. 1977. A Rumor of War.

- Al Santoli. 1981. Everything We Had: an Oral History of the Vietnam War by 33 American Soldiers Who Fought It.
- Robert C. Mason. 1983. Chickenhawk.
- Michael Herr. 1977. Dispatches.
- Joseph T. Ward. 1991. Dear Mom: a Sniper"s Vietnam.
- Hemphill, Robert. 1998. Platoon: Bravo Company.
- Noam Chomsky. 1967. The Responsibility of Intellectuals.
- Moore, Robin. 1965 The Green Berets (ISBN 0-312-98492-8)

- Robert Olen Butler. 1992.

Coalition	A Coalition is an alliance among individuals or groups, during which they cooperate in joint action, each in his own self-interest, joining forces together for a common cause. This alliance may be temporary or a matter of convenience. A Coalition thus differs from a more formal covenant.
Pro-life	Pro-life is a term representing a variety of perspectives and activist movements in medical ethics. It is most commonly used, especially in the media and popular discourse, to refer to opposition to abortion. More generally, the term describes a political and ethical view which maintains that human fetuses and embryos are persons and therefore have a right to live.
World Trade Organization	The World Trade Organization is an international organization designed by its founders to supervise and liberalize international trade. The organization officially commenced on January 1, 1995 under the Marrakesh Agreement, replacing the General agreements on Tariffs and Trade (GATT), wich commenced in 1947. The World Trade Organization deals with regulation of trade between participating countries; it provides a framework for negotiating and formalising trade agreements, and a dispute resolution process aimed at enforcing participants" adherence to World Trade Organization agreements which are signed by representatives of member governments and ratified by their parliaments.
International Monetary Fund	The International Monetary Fund is an international organization that oversees the global financial system by following the macroeconomic policies of its member countries, in particular those with an impact on exchange rates and the balance of payments. It is an organization formed to stabilize international exchange rates and facilitate development. It also offers highly leveraged loans mainly to poorer countries.
Iraq	Iraq , officially the Republic of Iraq JumhÅ«rÄ«yat Al-Ê¿IrÄ q, Kurdish: ÙƒÛÙ…Ø§Ø±ÛŒ Ø¹ÛŽØ±Ø§Ù‚â€Ž, Komara Iraqê), is a country in Western Asia spanning most of the northwestern end of the Zagros mountain range, the eastern part of the Syrian Desert and the northern part of the Arabian Desert. Iraq shares borders with Jordan to the west, Syria to the northwest, Turkey to the north, Iran to the east, and Kuwait and Saudi Arabia to the south. Iraq has a narrow section of coastline measuring 58 km between Umm Qasr and Al Faw on the Persian Gulf.
Anti-war	The term Anti-war usually refers to the opposition to a particular nation"s decision to start or carry on an armed conflict, unconditional of a maybe-existing just cause. The term can also refer to pacifism, which is the opposition to all use of military force during conflicts. Many activists distinguish between Anti-war movements and peace movements.
Axis of evil	"Axis of evil" is a term coined by United States President George W. Bush in his State of the Union Address on January 29, 2002 in order to describe governments that he accused of helping terrorism and seeking weapons of mass destruction. President Bush named Iran, Iraq and North Korea in his speech. President Bush"s presidency was marked by this notion as a justification for the War on Terror.
Summit	A Summit meeting (or Summit) is a meeting of heads of state or government, usually with considerable media exposure, tight security and a prearranged agenda.

Notable Summit meetings include those of Franklin D. Roosevelt, Winston Churchill and Joseph Stalin during World War II.

During the Cold War, when American presidents joined with Soviet or Chinese counterparts for one-on-one meetings, the media labelled the event as a "Summit,". The post-Cold War era has produced an increase in the number of "Summit" events.

Civil rights movement	The Civil rights movement was a worldwide political movement for equality before the law occurring between approximately 1950 and 1980. It was accompanied by much civil unrest and popular rebellion. The process was long and tenuous in many countries, and most of these movements did not achieve or fully achieve their objectives.
Strike	Strike is a Polish language film produced by a mainly German group, released in 2006 and directed by Volker Schlöndorff. The film is broadly a docudrama. It covers the formation of Solidarity.
Civil disobedience	Civil disobedience is the active refusal to obey certain laws, demands and commands of a government without resorting to physical violence. It is one of the primary tactics of nonviolent resistance. In its most nonviolent form (in India, known as ahimsa or satyagraha) it could be said that it is compassion in the form of respectful disagreement.
Sit-in	A Sit-in or sit-down is a form of direct action that involves one or more persons nonviolently occupying an area for a protest, often to promote political, social, or economic change.
	In a Sit-in, protesters usually seat themselves at some strategic location (inside a restaurant, in a street to block it, in a government or corporate office, and so on.) They remain until they are evicted, usually by force, or arrested, or until their requests have been met.
National Guard	The National Guard was the name given at the time of the French Revolution to the militias formed in each city, in imitation of the National Guard created in Paris. It was a military force separate from the regular army. Initially under the command of the Marquis de la Fayette, then briefly under the Marquis de Mandat, it was strongly identified until the summer of 1792 with the middle class and its support for constitutional monarchy.
Social Security	Social Security, in Australia, refers to a system of social welfare payments provided by Commonwealth Government of Australia. These payments are administered by a Government body named Centrelink. In Australia, most benefits are subject to a means test.
Judicial activism	Judicial activism is a critical term used to describe judicial rulings that are viewed as imposing a personal biased interpretation by a given court of what a law means as opposed to what a neutral, unbiased observer would naturally interpret a law to be. The term has most often been used to describe left-wing judges, however; the Supreme Court"s activity since the confirmation of justices Alito and Roberts under George W. Bush, and the ensuing perception that the conservative court was expanding the rights of corporations at the cost of the rights of citizens, has since led to conservative judges being labeled activists.

The term "Judicial activism" is frequently used in political debate without definition, which has created some confusion over its precise meaning or meanings.

Leadership

Leadership has been described as the "process of social influence in which one person can enlist the aid and support of others in the accomplishment of a common task". A definition more inclusive of followers comes from Alan Keith of Genentech who said "Leadership is ultimately about creating a way for people to contribute to making something extraordinary happen."

Leadership is one of the most salient aspects of the organizational context. However, defining Leadership has been challenging.

Ethnicity

Ethnicity plays a prominent role in pornography. Distinct genres of pornography focus on performers of specific ethnic groups, or on the depiction of interracial sexual activity. Ethnic pornography typically employs ethnic and racial stereotypes in its depiction of performers.

Civil service

The term Civil service has two distinct meanings:

- Branch of governmental service in which individuals are hired on the basis of merit which is proven by the use of competitive examinations.
- Body of employees in any government agency, except the military.

A civil servant or public servant is a civilian public sector employee working for a government department or agency. The term explicitly excludes the armed services, although civilian officials will work at "Defence Ministry" headquarters. The term always includes the (sovereign) state"s employees; whether regional, or sub-state, or even municipal employees are called "civil servants" varies from country to country. In the United Kingdom, for instance, only Crown employees are civil servants, county or city employees are not.

Minority

Minority, and the related concept of "becoming-minor," is a philosophical concept developed by Gilles Deleuze and Félix Guattari in their books Kafka: Towards a Minor Literature (1975), A Thousand Plateaus (1980), and elsewhere. In these texts, they criticize the concept of "majority" as being based on a form of domination that works by naturalizing a purely numerical conception. They argue that the concept of a "dominant Minority" is an oxymoron, because the term "majority" always refers to those who are in a position of dominance.

Politics

Politics are an integral part of the Unification Church"s concerns and activities, although the church itself largely remains aloof from Politics The degree of involvement of the movement, as well as some of its specific stances, have also been part of the reason for the movement"s controversial status over the years. The belief in the establishment of a literal Kingdom of Heaven on earth and Rev. Moon"s teaching that religion alone is not enough to bring this provides a motivation for political involvement.

Civil liberties

Civil liberties are freedoms that protect an individual from the government of the nation in which they reside. Civil liberties set limits for government so that it cannot abuse its power and interfere unduly with the lives of its citizens.

Common Civil liberties include the rights of people, freedom of religion, and freedom of speech, and additionally, the right to due process, to a fair trial, to own property, and to privacy.

Democratic party	Democratic Party was a political party in Gambia. The party was founded during the pre-independence period in the colony of Bathurst (currently the national capital Banjul.) Ahead of the 1962 election, the Democratic Party merged with the Muslim Congress Party to form the Democratic Congress Alliance.
Germany	Germany), officially the Federal Republic of Germany), is a country in Central Europe. It is bordered to the north by the North Sea, Denmark, and the Baltic Sea; to the east by Poland and the Czech Republic; to the south by Austria and Switzerland; and to the west by France, Luxembourg, Belgium, and the Netherlands. The territory of Germany covers 357,021 square kilometers and is influenced by a temperate seasonal climate.
Iraq	Iraq , officially the Republic of Iraq JumhÅ«rÄ«yat Al-Ê¿IrÄ q, Kurdish: ÙƒÙ†Ù…Ø§Ø±ÛŒ Ø¹ÛŽØ±Ø§Ù‚â€Ž, Komara Iraqê), is a country in Western Asia spanning most of the northwestern end of the Zagros mountain range, the eastern part of the Syrian Desert and the northern part of the Arabian Desert. Iraq shares borders with Jordan to the west, Syria to the northwest, Turkey to the north, Iran to the east, and Kuwait and Saudi Arabia to the south. Iraq has a narrow section of coastline measuring 58 km between Umm Qasr and Al Faw on the Persian Gulf.
Committee	A Committee (some of which are titled instead as a "Commission" larger deliberative assembly--which when organized so that action on Committee requires a vote by all its entitled members, is called the Committee of the Whole". Committee s often serve several different functions:
	• Governance: in organizations considered too large for all the members to participate in decisions affecting the organization as a whole, a Committee (such as a Board of Directors or "Executive Committee) is given the power to make decisions, spend money the Board of directors can frequently enter into binding contracts and make decisions which once taken or made, can"t be taken back or undone under the law.
	• Coordination: individuals from different parts of an organization (for example, all senior vice presidents) might meet regularly to discuss developments in their areas, review projects that cut across organizational boundaries, talk about future options, etc. Where there is a large Committee it is common to have smaller Committee s with more specialized functions - for example, Boards of Directors of large corporations typically have an (ongoing) audit Committee finance Committee compensation Committee etc. Large academic conferences are usually organized by a co-ordinating Committee drawn from the relevant professional body.
Intelligence	Intelligence refers to discrete information with currency and relevance, and the abstraction, evaluation, and understanding of such information for its accuracy and value.

Chapter 9. Political Parties

Politics	Politics are an integral part of the Unification Church"s concerns and activities, although the church itself largely remains aloof from Politics The degree of involvement of the movement, as well as some of its specific stances, have also been part of the reason for the movement"s controversial status over the years. The belief in the establishment of a literal Kingdom of Heaven on earth and Rev. Moon"s teaching that religion alone is not enough to bring this provides a motivation for political involvement.
Public Service of Canada	The Public Service of Canada is the staff of the federal government of Canada. Its function is to support the Canadian monarch, and to handle the hiring of employees for the federal government ministries. It is represented by the Governor General, and the appointed [[list of Canadian ministries | ministry].
Popular sovereignty	Popular sovereignty or the sovereignty of the people is the belief that the legitimacy of the state is created by the will or consent of its people, who are the source of all political power. It is closely associated with the social contract philosophers, among whom are Thomas Hobbes, John Locke, and Jean-Jacques Rousseau. Popular sovereignty expresses a concept and does not necessarily reflect or describe a political reality.
Two-party system	A Two-party system is a form of party system where two major political parties dominate voting in nearly all elections, at every level. As a result, all, or nearly all, elected offices end up being held by candidates endorsed by one of the two major parties. Coalition governments occur only rarely in Two-party system s.
Bill of Rights	A Bill of rights is a list or summary of rights that are considered important and essential by a nation. The purpose of these bills is to protect those rights against infringement by the government. The term "Bill of rights" originates from Britain, where it referred to a bill that was passed by Parliament in 1689.
Declaration of Independence	A Declaration of independence is an assertion of the independence of an aspiring state or states. Such places are usually declared from part or all of the territory of another nation or failed nation, or are breakaway territories from within the larger state. Not all declarations of independence were successful and resulted in independence for these regions.
Italy	Italy, in particular at the turn of the 20th century, had a strong anarcho-syndicalist movement. • 1891: Foundation of the Socialist Revolutionary Anarchist Party • 1912: Foundation of the Unione Sindacale Italiana trade-union (joined the International Workers Association founded in 1922) • 1920: Publication of the newspaper Umanità Nova (New Humanity) • 1936-1939: Sébastien Faure Century, contingent of the Durruti Column in the Spanish Civil War • 1986: Foundation in Italy of the Federation of Anarchist Communists .

Presidential election	A presidential election was held in Chile on 4 September 1970. A narrow plurality (36.6 percent of the total vote) was secured by Salvador Allende, the candidate of the Popular Unity coalition of leftist parties. Because he did not obtain an absolute majority, his election required a further vote by the National Congress of Chile which resulted in Allende assuming the presidency in accordance with the Chilean Constitution of 1925.
Right	A right is the legal or moral entitlement to do or refrain from doing something thing or recognition in civil society. Rights serve as rules of interaction between people, and, as such, they place constraints and obligations upon the actions of individuals or groups (for example, if one has a right to life, this means that others do not have the liberty to kill him.) Most modern conceptions of rights are universalist and egalitarian -- in other words, equal rights are granted to all people.
Constitution	A Constitution is set of rules for government -- often codified as a written document -- that establishes principles of an autonomous political entity. In the case of countries, this term refers specifically to a national Constitution defining the fundamental political principles, and establishing the structure, procedures, powers and duties, of a government. By limiting the government"s own reach, most Constitution s guarantee certain rights to the people.
Limited government	Limited government is a government where any more than minimal governmental intervention in personal liberties and the economy is not usually allowed by law, usually in a written Constitution. It is closely related to libertarianism, classical liberalism, and some tendencies of liberalism and conservatism in the United States. Limited government is a common practice through Western culture.
William Jennings Bryan	William Jennings Bryan was the Democratic Party nominee for President of the United States in 1896, 1900 and 1908, a lawyer, and the 41st United States Secretary of State under President Woodrow Wilson. One of the most popular speakers in American history, he was noted for a deep, commanding voice. Bryan was a devout Presbyterian, a supporter of popular democracy, a critic of banks and railroads, a leader of the silverite movement in the 1890s, a leading figure in the Democratic Party, a peace advocate, a prohibitionist, an opponent of Darwinism, and one of the most prominent leaders of populism in the late 19th - and early 20th century.
New Deal	The New Deal is a programme of active labour market policies introduced in the United Kingdom by the Labour government in 1998, initially funded by a one off Â£5bn windfall tax on privatised utility companies. The stated purpose is to reduce unemployment by providing training, subsidised employment and voluntary work to the unemployed. Spending on the New Deal was Â£1.3 billion in 2001.
Coalition	A Coalition is an alliance among individuals or groups, during which they cooperate in joint action, each in his own self-interest, joining forces together for a common cause. This alliance may be temporary or a matter of convenience. A Coalition thus differs from a more formal covenant.

Chapter 9. Political Parties

Dealignment	Dealignment, in political science, is a trend or process whereby a large portion of the electorate abandons its previous partisan affiliation, without developing a new one to replace it. It is contrasted with realignment.
	Many scholars argue that the trends in elections in the United States over the last several decades are best characterized as Dealignment.
Region	Region is most commonly a geographical term that is used in various ways among the different branches of geography. In general, a Region is a medium-scale area of land or water, smaller than the whole areas of interest (which could be, for example, the world, a nation, a river basin, mountain range, and so on), and larger than a specific site. A Region may be seen as a collection of smaller units (as in "the New England states") or as one part of a larger whole (as in "the New England Region of the United States".)
Israel	Israel officially the State of Israel , Medinat Yisra"el; Arabic: Ø¯ ÙŽÙˆˆÙ'Ù„ÙŽØ©Ù Ø¥Ù Ø³Ù'Ø±ÙŽØ§Ø¡Ù ÙˆÙ„ÙŽâ€Ž, Dawlat IsrÄ "Ä«l), is a country in Western Asia located on the eastern shore of the Mediterranean Sea. It borders Lebanon in the north, Syria in the northeast, Jordan in the east, and Egypt on the southwest, and contains geographically diverse features within its relatively small area. Also adjacent are the West Bank to the east and Gaza Strip to the southwest.
Netherlands	The Netherlands is known under various terms both in English and other languages. These are used to describe the different overlapping geographical, linguistic and political areas of the Netherlands. This is often a source of confusion for people from other parts of the world.
New Zealand	New Zealand is an island country in the south-western Pacific Ocean comprising two main landmasses (commonly called the North Island and the South Island), and numerous smaller islands, most notably Stewart Island/Rakiura and the Chatham Islands. The indigenous MÄ ori named New Zealand Aotearoa, commonly translated as The Land of the Long White Cloud. The Realm of New Zealand also includes the Cook Islands and Niue (self-governing but in free association); Tokelau; and the Ross Dependency (New Zealand"s territorial claim in Antarctica.)
Green	Green is a color, the perception of which is evoked by light having a spectrum dominated by energy with a wavelength of roughly 520-570 nanometres. In the subtractive color system, it is not a primary color, but is created out of a mixture of yellow and blue, or yellow and cyan; it is considered one of the additive primary colors. On the HSV color wheel, the complement of Green is magenta; that is, a purple color corresponding to an equal mixture of red and blue light.
Green party	A Green party or ecologist party is a formally organized political party based on the principles of Green politics. These principles include environmentalism, reliance on grassroots democracy, nonviolence, and support for social justice causes, including those related to the rights of indigenous peoples, among others. "Greens" believe that the exercise of these principles leads to the health of people, societies, and ecosystems.

Duke	A Duke is a member of the nobility, historically of highest rank below the monarch, and historically controlling a duchy. The title comes from the Latin Dux Bellorum, which had the sense of "military commander" and was employed by both the Germanic peoples themselves and by the Roman authors covering them to refer to their war leaders. In the Middle Ages the title signified first among the Germanic monarchies.
Boosterism	Boosterism is the act of "boosting," or promoting, one"s town, city with the goal of improving public perception of it. Boosting can be as simple as "talking up" the entity at a party or as elaborate as establishing a visitors" bureau. It is somewhat associated with American small towns.
Power	Power in international relations is defined in several different ways. Political scientists, historians, and practitioners of international relations (diplomats) have used the following concepts of political Power: • Power as a goal of states or leaders; • Power as a measure of influence or control over outcomes, events, actors and issues; • Power as reflecting victory in conflict and the attainment of security; and, • Power as control over resources and capabilities. Modern discourse generally speaks in terms of state Power, indicating both economic and military Power. Those states that have significant amounts of Power within the international system are referred to as middle powers, regional powers, great powers, superpowers, or hyperpowers, although there is no commonly accepted standard for what defines a powerful state. Entities other than states can also acquire and wield Power in international relations.
Ku Klux Klan	Ku Klux Klan , informally known as The Klan, is the name of several past and present hate group organizations in the United States whose avowed purpose was to protect the rights of and further the interests of white Americans by violence and intimidation. The first such organizations originated in the Southern states and eventually grew to national scope. They developed iconic white costumes consisting of robes, masks, and conical hats.
National party	The National Party of Belize was a political party established mainly to fight the anti-colonialist movement propagated by the People"s United Party (PUP.) It had only minimal success and was eventually deregistered. The Party was established on August 21, 1951 and dissolved on June 26, 1958.
Ethnicity	Ethnicity plays a prominent role in pornography. Distinct genres of pornography focus on performers of specific ethnic groups, or on the depiction of interracial sexual activity. Ethnic pornography typically employs ethnic and racial stereotypes in its depiction of performers.

Chapter 9. Political Parties

Party identification	Party identification is a political term to describe a voter"s underlying allegiance to a political party. The term was first used in the United States in the 1950s, but use of the term has decreased in usage as the process of party dealignment has accelerated.

According to modern theories of political socialization, partisanship is typically formed between the ages of 18 and 24, and is generally stable after that. |
| Public opinion | Public opinion is the aggregate of individual attitudes or beliefs held by the adult population. Public opinion can also be defined as the complex collection of opinions of many different people and the sum of all their views. The principle approaches to the study of Public opinion may be divided into 4 categories:

    a) quantitative measurement of opinion distributions;
    b) investigation of the internal relationships among the individual opinions that make up Public opinion on an issue;
    c) description or analysis of the public role of Public opinion;
    d) study both of the communication media that disseminate the ideas on which opinions are based and of the uses that propagandists and other manipulators make of these media.

Public opinion as a concept gained credence with the rise of "public" in the eighteenth century. |
| Leadership | Leadership has been described as the "process of social influence in which one person can enlist the aid and support of others in the accomplishment of a common task". A definition more inclusive of followers comes from Alan Keith of Genentech who said "Leadership is ultimately about creating a way for people to contribute to making something extraordinary happen."

Leadership is one of the most salient aspects of the organizational context. However, defining Leadership has been challenging. |
| Medicare | Medicare is a social insurance program administered by the United States government, providing health insurance coverage to people who are aged 65 and over, or who meet other special criteria. Medicare operates as a single-payer health care system. The Social Security Act of 1965 was passed by Congress in late-spring of 1965 and signed into law on July 30, 1965, by President Lyndon B. Johnson as amendments to Social Security legislation. |
| Prescription | In law, Prescription is the method of sovereignty transfer of a territory through international law analogous to the common law doctrine of adverse possession for private real-estate. Prescription involves the open encroachment by the new sovereign upon the territory in question for a prolonged period of time, acting as the sovereign, without protest or other contest by the original sovereign. This doctrine legalizes de jure the de facto transfer of sovereignty caused in part by the original sovereign"s extended negligence and/or neglect of the area in question. |

Divided government	In the United States, Divided government describes a situation in which one party controls the White House and another party controls one or both houses of the United States Congress. Divided government is suggested by some to be an undesirable product of the separation of powers in the United States" political system. Earlier in the 20th century, Divided government was rare.
Federalism	Federalism is a political philosophy in which a group of members are bound together ">covenant) with a governing representative head. The term Federalism is also used to describe a system of the government in which sovereignty is constitutionally divided between a central governing authority and constituent political units (like states or provinces.) Federalism is a system in which the power to govern is shared between national and central(state) governments, creating what is often called a federation.
Civil liberties	Civil liberties are freedoms that protect an individual from the government of the nation in which they reside. Civil liberties set limits for government so that it cannot abuse its power and interfere unduly with the lives of its citizens.

Common Civil liberties include the rights of people, freedom of religion, and freedom of speech, and additionally, the right to due process, to a fair trial, to own property, and to privacy. |

Fiscal policy	In economics, Fiscal policy is the use of government spending and revenue collection to influence the economy. Fiscal policy can be contrasted with the other main type of economic policy, monetary policy, which attempts to stabilize the economy by controlling interest rates and the supply of money. The two main instruments of Fiscal policy are government spending and taxation.
New Deal	The New Deal is a programme of active labour market policies introduced in the United Kingdom by the Labour government in 1998, initially funded by a one off Â£5bn windfall tax on privatised utility companies. The stated purpose is to reduce unemployment by providing training, subsidised employment and voluntary work to the unemployed. Spending on the New Deal was Â£1.3 billion in 2001.
Committee	A Committee (some of which are titled instead as a "Commission" larger deliberative assembly-- which when organized so that action on Committee requires a vote by all its entitled members, is called the Committee of the Whole". Committee s often serve several different functions: • Governance: in organizations considered too large for all the members to participate in decisions affecting the organization as a whole, a Committee (such as a Board of Directors or "Executive Committee) is given the power to make decisions, spend money the Board of directors can frequently enter into binding contracts and make decisions which once taken or made, can"t be taken back or undone under the law. • Coordination: individuals from different parts of an organization (for example, all senior vice presidents) might meet regularly to discuss developments in their areas, review projects that cut across organizational boundaries, talk about future options, etc. Where there is a large Committee it is common to have smaller Committee s with more specialized functions - for example, Boards of Directors of large corporations typically have an (ongoing) audit Committee finance Committee compensation Committee etc. Large academic conferences are usually organized by a co-ordinating Committee drawn from the relevant professional body.
Constitution	A Constitution is set of rules for government -- often codified as a written document -- that establishes principles of an autonomous political entity. In the case of countries, this term refers specifically to a national Constitution defining the fundamental political principles, and establishing the structure, procedures, powers and duties, of a government. By limiting the government"s own reach, most Constitution s guarantee certain rights to the people.
Presidential election	A presidential election was held in Chile on 4 September 1970. A narrow plurality (36.6 percent of the total vote) was secured by Salvador Allende, the candidate of the Popular Unity coalition of leftist parties. Because he did not obtain an absolute majority, his election required a further vote by the National Congress of Chile which resulted in Allende assuming the presidency in accordance with the Chilean Constitution of 1925.

Public Service of Canada	The Public Service of Canada is the staff of the federal government of Canada. Its function is to support the Canadian monarch, and to handle the hiring of employees for the federal government ministries. It is represented by the Governor General, and the appointed [[list of Canadian ministries | ministry].
Democratic party	Democratic Party was a political party in Gambia. The party was founded during the pre-independence period in the colony of Bathurst (currently the national capital Banjul.) Ahead of the 1962 election, the Democratic Party merged with the Muslim Congress Party to form the Democratic Congress Alliance.
Anti-Americanism	Dictionaries tend to define Anti-Americanism, often anti-American sentiment, as a widespread opposition or hostility to the people, government or policies of the United States. In practice, a broad range of attitudes and actions critical of or opposed to the United States have been labeled Anti-Americanism. Thus, the nature and applicability of the term is often disputed.
Civil service	The term Civil service has two distinct meanings: • Branch of governmental service in which individuals are hired on the basis of merit which is proven by the use of competitive examinations. • Body of employees in any government agency, except the military. A civil servant or public servant is a civilian public sector employee working for a government department or agency. The term explicitly excludes the armed services, although civilian officials will work at "Defence Ministry" headquarters. The term always includes the (sovereign) state"s employees; whether regional, or sub-state, or even municipal employees are called "civil servants" varies from country to country. In the United Kingdom, for instance, only Crown employees are civil servants, county or city employees are not.
Finland	Finland , officially the Republic of Finland), is a Nordic country situated in the Fennoscandian region of northern Europe. It borders Sweden on the west, Russia on the east, and Norway on the north, while Estonia lies to its south across the Gulf of Finland. The capital city is Helsinki.
France	France , officially the French Republic , is a country located in Western Europe, with several overseas islands and territories located on other continents. Metropolitan France extends from the Mediterranean Sea to the English Channel and the North Sea, and from the Rhine to the Atlantic Ocean. It is often referred to as L"Hexagone ("The Hexagon") because of the geometric shape of its territory.
Germany	Germany), officially the Federal Republic of Germany), is a country in Central Europe. It is bordered to the north by the North Sea, Denmark, and the Baltic Sea; to the east by Poland and the Czech Republic; to the south by Austria and Switzerland; and to the west by France, Luxembourg, Belgium, and the Netherlands. The territory of Germany covers 357,021 square kilometers and is influenced by a temperate seasonal climate.

Declaration of Independence	A Declaration of independence is an assertion of the independence of an aspiring state or states. Such places are usually declared from part or all of the territory of another nation or failed nation, or are breakaway territories from within the larger state. Not all declarations of independence were successful and resulted in independence for these regions.
Right	A right is the legal or moral entitlement to do or refrain from doing something thing or recognition in civil society. Rights serve as rules of interaction between people, and, as such, they place constraints and obligations upon the actions of individuals or groups (for example, if one has a right to life, this means that others do not have the liberty to kill him.)
	Most modern conceptions of rights are universalist and egalitarian -- in other words, equal rights are granted to all people.
Suffrage	Suffrage is the civil right to vote, or the exercise of that right. In that context, it is also called political franchise or simply the franchise. Suffrage is very valuable to the extent that there are opportunities to vote .
National party	The National Party of Belize was a political party established mainly to fight the anti-colonialist movement propagated by the People"s United Party (PUP.) It had only minimal success and was eventually deregistered.
	The Party was established on August 21, 1951 and dissolved on June 26, 1958.
Politics	Politics are an integral part of the Unification Church"s concerns and activities, although the church itself largely remains aloof from Politics The degree of involvement of the movement, as well as some of its specific stances, have also been part of the reason for the movement"s controversial status over the years. The belief in the establishment of a literal Kingdom of Heaven on earth and Rev. Moon"s teaching that religion alone is not enough to bring this provides a motivation for political involvement.
Complexity	In general usage, Complexity tends to be used to characterize something with many parts in intricate arrangement. The study of these complex linkages is the main goal of network theory and network science. In science there are at this time a number of approaches to characterizing Complexity, many of which are reflected in Seth Lloyd of M.I.T. writes that he once gave a presentation which set out 32 definitions of Complexity.
Ethnicity	Ethnicity plays a prominent role in pornography. Distinct genres of pornography focus on performers of specific ethnic groups, or on the depiction of interracial sexual activity. Ethnic pornography typically employs ethnic and racial stereotypes in its depiction of performers.

Federalism	Federalism is a political philosophy in which a group of members are bound together ">covenant) with a governing representative head. The term Federalism is also used to describe a system of the government in which sovereignty is constitutionally divided between a central governing authority and constituent political units (like states or provinces.) Federalism is a system in which the power to govern is shared between national and central(state) governments, creating what is often called a federation.
Leadership	Leadership has been described as the "process of social influence in which one person can enlist the aid and support of others in the accomplishment of a common task". A definition more inclusive of followers comes from Alan Keith of Genentech who said "Leadership is ultimately about creating a way for people to contribute to making something extraordinary happen." Leadership is one of the most salient aspects of the organizational context. However, defining Leadership has been challenging.
National convention	During the French Revolution, the National Convention or Convention, in France, comprised the constitutional and legislative assembly which sat from 20 September 1792 to 26 October 1795 . It held executive power in France during the first years of the French First Republic. It was succeeded by the Directory, commencing 2 November 1795.
Vietnam	Vietnam " href="/wiki/Battle_of_B%E1%BA%A1ch_%C4%90%E1%BA%B1ng_River_(938)">battle of Bá⁰ịch Ä á⁰±ng River. Successive dynasties flourished along with geographic and political expansion deeper into Southeast Asia, until it was colonized by the French in the mid-19th century. Efforts to resist the French eventually led to their expulsion from the country in the mid-20th century, leaving a nation divided politically into two countries.
Vietnam War	The Vietnam War was a military conflict that occurred in Vietnam, Laos and Cambodia from 1959 to 30 April 1975. The war was fought between the communist North Vietnam, supported by its communist allies, and the government of South Vietnam, supported by the United States and other member nations of the Southeast Asia Treaty Organization (SEATO.) The following outline is provided as an overview of and topical guide to the Vietnam War:

Listed by starting date:

- Operation 34A - (1964)
- Operation Starlite - August 18-24 1965
- Operation Hump- November 5 1965
- Operation Crimp - January 7, 1966
- Operation Birmingham - April 1966
- Operation Hastings - Late May 1966
- Operation Prairie - August 1966
- Operation Deckhouse Five - January 6, 1967
- Operation Cedar Falls - January 8, 1967
- Operation Junction City - February 21, 1967
- Operation Francis Marion - April 6 - April 30, 1967
- Operation Union - April 21-May 16, 1967
- Operations Malheur I and Malheur II - 11 May - July 1, 1967
- Operation Baker - May 11, 1967
- Operation Scotland - See Battle of Khe Sanh
- Operation Pegasus - August 8, 1968
- Operation Dewey Canyon - January 22, 1969
- Operation Twinkletoes - 1969
- Operation Apache Snow - May 10 - May 20, 1969
- Operation Chicago Peak - April 1970
- Operation Texas Star - April - September, 1970
- Operation Ivory Coast - November 21, 1970
- Operation Jefferson Glenn - 1970-1971
- Operation Lam Son 719 - February 8, 1971
- Ho Chi Minh Campaign January 24 - April 30, 1975
- Operation Frequent Wind - April, 1975

- Battle of Ap Bac - January 2, 1963
- Battle of Kien Long - April 11 - April 15, 1964
- Battle of Thanh Hóa - July 31, 1964
- Battle of Binh Gia - December 28, 1964 - January 1, 1965
- Battle of Dong Xoai - June 10, 1965
- Battle near Minh Thanh - October 25 - October 27, 1965
- Battle of Ia Drang - November 14 - November 16, 1965
- Battle of Cu Nghi - January 28 - January 31, 1966
- Battle of Kim Son Valley - February 16 - February 28, 1966
- Battle of A Shau - March 9 - March 10, 1966
- Battle of Xa Cam My - April 11 - April 12, 1966
- First Battle of Dong Ha - Late May - June, 1966
- Battle on Minh Thanh Road - July 9, 1966
- Battle of Ä   á»©c CÆ¡ - August 9, 1966
- Battle of Long Tá°§n - August 18- August 19, 1966
- Viet Cong attack on Tan Son Nhut airbase - December 4, 1966
- Battle of LZ Bird - December 27, 1966

- Battle of Tra Binh Dong - February 14 - February 15, 1967
- Battle of Hills 881 and 861 - April 24-May 9, 1967
- Nine Days in May - May 18 - May 28, 1967
- Battle of Vinh Huy - May 30 - June 2, 1967
- Battle of Con Thien - July 2 - July 3, 1967
- Battle of Dong Son - September 4, 1967
- Battle of Ong Thang - October 17, 1967
- First Battle of Loc Ninh - October 29 - November, 1967
- Battle of Dak To - November 3-November 22, 1967
- Battle in the Mekong Delta - December 4, 1967
- Battle of Tam Quan - December 6 - December 20, 1967
- Battle of Thom Tham Khe - December 27 - December 28, 1967
- Phoenix Program - 1967 - 1972
- Battle of Khe Sanh - January 21 - April 8, 1968
- Tet Offensive - January 30 - February 25, 1968
- Battle of Bien Hoa - January 31 - July 1, 1968
- Battle of Kham Duc - May 10 - May 12, 1968
- First Battle of Saigon - January 31, - February 3, 1968
- Battle of Hue - January 31, - February 25, 1968
- Tet 1969 - February 1969
- Battle of Hamburger Hill - May 10 - May 20, 1969
- Firebase Ripcord - March 12 - July 23, 1970
- Cambodian Incursion - April 29 - July 22, 1970
- Battle of Snoul - January 5 - May 30, 1971
- Easter Offensive - March 30 - October 22, 1972
- First Battle of Quang Tri - March 30 - May 1, 1972
- Battle of Loc Ninh - April 4 - April 7, 1972
- Battle of An Loc - April 20 - July 20, 1972
- Second Battle of Quang Tri - June 28 - September 16, 1972
- Battle of Phuoc Long - December 13, 1974 - January 6, 1975
- Battle of Buon Me Thuot - March 10 - March 12, 1975
- Battle of Xuan Loc - April 9 - April 20, 1975

- Operation Farm Gate
- Operation Chopper (1962)
- Operation Ranch Hand (1962-1971)
- Operation Pierce Arrow (1964)
- Operation Barrell Roll (1964-1972)
- Operation Pony Express (1965-1970)
- Operation Flaming Dart (1965)
- Operation Rolling Thunder (1965-1968)
- Operation Steel Tiger (1965-1968)
- Operation Arc Light (1965-1973)
- Operation Tiger Hound (1965-1968)
- Operation Shed Light (1966-1972)
- Operation Carolina Moon (1966)
- Operation Wahiawa (1966)
- Operation Bolo (1967)
- Operation Popeye (1967-1972)
- Operation Niagara (1968)
- Operation Igloo White (1968-1973

- Operation Giant Lance (1969)
- Operation Commando Hunt (1968-1972)
- Operation Menu (1969-1970)
- Operation Patio (1970)
- Operation Freedom Deal (1970-1973)
- Operation Linebacker (1972)
- Operation Enhance Plus (1972)
- Operation Linebacker II (1972)
- Operation Homecoming (1973)
- Operation Baby Lift (1975)
- Operation Eagle Pull (1975)
- Operation Frequent Wind (1975)

- National Order of Vietnam
- Vietnam Military Merit Medal
- Vietnam Distinguished Service Order
- Vietnam Meritorious Service Medal
- Vietnam Special Service Medal
- Vietnam Gallantry Cross
- Vietnam Air Gallantry Cross
- Vietnam Navy Gallantry Cross
- Vietnam Armed Forces Honor Medal
- Vietnam Civil Actions Medal
- Vietnam Staff Service Medal
- Vietnam Technical Service Medal
- Vietnam Wound Medal
- Vietnam Campaign Medal
- Presidential Unit Citation (Vietnam)
- Vietnam Gallantry Cross Unit Citation
- Vietnam Civil Actions Unit Citation

- Golden Star Medal
- Ho Chi Minh Order
- Defeat American Aggression Badge
- Vietnam Liberation Order
- Resolution for Victory Order

- Medal of Honor rare
- Distinguished Service Cross rare
- Navy Cross uncommon
- Air Force Cross uncommon
- Silver Star uncommon
- Purple Heart frequent
- Bronze Star frequent
- Presidential Unit Citation rare
- Vietnam Service Medal very common
- National Defense Service Medal very common
- Commendation Medal common

- "Fatigue Press" at Fort Hood,
- "Last Harass" at Fort Gordon, Georgia
- "Pawn"s Pawn" at Fort Leonard Wood, Missouri

- "Ultimate Weapon" at Fort Dix, New Jersey
- "Attitude Check" at Camp Pendleton, California
- "Green Machine" at Fort Greely, Alaska
- "Napalm" at Fort Campbell, Tennessee
- "Arctic Arsenal" at Fort Greely, Alaska
- "Black Voice" at Fort McClellan, Alabama
- "Fragging Action" at Fort Dix
- "Fort Polk Puke" at Fort Polk, Louisiana
- "Custer"s Last Stand" at Fort Riley, Kansas
- "Whack!" from the Women"s Army Corps School
- "Where Are We?" at Fort Huachuca, Arizona
- "Voice of the Lumpen" (affiliated with the Black Panther Party) in Frankfurt
- "Can You Bear McNair?" at McNair Barracks, Berlin
- "Seasick" at Subic Bay
- "The Man Can"t Win If You Grin" in Okinawa
- "Korea Free Press"
- "Semper Fi" in Japan
- "Stars and Bars" in England
- "Separated From Life" in England
- "Duck Power" in San Diego
- "Harass the Brass" at Canute Air Force Base, Illinois
- "All Hands Abandon Ship", Newport, Rhode Island
- "Now Hear This", Long Beach
- "Potemkin" on the USS Forestall
- "Star Spangled Bummer" at Wright-Patterson Air Force Base in Ohio
- "Fat Albert"s Death Ship" in Charlestown
- "Pig Boat Blues", USS Agerholm
- "Special Weapons", Kirtland AFB, New Mexico
- "I Will Fear No Evil", Kirtland AFB, New Mexico
- "Blows Against the Empire", Kirtland AFB, New Mexico

source: "The American War" - see references below

- Bao Dai
- Duong Van Minh
- Madame Ngo Dinh Nhu
- Ngo Dinh Diem
- Ngo Dinh Nhu
- Nguyen Cao Ky
- Nguyen Khanh
- Nguyen Van Thieu

- Creighton W. Abrams
- Dean Acheson
- Spiro Agnew
- Ellsworth Bunker
- McGeorge Bundy
- William Bundy
- William Calley
- Clark Clifford
- William Colby
- A. Peter Dewey
- John Foster Dulles
- Dwight D. Eisenhower
- Daniel Ellsberg
- J. William Fulbright
- Barry Goldwater
- David Hackworth
- Alexander Haig
- Paul D. Harkins
- Seymour Hersh
- Hubert Humphrey
- Lyndon Johnson
- John F. Kennedy
- John Kerry
- Henry Kissinger
- Melvin Laird
- Edward Lansdale
- Henry Cabot Lodge, Jr.
- Mike Mansfield
- Graham Martin
- Robert McNamara
- George McGovern
- Richard Nixon
- Pete Peterson
- Charika Pugh
- Dean Rusk

- Maxwell D. Taylor
- Hugh C. Thompson, Jr
- John Paul Vann
- Gary Varsel
- William Westmoreland

- Ho Chi Minh
- Le Duan
- Tran Van Tra
- Le Duc Tho
- Pham Van Dong
- General Giap
- Poewll Ward

- Lon Nol
- Pol Pot
- Norodom Sihanouk
- Sirik Matak
- Sosthene Fernandez

- David H. Hackworth. 1989 About Face
- A.J. Langguth. 2000. Our Vietnam: the War 1954-1975.
- Mann, Robert. 2002. Grand Delusion, A: America"s Descent Into Vietnam.
- Windrow, Martin. 2005. The Last Valley: Dien Bien Phu and the French Defeat in Vietnam.
- Bernard Fall. 1967. Hell in a Very Small Place: the Siege of Dien Bien Phu.
- Harvey Pekar. 2003. American Splendor: Unsung Hero
- Prados, John. 2000. The Blood Road: The Ho Chi Minh Trail and the Vietnam War.
- Prados, John. 1999. Valley of Decision: The Siege of Khe Sanh.
- Shultz, Robert H. Jr. 2000. The Secret War Against Hanoi: The Untold Story of Spies, Saboteurs, and Covert Warriors in North Vietnam.
- Plaster, John L. 1998. SOG: The Secret Wars of America"s Commandos in Vietnam.
- Murphy, Edward F. 1995. Dak To: America"s Sky Soldiers in South Vietnam"s Central Highlands.
- Nolan, Keith W. 1996. The Battle for Saigon: Tet 1968.
- Nolan, Keith W. 1996. Sappers in the Wire: The Life and Death of Firebase Mary Ann.
- Nolan, Keith W. 1992. Operation Buffalo: USMC Fight for the DMZ.
- Nolan, Keith W. 2003. Ripcord : Screaming Eagles Under Siege, Vietnam 1970.
- Robert S. McNamara. 1996. In Retrospect: The Tragedy and Lessons of Vietnam.
- Larry Berman. 2002. No Peace, No Honor: Nixon, Kissinger, and Betrayal in Vietnam.
- Bergerud, Eric M. 1994. Red Thunder, Tropic Lightning: The World of a Combat Division in Vietnam.
- Bernard Edelman. 2002. Dear America: Letters Home from Vietnam.
- Darrel D. Whitcomb. 1999. The Rescue of Bat 21.
- Oberdorfer, Don. 1971. Tet: the Story of a Battle and its Historic Aftermath.
- LTG Harold G. Moore and Joseph L. Galloway. 1992. We Were Soldiers Once ... And Young.
- Duiker, William J. 2002. Ho Chi Minh: A Life.
- John Laurence. 2002. The Cat from Hue: A Vietnam War Story.
- Emerson, Gloria. 1976. Winners and Losers: Battles, Retreats, Gains, Losses and Ruins from a Long War.
- Philip Caputo. 1977. A Rumor of War.

- Al Santoli. 1981. Everything We Had: an Oral History of the Vietnam War by 33 American Soldiers Who Fought It.
- Robert C. Mason. 1983. Chickenhawk.
- Michael Herr. 1977. Dispatches.
- Joseph T. Ward. 1991. Dear Mom: a Sniper"s Vietnam.
- Hemphill, Robert. 1998. Platoon: Bravo Company.
- Noam Chomsky. 1967. The Responsibility of Intellectuals.
- Moore, Robin. 1965 The Green Berets (ISBN 0-312-98492-8)

- Robert Olen Butler. 1992.

Chapter 10. Participation, Voting, and Elections

Foreign policy	A country"s Foreign policy is a set of goals outlining how the country will interact with other countries economically, politically, socially and militarily, and to a lesser extent, how the country will interact with non-state actors. The aforementioned interaction is evaluated and monitored in attempts to maximize benefits of multilateral international cooperation. Foreign policies are designed to help protect a country"s national interests, national security, ideological goals, and economic prosperity.
Coalition	A Coalition is an alliance among individuals or groups, during which they cooperate in joint action, each in his own self-interest, joining forces together for a common cause. This alliance may be temporary or a matter of convenience. A Coalition thus differs from a more formal covenant.
Public opinion	Public opinion is the aggregate of individual attitudes or beliefs held by the adult population. Public opinion can also be defined as the complex collection of opinions of many different people and the sum of all their views. The principle approaches to the study of Public opinion may be divided into 4 categories: a) quantitative measurement of opinion distributions; b) investigation of the internal relationships among the individual opinions that make up Public opinion on an issue; c) description or analysis of the public role of Public opinion; d) study both of the communication media that disseminate the ideas on which opinions are based and of the uses that propagandists and other manipulators make of these media. Public opinion as a concept gained credence with the rise of "public" in the eighteenth century.
Civil liberties	Civil liberties are freedoms that protect an individual from the government of the nation in which they reside. Civil liberties set limits for government so that it cannot abuse its power and interfere unduly with the lives of its citizens. Common Civil liberties include the rights of people, freedom of religion, and freedom of speech, and additionally, the right to due process, to a fair trial, to own property, and to privacy.

Politics	Politics are an integral part of the Unification Church"s concerns and activities, although the church itself largely remains aloof from Politics The degree of involvement of the movement, as well as some of its specific stances, have also been part of the reason for the movement"s controversial status over the years. The belief in the establishment of a literal Kingdom of Heaven on earth and Rev. Moon"s teaching that religion alone is not enough to bring this provides a motivation for political involvement.
Right	A right is the legal or moral entitlement to do or refrain from doing something thing or recognition in civil society. Rights serve as rules of interaction between people, and, as such, they place constraints and obligations upon the actions of individuals or groups (for example, if one has a right to life, this means that others do not have the liberty to kill him.) Most modern conceptions of rights are universalist and egalitarian -- in other words, equal rights are granted to all people.
Constitution	A Constitution is set of rules for government -- often codified as a written document -- that establishes principles of an autonomous political entity. In the case of countries, this term refers specifically to a national Constitution defining the fundamental political principles, and establishing the structure, procedures, powers and duties, of a government. By limiting the government"s own reach, most Constitution s guarantee certain rights to the people.
Bicameralism	In government, Bicameralism is the practice of having two legislative or parliamentary chambers. Thus, a bicameral parliament or bicameral legislature is a legislature which consists of two chambers or houses. Bicameralism is an essential and defining feature of the classical notion of mixed government.
Enumerated powers	The Enumerated powers are a list of specific responsibilities found in Article 1 Section 8 of the United States Constitution, which iterates the authority granted to the United States Congress. Congress may exercise only those powers that are granted to it by the Constitution, limited by the Bill of Rights and the other protections found in the Constitutional text. The classical statement of a government of Enumerated powers is that by Chief Justice Marshall in McCulloch v. Maryland: This government is acknowledged by all, to be one of Enumerated powers.

Ex post facto law	An Ex post facto law or retroactive law, is a law that retroactively changes the legal consequences of acts committed or the legal status of facts and relationships that existed prior to the enactment of the law. In reference to criminal law, it may criminalize actions that were legal when committed; or it may aggravate a crime by bringing it into a more severe category than it was in at the time it was committed; or it may change or increase the punishment prescribed for a crime, such as by adding new penalties or extending terms; or it may alter the rules of evidence in order to make conviction for a crime more likely than it would have been at the time of the action for which a defendant is prosecuted. Conversely, a form of Ex post facto law commonly known as an amnesty law may decriminalize certain acts or alleviate possible punishments retroactively.
Habeas corpus	Habeas corpus have the body) is a legal action through which a person can seek relief from the unlawful detention of him or herself or from being harmed by the judicial system. Of English origin, the writ of Habeas corpus has historically been an important instrument for the safeguarding of individual freedom against arbitrary state action.
Iraq	Iraq , officially the Republic of Iraq JumhÅ«rÄ«yat Al-Ê¿IrÄ q, Kurdish: ÙƒÛ†Ù…Ø§Ø±ÛŒ Ø¹ÛŽØ²Ø§Ù‚ÛŽ, Komara Iraqê), is a country in Western Asia spanning most of the northwestern end of the Zagros mountain range, the eastern part of the Syrian Desert and the northern part of the Arabian Desert. Iraq shares borders with Jordan to the west, Syria to the northwest, Turkey to the north, Iran to the east, and Kuwait and Saudi Arabia to the south. Iraq has a narrow section of coastline measuring 58 km between Umm Qasr and Al Faw on the Persian Gulf.
Power	Power in international relations is defined in several different ways. Political scientists, historians, and practitioners of international relations (diplomats) have used the following concepts of political Power: • Power as a goal of states or leaders; • Power as a measure of influence or control over outcomes, events, actors and issues; • Power as reflecting victory in conflict and the attainment of security; and, • Power as control over resources and capabilities. Modern discourse generally speaks in terms of state Power, indicating both economic and military Power. Those states that have significant amounts of Power within the international system are referred to as middle powers, regional powers, great powers, superpowers, or hyperpowers, although there is no commonly accepted standard for what defines a powerful state. Entities other than states can also acquire and wield Power in international relations.

Federalism	Federalism is a political philosophy in which a group of members are bound together ">covenant) with a governing representative head. The term Federalism is also used to describe a system of the government in which sovereignty is constitutionally divided between a central governing authority and constituent political units (like states or provinces.) Federalism is a system in which the power to govern is shared between national and central(state) governments, creating what is often called a federation.
Limited government	Limited government is a government where any more than minimal governmental intervention in personal liberties and the economy is not usually allowed by law, usually in a written Constitution. It is closely related to libertarianism, classical liberalism, and some tendencies of liberalism and conservatism in the United States. Limited government is a common practice through Western culture.
Public Service of Canada	The Public Service of Canada is the staff of the federal government of Canada. Its function is to support the Canadian monarch, and to handle the hiring of employees for the federal government ministries. It is represented by the Governor General, and the appointed [[list of Canadian ministries | ministry].
Civil rights movement	The Civil rights movement was a worldwide political movement for equality before the law occurring between approximately 1950 and 1980. It was accompanied by much civil unrest and popular rebellion. The process was long and tenuous in many countries, and most of these movements did not achieve or fully achieve their objectives.
Ethnicity	Ethnicity plays a prominent role in pornography. Distinct genres of pornography focus on performers of specific ethnic groups, or on the depiction of interracial sexual activity. Ethnic pornography typically employs ethnic and racial stereotypes in its depiction of performers.
Civil service	The term Civil service has two distinct meanings: • Branch of governmental service in which individuals are hired on the basis of merit which is proven by the use of competitive examinations. • Body of employees in any government agency, except the military. A civil servant or public servant is a civilian public sector employee working for a government department or agency. The term explicitly excludes the armed services, although civilian officials will work at "Defence Ministry" headquarters. The term always includes the (sovereign) state"s employees; whether regional, or sub-state, or even municipal employees are called "civil servants" varies from country to country. In the United Kingdom, for instance, only Crown employees are civil servants, county or city employees are not.

Minority	Minority, and the related concept of "becoming-minor," is a philosophical concept developed by Gilles Deleuze and Félix Guattari in their books Kafka: Towards a Minor Literature (1975), A Thousand Plateaus (1980), and elsewhere. In these texts, they criticize the concept of "majority" as being based on a form of domination that works by naturalizing a purely numerical conception. They argue that the concept of a "dominant Minority" is an oxymoron, because the term "majority" always refers to those who are in a position of dominance.
Germany	Germany), officially the Federal Republic of Germany), is a country in Central Europe. It is bordered to the north by the North Sea, Denmark, and the Baltic Sea; to the east by Poland and the Czech Republic; to the south by Austria and Switzerland; and to the west by France, Luxembourg, Belgium, and the Netherlands. The territory of Germany covers 357,021 square kilometers and is influenced by a temperate seasonal climate.
Judicial activism	Judicial activism is a critical term used to describe judicial rulings that are viewed as imposing a personal biased interpretation by a given court of what a law means as opposed to what a neutral, unbiased observer would naturally interpret a law to be. The term has most often been used to describe left-wing judges, however; the Supreme Court"s activity since the confirmation of justices Alito and Roberts under George W. Bush, and the ensuing perception that the conservative court was expanding the rights of corporations at the cost of the rights of citizens, has since led to conservative judges being labeled activists.

The term "Judicial activism" is frequently used in political debate without definition, which has created some confusion over its precise meaning or meanings. |
| Netherlands | The Netherlands is known under various terms both in English and other languages. These are used to describe the different overlapping geographical, linguistic and political areas of the Netherlands. This is often a source of confusion for people from other parts of the world. |
| Norway | Norway , Noreg (Nynorsk)) or Norga (North Sami), officially the Kingdom of Norway, is a country in Northern Europe occupying the western portion of the Scandinavian Peninsula, as well as Jan Mayen and the Arctic archipelago of Svalbard under the Spitsbergen Treaty. The majority of the country shares a border to the east with Sweden; its northernmost region is bordered by Finland to the south and Russia to the east. The United Kingdom and Faroe Islands lie to its west across the North Sea, Iceland and Greenland lies to its west across the Norwegian Sea, and Denmark lies south of its southern tip across the Skagerrak Strait. |
| Sweden | Sweden , officially the Kingdom of Sweden), is a Nordic country on the Scandinavian Peninsula in Northern Europe. Sweden has land borders with Norway to the west and Finland to the northeast, and it is connected to Denmark by the Öresund Bridge in the south.

At 450,000 km^2 (173,746 sq mi), Sweden is the third largest country in the European Union in terms of area, and it has a total population of over 9.2 million. |

New Deal	The New Deal is a programme of active labour market policies introduced in the United Kingdom by the Labour government in 1998, initially funded by a one off Â£5bn windfall tax on privatised utility companies. The stated purpose is to reduce unemployment by providing training, subsidised employment and voluntary work to the unemployed. Spending on the New Deal was Â£1.3 billion in 2001.
Presidential election	A presidential election was held in Chile on 4 September 1970. A narrow plurality (36.6 percent of the total vote) was secured by Salvador Allende, the candidate of the Popular Unity coalition of leftist parties. Because he did not obtain an absolute majority, his election required a further vote by the National Congress of Chile which resulted in Allende assuming the presidency in accordance with the Chilean Constitution of 1925.
Committee	A Committee (some of which are titled instead as a "Commission" larger deliberative assembly-- which when organized so that action on Committee requires a vote by all its entitled members, is called the Committee of the Whole". Committee s often serve several different functions:

- Governance: in organizations considered too large for all the members to participate in decisions affecting the organization as a whole, a Committee (such as a Board of Directors or "Executive Committee) is given the power to make decisions, spend money the Board of directors can frequently enter into binding contracts and make decisions which once taken or made, can"t be taken back or undone under the law.

- Coordination: individuals from different parts of an organization (for example, all senior vice presidents) might meet regularly to discuss developments in their areas, review projects that cut across organizational boundaries, talk about future options, etc. Where there is a large Committee it is common to have smaller Committee s with more specialized functions - for example, Boards of Directors of large corporations typically have an (ongoing) audit Committee finance Committee compensation Committee etc. Large academic conferences are usually organized by a co-ordinating Committee drawn from the relevant professional body.

Australia	Australia , officially the Commonwealth of Australia is a country in the southern hemisphere comprising the mainland, which is both the world"s smallest continent and the world"s largest island, the island of Tasmania, and numerous other islands in the Indian and Pacific Oceans.[N4] Australia is the only place that is simultaneously considered a continent, a country and an island. Neighbouring countries include Indonesia, East Timor and Papua New Guinea to the north, the Solomon Islands, Vanuatu and New Caledonia to the north-east and New Zealand to the southeast.

For around 40,000 years before European settlement commenced in the late 18th century, the Australia n mainland and Tasmania were inhabited by around 250 individual nations of indigenous Australia ns.

Democratic party	Democratic Party was a political party in Gambia. The party was founded during the pre-independence period in the colony of Bathurst (currently the national capital Banjul.) Ahead of the 1962 election, the Democratic Party merged with the Muslim Congress Party to form the Democratic Congress Alliance.
Parliamentary system	A Parliamentary system is a system of government wherein the ministers of the executive branch are drawn from the legislature, and are accountable to that body, such that the executive and legislative branches are intertwined. In such a system, the head of government is both de facto chief executive and chief legislator.
	Parliamentary system s are characterized by no clear-cut separation of powers between the executive and legislative branches, leading to a different set of checks and balances compared to those found in presidential systems.
Contract	Agreement is said to be reached when an offer capable of immediate acceptance is met with a "mirror image" acceptance (ie, an unqualified acceptance.) The parties must have the necessary capacity to Contract and the Contract must not be either trifling, indeterminate, impossible or illegal. Contract law is based on the principle expressed in the Latin phrase pacta sunt servanda .
Privatization	Privatization is the incidence or process of transferring ownership of a business, enterprise, agency or public service from the public sector (government) to the private sector (business.) In a broader sense, Privatization refers to transfer of any government function to the private sector including governmental functions like revenue collection and law enforcement.
	The term "Privatization" also has been used to describe two unrelated transactions.
Property right	A Property right is the exclusive authority to determine how a resource is used, whether that resource is owned by government or by individuals. All economic goods have a property rights attribute. This attribute has three broad components
	1. The right to use the good
	2. The right to earn income from the good
	3. The right to transfer the good to others
	The concept of property rights as used by economists and legal scholars are related but distinct. The distinction is largely seen in the economists" focus on the ability of an individual or collective to control the use of the good.
Social Security	Social Security, in Australia, refers to a system of social welfare payments provided by Commonwealth Government of Australia. These payments are administered by a Government body named Centrelink. In Australia, most benefits are subject to a means test.

K street project	The K Street Project is an effort by the Republican Party (GOP) to pressure Washington lobbying firms to hire Republicans in top positions, and to reward loyal GOP lobbyists with access to influential officials. It was launched in 1995 by Republican strategist Grover Norquist and then-House majority whip Tom DeLay. It has been criticized as being part of a "coziness" between the GOP and large corporations which has allegedly allowed business to rewrite government regulations affecting their own industries in some cases
Leadership	Leadership has been described as the "process of social influence in which one person can enlist the aid and support of others in the accomplishment of a common task". A definition more inclusive of followers comes from Alan Keith of Genentech who said "Leadership is ultimately about creating a way for people to contribute to making something extraordinary happen."
	Leadership is one of the most salient aspects of the organizational context. However, defining Leadership has been challenging.
Iran-Contra Affair	The Iran-Contra affair was a political scandal in the United States which came to light in November 1986, during the Reagan administration, in which senior US figures agreed to facilitate the sale of arms to Iran, the subject of an arms embargo, to secure the release of hostages and to fund Nicaraguan contras.
	It began as an operation to improve U.S.-Iranian relations, wherein Israel would ship weapons to a relatively moderate, politically influential group of Iranians; the U.S. would then resupply Israel and receive the Israeli payment. The Iranian recipients promised to do everything in their power to achieve the release of six U.S. hostages, who were being held by the Lebanese Shia Islamist group Hezbollah, who were unknowingly connected to the Army of the Guardians of the Islamic Revolution.
Intelligence	Intelligence refers to discrete information with currency and relevance, and the abstraction, evaluation, and understanding of such information for its accuracy and value.
Appropriation	Appropriation is a non-violent process by which previously unowned natural resources, particularly land, become the property of a person or group of persons. The term is widely used in economics in this sense. In certain cases, it proceeds under very specifically defined forms, such as driving stakes or other such markers into the land claimed, which form gave rise to the term "staking a claim." "Squatter"s rights" are another form of Appropriation, but are usually asserted against land to which ownership rights of another party have been recognized.
Reciprocity	In international relations and treaties, the principle of Reciprocity states that favours, benefits should be returned in kind.
	For example, Reciprocity has been used in the reduction of tariffs, the grant of copyrights to foreign authors, the mutual recognition and enforcement of judgments, and the relaxation of travel restrictions and visa requirements.

The principle of Reciprocity also governs agreements on extradition.

Norm

In the general sense of meaning, a Norm is something to help depict a phenomenon or system by means of averaging or bordering e.g. people are normally heterosexual, or good people live without sin. Comparison, classification and measurement all require some normative factor, e.g. altitude normal to sea level.

Norms are sentences or sentence meanings with practical, i. e. action-oriented (rather than descriptive, explanatory, or expressive) import, the most common of which are commands, permissions, and prohibitions.

Nation

A nation are regional corporations of students at university, once widespread across central and northern Europe in medieval times, they are now largely restricted to the two ancient universities of Sweden. The students, who were all born within the same region, usually spoke the same language, and expected to be ruled by their own familiar law. The most similar comparison in the Anglo-world to the nation system is in the collegiate system of older British universities or fraternities at American universities; however, both of these comparisons are imperfect.

United Nations

The United Nations is an international organization whose stated aims are facilitating cooperation in international law, international security, economic development, social progress, human rights, and the achieving of world peace. The United Nations was founded in 1945 after World War II to replace the League of Nations, to stop wars between countries, and to provide a platform for dialogue. It contains multiple subsidiary organizations to carry out its missions.

International Relations

International relations or International Studies (IS) represents the study of foreign affairs and global issues among states within the international system, including the roles of states, inter-governmental organizations (IGOs), non-governmental organizations (NGOs), and multinational corporations (MNCs.) It is both an academic and public policy field, and can be either positive or normative as it both seeks to analyze as well as formulate the foreign policy of particular states. It is often considered a branch of political science.

Public opinion

Public opinion is the aggregate of individual attitudes or beliefs held by the adult population. Public opinion can also be defined as the complex collection of opinions of many different people and the sum of all their views. The principle approaches to the study of Public opinion may be divided into 4 categories:

a) quantitative measurement of opinion distributions;
b) investigation of the internal relationships among the individual opinions that make up Public opinion on an issue;
c) description or analysis of the public role of Public opinion;
d) study both of the communication media that disseminate the ideas on which opinions are based and of the uses that propagandists and other manipulators make of these media.

Public opinion as a concept gained credence with the rise of "public" in the eighteenth century.

Civil liberties

Civil liberties are freedoms that protect an individual from the government of the nation in which they reside. Civil liberties set limits for government so that it cannot abuse its power and interfere unduly with the lives of its citizens.

Common Civil liberties include the rights of people, freedom of religion, and freedom of speech, and additionally, the right to due process, to a fair trial, to own property, and to privacy.

Chapter 12. The Presidency

Iraq	Iraq , officially the Republic of Iraq JumhÅ«rÄ«yat Al-Ê¿IrÄ q, Kurdish: ÙƒÛ†Ù…Ø§Ø±ÛŒ Ø¹ÛŽØ±Ø§Ù‚â‚, Komara Iraqê), is a country in Western Asia spanning most of the northwestern end of the Zagros mountain range, the eastern part of the Syrian Desert and the northern part of the Arabian Desert. Iraq shares borders with Jordan to the west, Syria to the northwest, Turkey to the north, Iran to the east, and Kuwait and Saudi Arabia to the south. Iraq has a narrow section of coastline measuring 58 km between Umm Qasr and Al Faw on the Persian Gulf.
National Security	National security refers to the requirement to maintain the survival of the nation-state through the use of economic, military and political power and the exercise of diplomacy.

Measures taken to ensure National security include:

- using diplomacy to rally allies and isolate threats
- marshalling economic power to facilitate or compel cooperation
- maintaining effective armed forces
- implementing civil defense and emergency preparedness measures (including anti-terrorism legislation)
- ensuring the resilience and redundancy of critical infrastructure
- using intelligence services to detect and defeat or avoid threats and espionage, and to protect classified information
- using counterintelligence services or secret police to protect the nation from internal threats

The relatively new concept of National security was first introduced in the United States after World War II, and has to some degree replaced other concepts that describe the struggle of states to overcome various external and internal threats.

The concept of National security became an official guiding principle of foreign policy in the United States when the National security Act of 1947 was signed on July 26, 1947 by U.S. President Harry S. Truman.

The majority of the provisions of the Act took effect on 18 September 1947, the day after the Senate confirmed James V. Forrestal as the first Secretary of Defense.

Presidential election	A presidential election was held in Chile on 4 September 1970. A narrow plurality (36.6 percent of the total vote) was secured by Salvador Allende, the candidate of the Popular Unity coalition of leftist parties. Because he did not obtain an absolute majority, his election required a further vote by the National Congress of Chile which resulted in Allende assuming the presidency in accordance with the Chilean Constitution of 1925.
Security Agency	A Security agency is an organization which conducts intelligence activities for the internal security of a nation, state or organization. They are the domestic cousins of foreign intelligence agencies.

Chapter 12. The Presidency

Axis of evil	"Axis of evil" is a term coined by United States President George W. Bush in his State of the Union Address on January 29, 2002 in order to describe governments that he accused of helping terrorism and seeking weapons of mass destruction. President Bush named Iran, Iraq and North Korea in his speech. President Bush"s presidency was marked by this notion as a justification for the War on Terror.
Public Service of Canada	The Public Service of Canada is the staff of the federal government of Canada. Its function is to support the Canadian monarch, and to handle the hiring of employees for the federal government ministries. It is represented by the Governor General, and the appointed [[list of Canadian ministries | ministry].
Intelligence	Intelligence refers to discrete information with currency and relevance, and the abstraction, evaluation, and understanding of such information for its accuracy and value.
Regime	The word dub korp Regime (occasionally spelled "régime", particularly in older texts) refers to a set of conditions, most often of a political nature. It may also be used synonymously with " Regime n", for example in the phrases "exercise Regime or "medical Regime . In politics, a Regime is the form of government: the set of rules, cultural or social norms, etc.
Germany	Germany), officially the Federal Republic of Germany), is a country in Central Europe. It is bordered to the north by the North Sea, Denmark, and the Baltic Sea; to the east by Poland and the Czech Republic; to the south by Austria and Switzerland; and to the west by France, Luxembourg, Belgium, and the Netherlands. The territory of Germany covers 357,021 square kilometers and is influenced by a temperate seasonal climate.
Limited government	Limited government is a government where any more than minimal governmental intervention in personal liberties and the economy is not usually allowed by law, usually in a written Constitution. It is closely related to libertarianism, classical liberalism, and some tendencies of liberalism and conservatism in the United States. Limited government is a common practice through Western culture.
Vietnam	Vietnam " href="/wiki/Battle_of_B%E1%BA%A1ch_%C4%90%E1%BA%B1ng_River_(938)">battle of Bá⁰ich Ä á⁰±ng River. Successive dynasties flourished along with geographic and political expansion deeper into Southeast Asia, until it was colonized by the French in the mid-19th century. Efforts to resist the French eventually led to their expulsion from the country in the mid-20th century, leaving a nation divided politically into two countries.
Vietnam War	The Vietnam War was a military conflict that occurred in Vietnam, Laos and Cambodia from 1959 to 30 April 1975. The war was fought between the communist North Vietnam, supported by its communist allies, and the government of South Vietnam, supported by the United States and other member nations of the Southeast Asia Treaty Organization (SEATO.) The following outline is provided as an overview of and topical guide to the Vietnam War:

Listed by starting date:

- Operation 34A - (1964)
- Operation Starlite - August 18-24 1965
- Operation Hump- November 5 1965
- Operation Crimp - January 7, 1966
- Operation Birmingham - April 1966
- Operation Hastings - Late May 1966
- Operation Prairie - August 1966
- Operation Deckhouse Five - January 6, 1967
- Operation Cedar Falls - January 8, 1967
- Operation Junction City - February 21, 1967
- Operation Francis Marion - April 6 - April 30, 1967
- Operation Union - April 21-May 16, 1967
- Operations Malheur I and Malheur II - 11 May - July 1, 1967
- Operation Baker - May 11, 1967
- Operation Scotland - See Battle of Khe Sanh
- Operation Pegasus - August 8, 1968
- Operation Dewey Canyon - January 22, 1969
- Operation Twinkletoes - 1969
- Operation Apache Snow - May 10 - May 20, 1969
- Operation Chicago Peak - April 1970
- Operation Texas Star - April - September, 1970
- Operation Ivory Coast - November 21, 1970
- Operation Jefferson Glenn - 1970-1971
- Operation Lam Son 719 - February 8, 1971
- Ho Chi Minh Campaign January 24 - April 30, 1975
- Operation Frequent Wind - April, 1975

- Battle of Ap Bac - January 2, 1963
- Battle of Kien Long - April 11 - April 15, 1964
- Battle of Thanh Hóa - July 31, 1964
- Battle of Binh Gia - December 28, 1964 - January 1, 1965
- Battle of Dong Xoai - June 10, 1965
- Battle near Minh Thanh - October 25 - October 27, 1965
- Battle of Ia Drang - November 14 - November 16, 1965
- Battle of Cu Nghi - January 28 - January 31, 1966
- Battle of Kim Son Valley - February 16 - February 28, 1966
- Battle of A Shau - March 9 - March 10, 1966
- Battle of Xa Cam My - April 11 - April 12, 1966
- First Battle of Dong Ha - Late May - June, 1966
- Battle on Minh Thanh Road - July 9, 1966
- Battle of Ä á»©c CÆ¡ - August 9, 1966
- Battle of Long Tá°§n - August 18- August 19, 1966
- Viet Cong attack on Tan Son Nhut airbase - December 4, 1966
- Battle of LZ Bird - December 27, 1966

- Battle of Tra Binh Dong - February 14 - February 15, 1967
- Battle of Hills 881 and 861 - April 24-May 9, 1967
- Nine Days in May - May 18 - May 28, 1967
- Battle of Vinh Huy - May 30 - June 2, 1967
- Battle of Con Thien - July 2 - July 3, 1967
- Battle of Dong Son - September 4, 1967
- Battle of Ong Thang - October 17, 1967
- First Battle of Loc Ninh - October 29 - November, 1967
- Battle of Dak To - November 3-November 22, 1967
- Battle in the Mekong Delta - December 4, 1967
- Battle of Tam Quan - December 6 - December 20, 1967
- Battle of Thom Tham Khe - December 27 - December 28, 1967
- Phoenix Program - 1967 - 1972
- Battle of Khe Sanh - January 21 - April 8, 1968
- Tet Offensive - January 30 - February 25, 1968
- Battle of Bien Hoa - January 31 - July 1, 1968
- Battle of Kham Duc - May 10 - May 12, 1968
- First Battle of Saigon - January 31, - February 3, 1968
- Battle of Hue - January 31, - February 25, 1968
- Tet 1969 - February 1969
- Battle of Hamburger Hill - May 10 - May 20, 1969
- Firebase Ripcord - March 12 - July 23, 1970
- Cambodian Incursion - April 29 - July 22, 1970
- Battle of Snoul - January 5 - May 30, 1971
- Easter Offensive - March 30 - October 22, 1972
- First Battle of Quang Tri - March 30 - May 1, 1972
- Battle of Loc Ninh - April 4 - April 7, 1972
- Battle of An Loc - April 20 - July 20, 1972
- Second Battle of Quang Tri - June 28 - September 16, 1972
- Battle of Phuoc Long - December 13, 1974 - January 6, 1975
- Battle of Buon Me Thuot - March 10 - March 12, 1975
- Battle of Xuan Loc - April 9 - April 20, 1975

- Operation Farm Gate
- Operation Chopper (1962)
- Operation Ranch Hand (1962-1971)
- Operation Pierce Arrow (1964)
- Operation Barrell Roll (1964-1972)
- Operation Pony Express (1965-1970)
- Operation Flaming Dart (1965)
- Operation Rolling Thunder (1965-1968)
- Operation Steel Tiger (1965-1968)
- Operation Arc Light (1965-1973)
- Operation Tiger Hound (1965-1968)
- Operation Shed Light (1966-1972)
- Operation Carolina Moon (1966)
- Operation Wahiawa (1966)
- Operation Bolo (1967)
- Operation Popeye (1967-1972
- Operation Niagara (1968)
- Operation Igloo White (1968-1973

- Operation Giant Lance (1969)
- Operation Commando Hunt (1968-1972)
- Operation Menu (1969-1970)
- Operation Patio (1970)
- Operation Freedom Deal (1970-1973)
- Operation Linebacker (1972)
- Operation Enhance Plus (1972)
- Operation Linebacker II (1972)
- Operation Homecoming (1973)
- Operation Baby Lift (1975)
- Operation Eagle Pull (1975)
- Operation Frequent Wind (1975)

- National Order of Vietnam
- Vietnam Military Merit Medal
- Vietnam Distinguished Service Order
- Vietnam Meritorious Service Medal
- Vietnam Special Service Medal
- Vietnam Gallantry Cross
- Vietnam Air Gallantry Cross
- Vietnam Navy Gallantry Cross
- Vietnam Armed Forces Honor Medal
- Vietnam Civil Actions Medal
- Vietnam Staff Service Medal
- Vietnam Technical Service Medal
- Vietnam Wound Medal
- Vietnam Campaign Medal
- Presidential Unit Citation (Vietnam)
- Vietnam Gallantry Cross Unit Citation
- Vietnam Civil Actions Unit Citation

- Golden Star Medal
- Ho Chi Minh Order
- Defeat American Aggression Badge
- Vietnam Liberation Order
- Resolution for Victory Order

- Medal of Honor rare
- Distinguished Service Cross rare
- Navy Cross uncommon
- Air Force Cross uncommon
- Silver Star uncommon
- Purple Heart frequent
- Bronze Star frequent
- Presidential Unit Citation rare
- Vietnam Service Medal very common
- National Defense Service Medal very common
- Commendation Medal common

- "Fatigue Press" at Fort Hood,
- "Last Harass" at Fort Gordon, Georgia
- "Pawn"s Pawn" at Fort Leonard Wood, Missouri

- "Ultimate Weapon" at Fort Dix, New Jersey
- "Attitude Check" at Camp Pendleton, California
- "Green Machine" at Fort Greely, Alaska
- "Napalm" at Fort Campbell, Tennessee
- "Arctic Arsenal" at Fort Greely, Alaska
- "Black Voice" at Fort McClellan, Alabama
- "Fragging Action" at Fort Dix
- "Fort Polk Puke" at Fort Polk, Louisiana
- "Custer"s Last Stand" at Fort Riley, Kansas
- "Whack!" from the Women"s Army Corps School
- "Where Are We?" at Fort Huachuca, Arizona
- "Voice of the Lumpen" (affiliated with the Black Panther Party) in Frankfurt
- "Can You Bear McNair?" at McNair Barracks, Berlin
- "Seasick" at Subic Bay
- "The Man Can"t Win If You Grin" in Okinawa
- "Korea Free Press"
- "Semper Fi" in Japan
- "Stars and Bars" in England
- "Separated From Life" in England
- "Duck Power" in San Diego
- "Harass the Brass" at Canute Air Force Base, Illinois
- "All Hands Abandon Ship", Newport, Rhode Island
- "Now Hear This", Long Beach
- "Potemkin" on the USS Forestall
- "Star Spangled Bummer" at Wright-Patterson Air Force Base in Ohio
- "Fat Albert"s Death Ship" in Charlestown
- "Pig Boat Blues", USS Agerholm
- "Special Weapons", Kirtland AFB, New Mexico
- "I Will Fear No Evil", Kirtland AFB, New Mexico
- "Blows Against the Empire", Kirtland AFB, New Mexico

source: "The American War" - see references below

- Bao Dai
- Duong Van Minh
- Madame Ngo Dinh Nhu
- Ngo Dinh Diem
- Ngo Dinh Nhu
- Nguyen Cao Ky
- Nguyen Khanh
- Nguyen Van Thieu

- Creighton W. Abrams
- Dean Acheson
- Spiro Agnew
- Ellsworth Bunker
- McGeorge Bundy
- William Bundy
- William Calley
- Clark Clifford
- William Colby
- A. Peter Dewey
- John Foster Dulles
- Dwight D. Eisenhower
- Daniel Ellsberg
- J. William Fulbright
- Barry Goldwater
- David Hackworth
- Alexander Haig
- Paul D. Harkins
- Seymour Hersh
- Hubert Humphrey
- Lyndon Johnson
- John F. Kennedy
- John Kerry
- Henry Kissinger
- Melvin Laird
- Edward Lansdale
- Henry Cabot Lodge, Jr.
- Mike Mansfield
- Graham Martin
- Robert McNamara
- George McGovern
- Richard Nixon
- Pete Peterson
- Charika Pugh
- Dean Rusk

- Maxwell D. Taylor
- Hugh C. Thompson, Jr
- John Paul Vann
- Gary Varsel
- William Westmoreland

- Ho Chi Minh
- Le Duan
- Tran Van Tra
- Le Duc Tho
- Pham Van Dong
- General Giap
- Poewll Ward

- Lon Nol
- Pol Pot
- Norodom Sihanouk
- Sirik Matak
- Sosthene Fernandez

- David H. Hackworth. 1989 About Face
- A.J. Langguth. 2000. Our Vietnam: the War 1954-1975.
- Mann, Robert. 2002. Grand Delusion, A: America"s Descent Into Vietnam.
- Windrow, Martin. 2005. The Last Valley: Dien Bien Phu and the French Defeat in Vietnam.
- Bernard Fall. 1967. Hell in a Very Small Place: the Siege of Dien Bien Phu.
- Harvey Pekar. 2003. American Splendor: Unsung Hero
- Prados, John. 2000. The Blood Road: The Ho Chi Minh Trail and the Vietnam War.
- Prados, John. 1999. Valley of Decision: The Siege of Khe Sanh.
- Shultz, Robert H. Jr. 2000. The Secret War Against Hanoi: The Untold Story of Spies, Saboteurs, and Covert Warriors in North Vietnam.
- Plaster, John L. 1998. SOG: The Secret Wars of America"s Commandos in Vietnam.
- Murphy, Edward F. 1995. Dak To: America"s Sky Soldiers in South Vietnam"s Central Highlands.
- Nolan, Keith W. 1996. The Battle for Saigon: Tet 1968.
- Nolan, Keith W. 1996. Sappers in the Wire: The Life and Death of Firebase Mary Ann.
- Nolan, Keith W. 1992. Operation Buffalo: USMC Fight for the DMZ.
- Nolan, Keith W. 2003. Ripcord : Screaming Eagles Under Siege, Vietnam 1970.
- Robert S. McNamara. 1996. In Retrospect: The Tragedy and Lessons of Vietnam.
- Larry Berman. 2002. No Peace, No Honor: Nixon, Kissinger, and Betrayal in Vietnam.
- Bergerud, Eric M. 1994. Red Thunder, Tropic Lightning: The World of a Combat Division in Vietnam.
- Bernard Edelman. 2002. Dear America: Letters Home from Vietnam.
- Darrel D. Whitcomb. 1999. The Rescue of Bat 21.
- Oberdorfer, Don. 1971. Tet: the Story of a Battle and its Historic Aftermath.
- LTG Harold G. Moore and Joseph L. Galloway. 1992. We Were Soldiers Once ... And Young.
- Duiker, William J. 2002. Ho Chi Minh: A Life.
- John Laurence. 2002. The Cat from Hue: A Vietnam War Story.
- Emerson, Gloria. 1976. Winners and Losers: Battles, Retreats, Gains, Losses and Ruins from a Long War.
- Philip Caputo. 1977. A Rumor of War.

- Al Santoli. 1981. Everything We Had: an Oral History of the Vietnam War by 33 American Soldiers Who Fought It.
- Robert C. Mason. 1983. Chickenhawk.
- Michael Herr. 1977. Dispatches.
- Joseph T. Ward. 1991. Dear Mom: a Sniper"s Vietnam.
- Hemphill, Robert. 1998. Platoon: Bravo Company.
- Noam Chomsky. 1967. The Responsibility of Intellectuals.
- Moore, Robin. 1965 The Green Berets (ISBN 0-312-98492-8)

- Robert Olen Butler. 1992.

Power	Power in international relations is defined in several different ways. Political scientists, historians, and practitioners of international relations (diplomats) have used the following concepts of political Power:

- Power as a goal of states or leaders;
- Power as a measure of influence or control over outcomes, events, actors and issues;
- Power as reflecting victory in conflict and the attainment of security; and,
- Power as control over resources and capabilities.

Modern discourse generally speaks in terms of state Power, indicating both economic and military Power. Those states that have significant amounts of Power within the international system are referred to as middle powers, regional powers, great powers, superpowers, or hyperpowers, although there is no commonly accepted standard for what defines a powerful state.

Entities other than states can also acquire and wield Power in international relations. |
| Public opinion | Public opinion is the aggregate of individual attitudes or beliefs held by the adult population. Public opinion can also be defined as the complex collection of opinions of many different people and the sum of all their views. The principle approaches to the study of Public opinion may be divided into 4 categories:

a) quantitative measurement of opinion distributions;
b) investigation of the internal relationships among the individual opinions that make up Public opinion on an issue;
c) description or analysis of the public role of Public opinion;
d) study both of the communication media that disseminate the ideas on which opinions are based and of the uses that propagandists and other manipulators make of these media.

Public opinion as a concept gained credence with the rise of "public" in the eighteenth century. |
| Foreign policy | A country"s Foreign policy is a set of goals outlining how the country will interact with other countries economically, politically, socially and militarily, and to a lesser extent, how the country will interact with non-state actors. The aforementioned interaction is evaluated and monitored in attempts to maximize benefits of multilateral international cooperation. Foreign policies are designed to help protect a country"s national interests, national security, ideological goals, and economic prosperity. |
| Constitution | A Constitution is set of rules for government -- often codified as a written document -- that establishes principles of an autonomous political entity. In the case of countries, this term refers specifically to a national Constitution defining the fundamental political principles, and establishing the structure, procedures, powers and duties, of a government. By limiting the government"s own reach, most Constitution s guarantee certain rights to the people. |

Chapter 12. The Presidency

Habeas corpus	Habeas corpus have the body) is a legal action through which a person can seek relief from the unlawful detention of him or herself or from being harmed by the judicial system. Of English origin, the writ of Habeas corpus has historically been an important instrument for the safeguarding of individual freedom against arbitrary state action.
Theodore Roosevelt	Theodore Roosevelt was the 26th (1901-1909) President of the United States. He had been the 25th Vice President before becoming President upon the assassination of President William McKinley. Owing to his charismatic personality and reformist policies, which he called the "Square Deal", Roosevelt is considered one of the ablest presidents and an icon of the Progressive Era.
Democratic party	Democratic Party was a political party in Gambia. The party was founded during the pre-independence period in the colony of Bathurst (currently the national capital Banjul.) Ahead of the 1962 election, the Democratic Party merged with the Muslim Congress Party to form the Democratic Congress Alliance.
Federal Trade Commission	The Federal Trade Commission is an independent agency of the United States government, established in 1914 by the Federal Trade Commission Act. Its principal mission is the promotion of "consumer protection" and the elimination and prevention of what regulators perceive to be harmfully "anti-competitive" business practices, such as coercive monopoly. The Federal Trade Commission Act was one of President Wilson"s major acts against trusts.
Freedom	Freedom is the right to act according to ones will without being held up by the power of others. From a philosophical point of view, it can be defined as the capacity to determine your own choices. It can be defined negatively as an absence of subordination, servitude and constraint.
New Deal	The New Deal is a programme of active labour market policies introduced in the United Kingdom by the Labour government in 1998, initially funded by a one off Â£5bn windfall tax on privatised utility companies. The stated purpose is to reduce unemployment by providing training, subsidised employment and voluntary work to the unemployed. Spending on the New Deal was Â£1.3 billion in 2001.
Progressive Era	The Progressive Era in the United States was a period of reform which lasted from the 1890s to the 1920s. Responding to the changes brought about by industrialization, the Progressives advocated a wide range of economic, political, social, and moral reforms. Initially the movement was successful at local level, and then it progressed to state and gradually national.
Soviet	A Soviet originally was a workers" local council in late Imperial Russia. According to the official historiography of the Soviet Union, the first Soviet was organized during the 1905 Russian Revolution in Ivanovo (Ivanovo region) in May 1905. However in his memoirs Volin claims that he witnessed the creation of the St Petersburg Soviet in Saint Petersburg in January 1905.

| Union of Soviet Socialist Republics | The Union of Soviet Socialist Republics, occasionally called the United Soviet Socialist Republic, was a constitutionally socialist state that existed in Eurasia from 1922 to 1991. The name is a translation of the Russian: Â·), tr. Soyuz Sovetskikh Sotsialisticheskikh Respublik, abbreviated Ð¡Ð¡Ð¡Ð , SSSR. The common short name is Soviet Union, from Ð¡Ð¾Ð²ÐµÑ‚ÑÐºÐ¸Ð¹ Ð¡Ð¾ÑŽÐ·, Sovetskiy Soyuz. |

Chapter 12. The Presidency

Countries

This is a list of articles on the constitutions of contemporary countries, states and dependencies.

- Constitution of Abkhazia - Republic of Abkhazia
- Constitution of Afghanistan - Islamic Republic of Afghanistan
- Constitution of Akrotiri - Sovereign Base Area of Akrotiri (UK overseas territory)
- Constitution of Åland - Åland (Autonomous province of Finland)
- Constitution of Albania - Republic of Albania
- Constitution of Algeria - People"s Democratic Republic of Algeria
- Constitution of American Samoa - Territory of American Samoa (US overseas territory)
- Constitution of Andorra - Principality of Andorra
- Constitution of Angola - Republic of Angola
- Constitution of Anguilla - Anguilla (UK overseas territory)
- Constitution of Antigua and Barbuda - Antigua and Barbuda
- Constitution of Argentina - Argentine Republic
- Constitution of Armenia - Republic of Armenia
- Constitution of Aruba - Aruba (Self-governing country in the Kingdom of the Netherlands)
- Constitution of Ascension Island - Ascension Island (Dependency of the UK overseas territory of Saint Helena)
- Constitution of Australia - Commonwealth of Australia
- Constitution of Austria - Republic of Austria
- Constitution of Azerbaijan - Republic of Azerbaijan

- Constitution of The Bahamas - Commonwealth of The Bahamas
- Constitution of Bahrain - Kingdom of Bahrain
- Constitution of Bangladesh - People"s Republic of Bangladesh
- Constitution of Barbados - Barbados
- Constitution of Belarus - Republic of Belarus
- Constitution of Belgium - Kingdom of Belgium
- Constitution of Belize - Belize
- Constitution of Benin - Republic of Benin
- Constitution of Bermuda - Bermuda (UK overseas territory)
- Constitution of Bhutan - Kingdom of Bhutan
- Constitution of Bolivia - Plurinational State of Bolivia
- Constitution of Bosnia and Herzegovina - Bosnia and Herzegovina
- Constitution of Botswana - Republic of Botswana
- Constitution of Brazil - Federative Republic of Brazil
- Constitution of Brunei - Negara Brunei Darussalam
- Constitution of Bulgaria - Republic of Bulgaria
- Constitution of Burkina Faso - Burkina Faso
- Constitution of Burma - Burma (Union of Myanmar)
- Constitution of Burundi - Republic of Burundi

- Constitution of Cambodia - Kingdom of Cambodia
- Constitution of Cameroon - Republic of Cameroon
- Constitution of Canada - Canada
- Constitution of Cape Verde - Republic of Cape Verde
- Constitution of the Cayman Islands - Cayman Islands (UK overseas territory)

- Constitution of the Central African Republic - Central African Republic
- Constitution of Chad - Republic of Chad
- Constitution of Chile - Republic of Chile
- Constitution of the People"s Republic of China - People"s Republic of China
- Constitution of the Republic of China - Republic of China
- Constitution of Christmas Island - Territory of Christmas Island (Australian overseas territory)
- Constitution of the Cocos (Keeling) Islands - Territory of Cocos (Keeling) Islands (Australian overseas territory)
- Constitution of Colombia - Republic of Colombia
- Constitution of Comoros - Union of the Comoros
- Constitution of the Democratic Republic of the Congo - Democratic Republic of the Congo
- Constitution of the Republic of the Congo - Republic of the Congo
- Constitution of the Cook Islands - Cook Islands (Associated state of New Zealand)
- Constitution of Costa Rica - Republic of Costa Rica
- Constitution of Côte d"Ivoire - Republic of Côte d"Ivoire
- Constitution of Croatia - Republic of Croatia
- Constitution of Cuba - Republic of Cuba
- Constitution of Cyprus - Republic of Cyprus
- Constitution of the Czech Republic - Czech Republic

- Constitution of Denmark - Kingdom of Denmark
- Constitution of Dhekelia - Sovereign Base Areas of Dhekelia (UK overseas territory)
- Constitution of Djibouti - Republic of Djibouti
- Constitution of Dominica - Commonwealth of Dominica
- Constitution of the Dominican Republic - Dominican Republic

- Constitution of East Timor (Timor-Leste) - Democratic Republic of Timor-Leste
- Constitution of Ecuador - Republic of Ecuador
- Constitution of Egypt - Arab Republic of Egypt
- Constitution of El Salvador - Republic of El Salvador
- Constitution of Equatorial Guinea - Republic of Equatorial Guinea
- Constitution of Eritrea - State of Eritrea
- Constitution of Estonia - Republic of Estonia
- Constitution of Ethiopia - Federal Democratic Republic of Ethiopia

- Constitution of the Falkland Islands - Falkland Islands (UK overseas territory)
- Constitution of the Faroe Islands - Faroe Islands (Self-governing country in the Kingdom of Denmark)
- Constitution of Fiji - Republic of the Fiji Islands
- Constitution of Finland - Republic of Finland
- Constitution of France - French Republic
- Constitution of French Polynesia - French Polynesia

- Constitution of Gabon - Gabonese Republic
- Constitution of Gambia - Republic of The Gambia
- Constitution of Georgia - Georgia
- Constitution of Germany - Federal Republic of Germany
- Constitution of Ghana - Republic of Ghana
- Constitution of Gibraltar - Gibraltar
- Constitution of Greece - Hellenic Republic
- Constitution of Greenland - Greenland (Self-governing country in the Kingdom of Denmark)

Right	A right is the legal or moral entitlement to do or refrain from doing something thing or recognition in civil society. Rights serve as rules of interaction between people, and, as such, they place constraints and obligations upon the actions of individuals or groups (for example, if one has a right to life, this means that others do not have the liberty to kill him.)
	Most modern conceptions of rights are universalist and egalitarian -- in other words, equal rights are granted to all people.
Committee	A Committee (some of which are titled instead as a "Commission" larger deliberative assembly-- which when organized so that action on Committee requires a vote by all its entitled members, is called the Committee of the Whole". Committee s often serve several different functions:
	• Governance: in organizations considered too large for all the members to participate in decisions affecting the organization as a whole, a Committee (such as a Board of Directors or "Executive Committee) is given the power to make decisions, spend money the Board of directors can frequently enter into binding contracts and make decisions which once taken or made, can"t be taken back or undone under the law.
	• Coordination: individuals from different parts of an organization (for example, all senior vice presidents) might meet regularly to discuss developments in their areas, review projects that cut across organizational boundaries, talk about future options, etc. Where there is a large Committee it is common to have smaller Committee s with more specialized functions - for example, Boards of Directors of large corporations typically have an (ongoing) audit Committee finance Committee compensation Committee etc. Large academic conferences are usually organized by a co-ordinating Committee drawn from the relevant professional body.
Leadership	Leadership has been described as the "process of social influence in which one person can enlist the aid and support of others in the accomplishment of a common task". A definition more inclusive of followers comes from Alan Keith of Genentech who said "Leadership is ultimately about creating a way for people to contribute to making something extraordinary happen."
	Leadership is one of the most salient aspects of the organizational context. However, defining Leadership has been challenging.
Globalization	Globalization or (globalisation) is the process by which the people of the world are unified into a single society and function together. Globalization is often used to refer to economic Globalization: the integration of national economies into the international economy through trade, foreign direct investment, capital flows, migration, and the spread of technology. This process is usually recognized as being driven by a combination of economic, technological, sociocultural, political and biological factors.

Mexico	The United Mexican States), commonly known as Mexico [Ĕˆmexiko]), is a federal constitutional republic in North America. It is bordered on the north by the United States; on the south and west by the Pacific Ocean; on the southeast by Guatemala, Belize, and the Caribbean Sea; and on the east by the Gulf of Mexico. Covering almost 2 million square kilometres, Mexico is the fifth-largest country in the Americas by total area and the 14th largest independent nation in the world.
Communism	Communism is a socioeconomic structure and political ideology that promotes the establishment of an egalitarian, classless, stateless society based on common ownership and control of the means of production and property in general. In political science, however, the term "Communism", usually spelled with the capital letter C is often used to refer to the Communist states, a form of government in which the state operates under a one-party system and declares allegiance to Marxism-Leninism or a derivative thereof, even if the party does not actually claim that it has already reached Communism. Forerunners of communist ideas existed in antiquity and particularly in the 18th and early 19th century France, with thinkers such as Jean-Jacques Rousseau and the more radical Gracchus Babeuf.
Ethnic cleansing	Ethnic Cleansing is a controversial computer game developed by Resistance Records, an underground music label specializing in Neo-Nazi and white supremacist bands. In the game, the protagonist (the player can choose either a skinhead or a Klansman) runs through a ghetto killing black people and Latinos, before descending into a subway system to kill Jews. Finally he reaches the "Jewish Control Center", where Ariel Sharon, former Prime Minister of Israel, is directing plans for world domination.
Grenada	Grenada is an island nation and sovereign state consisting of the island of Grenada and six smaller islands at the southern end of the Grenadines in the southeastern Caribbean Sea. Grenada is located northwest of Trinidad and Tobago, northeast of Venezuela, and southwest of Saint Vincent and the Grenadines. Its size is 344 km^2 with an estimated population of 110,000.
Libya	Libya ; Libya n vernacular: LÄ«bya Â·); Amazigh:), officially the Great Socialist People"s Libya n Arab Jamahiriya), is a country located in North Africa. Bordering the Mediterranean Sea to the north, Libya lies between Egypt to the east, Sudan to the southeast, Chad and Niger to the south, and Algeria and Tunisia to the west. With an area of almost 1.8 million square kilometres (700,000 sq mi), 90% of which is desert, Libya is the fourth largest country in Africa by area, and the 17th largest in the world.
Panama	Panama, officially the Republic of Panama , is the southernmost country of both Central America and, in turn, North America. Situated on the isthmus connecting North and South America, it is bordered by Costa Rica to the northwest, Colombia to the southeast, the Caribbean Sea to the north and the Pacific Ocean to the south. The capital is Panama City.

Chapter 12. The Presidency

Serbia	Serbia (Serbia n: Đ¡Ñ€Đ±Đ¸Ñ˜Đ°, Srbija), officially the Republic of Serbia (Serbia n: Đ ĐµĐ¿ÑƒĐ±Đ»Đ¸ĐºĐ° Đ¡Ñ€Đ±Đ¸Ñ˜Đ°, Republika Srbija), is a country located in both Central and Southeastern Europe. Its territory covers southern part of the Pannonian Plain and central part of the Balkans. Serbia borders Hungary to the north; Romania and Bulgaria to the east; the Republic of Macedonia and Albania to the south; and Croatia, Bosnia and Herzegovina and Montenegro to the west.
National Security Council	The White House National Security Council in the United States is the principal forum used by the President for considering national security and foreign policy matters with his senior national security advisors and Cabinet officials and is part of the Executive Office of the President of the United States. Since its inception under President Harry S. Truman, the function of the Council has been to advise and assist the President on national security and foreign policies. The Council also serves as the President"s principal arm for coordinating these policies among various government agencies.
Homeland	A Homeland is the concept of the place (cultural geography) to which an ethnic group holds a long history and a deep cultural association with --the country in which a particular national identity began. As a common noun, it simply connotes the country of one"s origin.
Iran-Contra Affair	The Iran-Contra affair was a political scandal in the United States which came to light in November 1986, during the Reagan administration, in which senior US figures agreed to facilitate the sale of arms to Iran, the subject of an arms embargo, to secure the release of hostages and to fund Nicaraguan contras.
	It began as an operation to improve U.S.-Iranian relations, wherein Israel would ship weapons to a relatively moderate, politically influential group of Iranians; the U.S. would then resupply Israel and receive the Israeli payment. The Iranian recipients promised to do everything in their power to achieve the release of six U.S. hostages, who were being held by the Lebanese Shia Islamist group Hezbollah, who were unknowingly connected to the Army of the Guardians of the Islamic Revolution.
Executive order	An Executive order in the United States is an order issued by the President, the head of the executive branch of the federal government. In other countries, similar edicts may be known as decrees, or orders-in-council. Executive orders may also be issued at the state level by a state"s Governor.
Cuban Missile Crisis	The Cuban Missile Crisis was a confrontation between the United States, the Soviet Union, and Cuba in October 1962, during the Cold War. In Russia, it is termed the "Caribbean Crisis" , while in Cuba it is called the "October Crisis." The Cuban and Soviet governments decided in September 1962 to place nuclear missiles on Cuba in order to protect it from United States harassment. When United States intelligence discovered the weapons its government decided to do all they could to ensure the removal of them.

Social Security	Social Security, in Australia, refers to a system of social welfare payments provided by Commonwealth Government of Australia. These payments are administered by a Government body named Centrelink. In Australia, most benefits are subject to a means test.
Turkey	Turkey , known officially as the Republic of Turkey Â·)), is a Eurasian country that stretches across the Anatolian peninsula in western Asia and Thrace in the Balkan region of southeastern Europe. Turkey is bordered by eight countries: Bulgaria to the northwest; Greece to the west; Georgia to the northeast; Armenia, Azerbaijan (the exclave of Nakhichevan) and Iran to the east; and Iraq and Syria to the southeast. The Mediterranean Sea and Cyprus are to the south; the Aegean Sea and Archipelago are to the west; and the Black Sea is to the north.
Argentina	Argentina is one of the world"s largest producers of beef. It is also the third-largest exporter (after Brazil and Australia), and has the world"s highest consumption rate (an average of 68 kg per person per year.) On 8 March 2006, President Néstor Kirchner took the drastic measure of banning all exports of beef for a period of 180 days, in order to stop continuous price rises.
Bill of Rights	A Bill of rights is a list or summary of rights that are considered important and essential by a nation. The purpose of these bills is to protect those rights against infringement by the government. The term "Bill of rights" originates from Britain, where it referred to a bill that was passed by Parliament in 1689.
Free Trade	Free trade is a type of trade policy that allows traders to act and transact without interference from government. Thus, the policy permits trading partners mutual gains from trade, with goods and services produced according to the theory of comparative advantage. Under a Free trade policy, prices are a reflection of true supply and demand, and are the sole determinant of resource allocation.
Japan	Japan is an island nation in East Asia. Located in the Pacific Ocean, it lies to the east of the Sea of Japan, People"s Republic of China, North Korea, South Korea and Russia, stretching from the Sea of Okhotsk in the north to the East China Sea and Taiwan in the south. The characters which make up Japan"s name mean "sun-origin", which is why Japan is sometimes identified as the "Land of the Rising Sun".
Parliamentary system	A Parliamentary system is a system of government wherein the ministers of the executive branch are drawn from the legislature, and are accountable to that body, such that the executive and legislative branches are intertwined. In such a system, the head of government is both de facto chief executive and chief legislator. Parliamentary system s are characterized by no clear-cut separation of powers between the executive and legislative branches, leading to a different set of checks and balances compared to those found in presidential systems.

Chapter 12. The Presidency

Separation of powers	The Separation of powers is a model for the governance of democratic states. The model was first developed in ancient Greece and came into widespread use by the Roman Republic as part of the uncodified Constitution of the Roman Republic. Under this model, the state is divided into branches or estates, each with separate and independent powers and areas of responsibility.
Sweden	Sweden , officially the Kingdom of Sweden), is a Nordic country on the Scandinavian Peninsula in Northern Europe. Sweden has land borders with Norway to the west and Finland to the northeast, and it is connected to Denmark by the Öresund Bridge in the south. At 450,000 km^2 (173,746 sq mi), Sweden is the third largest country in the European Union in terms of area, and it has a total population of over 9.2 million.
Balance	Balance is sometimes used in reference to political content in the mass media. This usage began in Britain in the early part of the 20th century when the conservative Tories were unpopular and receiving little coverage through the BBC. In order to provide an intellectual rationalization for an increased level of Conservative content, Lord John Reith, the BBC"s founding General Manager and later Chairman, promoted a concept called Balance. In practise Balance means ensuring that statements by those challenging the establishment are balanced with statements of those whom they are criticising, though not necessarily the other way round.

Led by Lorrin A. Thurston and Sanford B. Dole, the Provisional Government ruled over HawaiÊ»i until the formal establishment of a republic. Pictured above is the cabinet, (Left to Right) James A. King, Sanford B. Dole, William O. Smith and Peter C. Jones.

Capital	Flag

Capital	Honolulu
Language(s)	Hawaiian, English
Government	Not specified
Provisional Government	
- 1893-1894	Committee of Safety
Historical era	New Imperialism
- Monarchy overthrown	January 17, 1893
- Republic declared	July 4, 1894
Currency	U.S. dollar, Hawaiian dollar

The Provisional Government of HawaiÊ»i was proclaimed on January 17, 1893 by the 13 member Committee of Safety under the leadership of Lorrin A. Thurston and Sanford B. Dole. It governed the Kingdom of HawaiÊ»i after the overthrow of Queen LiliÊ»uokalani until the Republic of HawaiÊ»i was established on July 4, 1894.

Capital punishment	Capital punishment, the death penalty or execution, is the killing of a person by judicial process for retribution, general deterrence, and incapacitation. Crimes that can result in a death penalty are known as capital crimes or capital offences. The term capital originates from Latin capitalis, literally "regarding the head" .
Privatization	Privatization is the incidence or process of transferring ownership of a business, enterprise, agency or public service from the public sector (government) to the private sector (business.) In a broader sense, Privatization refers to transfer of any government function to the private sector including governmental functions like revenue collection and law enforcement. The term "Privatization" also has been used to describe two unrelated transactions.
Property right	A Property right is the exclusive authority to determine how a resource is used, whether that resource is owned by government or by individuals. All economic goods have a property rights attribute. This attribute has three broad components 1. The right to use the good 2. The right to earn income from the good 3. The right to transfer the good to others The concept of property rights as used by economists and legal scholars are related but distinct. The distinction is largely seen in the economists" focus on the ability of an individual or collective to control the use of the good.
Haiti	Haiti , officially the Republic of Haiti , is a Creole- and French-speaking Caribbean country. Along with the Dominican Republic, it occupies the island of Hispaniola, in the Greater Antillean archipelago. Ayiti (Land of high mountains) was the indigenous Taíno or Amerindian name for the mountainous western side of the island.
Pakistan	Pakistan), officially the Islamic Republic of Pakistan, is a country located in South Asia. It has a 1,046 kilometre coastline along the Arabian Sea and Gulf of Oman in the south, and is bordered by Afghanistan and Iran in the west, the Republic of India in the east and the People"s Republic of China in the far northeast. Tajikistan also lies adjacent to Pakistan but is separated by the narrow Wakhan Corridor.
Two-party system	A Two-party system is a form of party system where two major political parties dominate voting in nearly all elections, at every level. As a result, all, or nearly all, elected offices end up being held by candidates endorsed by one of the two major parties. Coalition governments occur only rarely in Two-party system s.
Civil liberties	Civil liberties are freedoms that protect an individual from the government of the nation in which they reside. Civil liberties set limits for government so that it cannot abuse its power and interfere unduly with the lives of its citizens.

Common Civil liberties include the rights of people, freedom of religion, and freedom of speech, and additionally, the right to due process, to a fair trial, to own property, and to privacy.

Somalia	Somalia, since 1991, is cited as a real-world example of a stateless society and legal system. Since the fall of Siad Barre"s government in January 1991 , there has been no permanent national government in Somalia. Large areas of the country such as Somaliland, Puntland, Awdal and Galmudug are internationally unrecognized autonomous regions.
Anti-Americanism	Dictionaries tend to define Anti-Americanism, often anti-American sentiment, as a widespread opposition or hostility to the people, government or policies of the United States. In practice, a broad range of attitudes and actions critical of or opposed to the United States have been labeled Anti-Americanism. Thus, the nature and applicability of the term is often disputed.
Bureaucrat	A Bureaucrat is a member of a bureaucracy and can comprise the administration of any organization of any size, though the term usually connotes someone within an institution of a government. Bureaucrat jobs were often "desk jobs" , though the modern Bureaucrat may be found "in the field" as well as in an office.

The term "Bureaucrat" today has largely accepted negative connotations, so those who are the members of a governmental bureaucracy usually prefer terms such as civil servant or public servant to describe their jobs.

Civil service	The term Civil service has two distinct meanings:

- Branch of governmental service in which individuals are hired on the basis of merit which is proven by the use of competitive examinations.
- Body of employees in any government agency, except the military.

A civil servant or public servant is a civilian public sector employee working for a government department or agency. The term explicitly excludes the armed services, although civilian officials will work at "Defence Ministry" headquarters. The term always includes the (sovereign) state"s employees; whether regional, or sub-state, or even municipal employees are called "civil servants" varies from country to country. In the United Kingdom, for instance, only Crown employees are civil servants, county or city employees are not.

France	France , officially the French Republic , is a country located in Western Europe, with several overseas islands and territories located on other continents. Metropolitan France extends from the Mediterranean Sea to the English Channel and the North Sea, and from the Rhine to the Atlantic Ocean. It is often referred to as L"Hexagone ("The Hexagon") because of the geometric shape of its territory.

Political culture	Political culture can be defined as "The orientation of the citizens of a nation toward politics, and their perceptions of political legitimacy and the traditions of political practice," and the feelings expressed by individuals in the position of the elected offices that allow for the nurture of a political society.

- Dennis Kavanagh defines Political culture as "A shorthand expression to denote the set of values within which the political system operates".

- Lucian Pye describes it as "the sum of the fundamental values, sentiments and knowledge that give form and substance to political process".

Political culture is how we think government should be carried out. It is different from ideology because people can disagree on ideology, but still have a common Political culture.

Boosterism	Boosterism is the act of "boosting," or promoting, one"s town, city with the goal of improving public perception of it. Boosting can be as simple as "talking up" the entity at a party or as elaborate as establishing a visitors" bureau. It is somewhat associated with American small towns.

Secret Service	Because of both the secrecy of Secret service s and the controversial nature of the issues involved, there is some difficulty in separating the definitions of Secret service secret police, intelligence agency etc. For instance a country may establish a Secret service which has some policing powers (such as surveillance) but not others. A secret police may also be said to be a Secret service
Public Service of Canada	The Public Service of Canada is the staff of the federal government of Canada. Its function is to support the Canadian monarch, and to handle the hiring of employees for the federal government ministries. It is represented by the Governor General, and the appointed [[list of Canadian ministries | ministry].
Individualism	Individualism is the moral stance, political philosophy, ideology, or social outlook that stresses independence and self-reliance. Individualists promote the exercise of one"s goals and desires, while opposing most external interference upon one"s choices, whether by society, or any other group or institution. Individualism is opposed to collectivism, which stress that communal, community, group, societal, or national goals should take priority over individual goals.
Boosterism	Boosterism is the act of "boosting," or promoting, one"s town, city with the goal of improving public perception of it. Boosting can be as simple as "talking up" the entity at a party or as elaborate as establishing a visitors" bureau. It is somewhat associated with American small towns.
Leadership	Leadership has been described as the "process of social influence in which one person can enlist the aid and support of others in the accomplishment of a common task". A definition more inclusive of followers comes from Alan Keith of Genentech who said "Leadership is ultimately about creating a way for people to contribute to making something extraordinary happen." Leadership is one of the most salient aspects of the organizational context. However, defining Leadership has been challenging.
Foundation	A Foundation in the United States is a type of charitable organization. However, the Internal Revenue Code distinguishes between private foundations (usually funded by an individual, family, or corporation) and public charities (community foundations and other nonprofit groups that raise money from the general public.) Private foundations have more restrictions and fewer tax benefits than public charities like community foundations.
Bicameralism	In government, Bicameralism is the practice of having two legislative or parliamentary chambers. Thus, a bicameral parliament or bicameral legislature is a legislature which consists of two chambers or houses. Bicameralism is an essential and defining feature of the classical notion of mixed government.
Bureaucrat	A Bureaucrat is a member of a bureaucracy and can comprise the administration of any organization of any size, though the term usually connotes someone within an institution of a government. Bureaucrat jobs were often "desk jobs" , though the modern Bureaucrat may be found "in the field" as well as in an office.

The term "Bureaucrat" today has largely accepted negative connotations, so those who are the members of a governmental bureaucracy usually prefer terms such as civil servant or public servant to describe their jobs.

| Environmental Protection Agency | The Environmental Protection Agency (Irish: An Ghníomhaireacht um Chaomhnú Comhshaoil) has responsibilities for a wide range of licensing, enforcement, monitoring and assessment activities associated with environmental protection. |

Cost-benefit analysis

Cost-benefit analysis is a term that refers both to:

to help appraise, or assess, the case for a project or proposal, which itself is a process known as project appraisal; and

- an informal approach to making decisions of any kind.

Under both definitions the process involves, whether explicitly or implicitly, weighing the total expected costs against the total expected benefits of one or more actions in order to choose the best or most profitable option. The formal process is often referred to as either CBA Cost-benefit analysis or B Cost-benefit analysis (Benefit-Cost Analysis.)

A hallmark of CBA is that all benefits and all costs are expressed in money terms, and are adjusted for the time value of money, so that all flows of benefits and flows of project costs over time (which tend to occur at different points in time) are expressed on a common basis in terms of their "present value." Closely related, but slightly different, formal techniques include Cost-effectiveness analysis, Economic impact analysis, Fiscal impact analysis and Social Return on Investment(SROI) analysis. The latter builds upon the logic of Cost-benefit analysis but differs in that it is explicitly designed to inform the practical decision-making of enterprise managers and investors focused on optimising their social and environmental impacts.

Power

Power in international relations is defined in several different ways. Political scientists, historians, and practitioners of international relations (diplomats) have used the following concepts of political Power:

- Power as a goal of states or leaders;
- Power as a measure of influence or control over outcomes, events, actors and issues;
- Power as reflecting victory in conflict and the attainment of security; and,
- Power as control over resources and capabilities.

Modern discourse generally speaks in terms of state Power, indicating both economic and military Power. Those states that have significant amounts of Power within the international system are referred to as middle powers, regional powers, great powers, superpowers, or hyperpowers, although there is no commonly accepted standard for what defines a powerful state.

Entities other than states can also acquire and wield Power in international relations.

Civil Service	The term Civil service has two distinct meanings: • Branch of governmental service in which individuals are hired on the basis of merit which is proven by the use of competitive examinations. • Body of employees in any government agency, except the military. A civil servant or public servant is a civilian public sector employee working for a government department or agency. The term explicitly excludes the armed services, although civilian officials will work at "Defence Ministry" headquarters. The term always includes the (sovereign) state"s employees; whether regional, or sub-state, or even municipal employees are called "civil servants" varies from country to country. In the United Kingdom, for instance, only Crown employees are civil servants, county or city employees are not.
Civil rights movement	The Civil rights movement was a worldwide political movement for equality before the law occurring between approximately 1950 and 1980. It was accompanied by much civil unrest and popular rebellion. The process was long and tenuous in many countries, and most of these movements did not achieve or fully achieve their objectives.
Ethnicity	Ethnicity plays a prominent role in pornography. Distinct genres of pornography focus on performers of specific ethnic groups, or on the depiction of interracial sexual activity. Ethnic pornography typically employs ethnic and racial stereotypes in its depiction of performers.
Minority	Minority, and the related concept of "becoming-minor," is a philosophical concept developed by Gilles Deleuze and Félix Guattari in their books Kafka: Towards a Minor Literature (1975), A Thousand Plateaus (1980), and elsewhere. In these texts, they criticize the concept of "majority" as being based on a form of domination that works by naturalizing a purely numerical conception. They argue that the concept of a "dominant Minority" is an oxymoron, because the term "majority" always refers to those who are in a position of dominance.
Right	A right is the legal or moral entitlement to do or refrain from doing something thing or recognition in civil society. Rights serve as rules of interaction between people, and, as such, they place constraints and obligations upon the actions of individuals or groups (for example, if one has a right to life, this means that others do not have the liberty to kill him.) Most modern conceptions of rights are universalist and egalitarian -- in other words, equal rights are granted to all people.

Arthur Andersen	Arthur Andersen LLP, based in Chicago, was once one of the "Big Five" accounting firms among PricewaterhouseCoopers, Deloitte Touche Tohmatsu, Ernst ' Young and KPMG, providing auditing, tax, and consulting services to large corporations. In 2002, the firm voluntarily surrendered its licenses to practice as Certified Public Accountants in the United States after being found guilty of criminal charges relating to the firm"s handling of the auditing of Enron, the energy corporation, resulting in the loss of 85,000 jobs. Although the verdict was subsequently overturned by the Supreme Court of the United States, it has not returned as a viable business.
Intelligence	Intelligence refers to discrete information with currency and relevance, and the abstraction, evaluation, and understanding of such information for its accuracy and value.
Popular sovereignty	Popular sovereignty or the sovereignty of the people is the belief that the legitimacy of the state is created by the will or consent of its people, who are the source of all political power. It is closely associated with the social contract philosophers, among whom are Thomas Hobbes, John Locke, and Jean-Jacques Rousseau. Popular sovereignty expresses a concept and does not necessarily reflect or describe a political reality.
Public opinion	Public opinion is the aggregate of individual attitudes or beliefs held by the adult population. Public opinion can also be defined as the complex collection of opinions of many different people and the sum of all their views. The principle approaches to the study of Public opinion may be divided into 4 categories: a) quantitative measurement of opinion distributions; b) investigation of the internal relationships among the individual opinions that make up Public opinion on an issue; c) description or analysis of the public role of Public opinion; d) study both of the communication media that disseminate the ideas on which opinions are based and of the uses that propagandists and other manipulators make of these media. Public opinion as a concept gained credence with the rise of "public" in the eighteenth century.

Committee	A Committee (some of which are titled instead as a "Commission" larger deliberative assembly--which when organized so that action on Committee requires a vote by all its entitled members, is called the Committee of the Whole". Committee s often serve several different functions: • Governance: in organizations considered too large for all the members to participate in decisions affecting the organization as a whole, a Committee (such as a Board of Directors or "Executive Committee) is given the power to make decisions, spend money the Board of directors can frequently enter into binding contracts and make decisions which once taken or made, can"t be taken back or undone under the law. • Coordination: individuals from different parts of an organization (for example, all senior vice presidents) might meet regularly to discuss developments in their areas, review projects that cut across organizational boundaries, talk about future options, etc. Where there is a large Committee it is common to have smaller Committee s with more specialized functions - for example, Boards of Directors of large corporations typically have an (ongoing) audit Committee finance Committee compensation Committee etc. Large academic conferences are usually organized by a co-ordinating Committee drawn from the relevant professional body.
Theodore Roosevelt	Theodore Roosevelt was the 26th (1901-1909) President of the United States. He had been the 25th Vice President before becoming President upon the assassination of President William McKinley. Owing to his charismatic personality and reformist policies, which he called the "Square Deal", Roosevelt is considered one of the ablest presidents and an icon of the Progressive Era.
Homeland	A Homeland is the concept of the place (cultural geography) to which an ethnic group holds a long history and a deep cultural association with --the country in which a particular national identity began. As a common noun, it simply connotes the country of one"s origin.
Appropriation	Appropriation is a non-violent process by which previously unowned natural resources, particularly land, become the property of a person or group of persons. The term is widely used in economics in this sense. In certain cases, it proceeds under very specifically defined forms, such as driving stakes or other such markers into the land claimed, which form gave rise to the term "staking a claim." "Squatter"s rights" are another form of Appropriation, but are usually asserted against land to which ownership rights of another party have been recognized.
Procedure	In all lawsuits involving Conflict of Laws, questions of Procedure as opposed to substance are always determined by the lex fori, i.e. the law of the state in which the case is being litigated.

This is a part of the process called characterisation. Issues identified as procedural include the following:

- By initiating the action before the forum court, the plaintiff is asking for the grant of the local remedies. This will not be a problem so long as the form of the relief is broadly similar to the relief available under the lex causae, i.e. the law selected under the choice of law rules. But forum courts may refuse a remedy in two situations:

    if the effect of granting the relief sought would offend against the public policy of the forum court;

    if the effect of the relief would be so different from that available under the lex causae that it makes the right sought to be enforced a different right. For example, in English law, the court was asked in Phrantzes v Argenti 2 QB 19 to enforce a Greek marriage dowry agreement.

Citizenship	Citizenship is an act of being a citizen of one community.
	Citizenship status, under social contract theory, carries with it both rights and responsibilities. "Active Citizenship" is the philosophy that citizens should work towards the betterment of their community through economic participation, public service, volunteer work, and other such efforts to improve life for all citizens.
Due process	Due process is the principle that the government must respect all of the legal rights that are owed to a person according to the law of the land. As developed through a large body of case law in the United States, this principle gives individuals a varying ability to enforce their rights against alleged violations by governments and their agents (that is, state actors), but normally not against other private citizens.
	Due process has also been frequently interpreted as placing limitations on laws and legal proceedings, in order for judges instead of legislators to define and guarantee fundamental fairness, justice, and liberty.
Demographic	Demographic s or Demographic data refers to selected population characteristics as used in government, marketing or opinion research, or the Demographic profiles used in such research. Note the distinction from the term "demography" Commonly-used Demographic s include race, age, income, disabilities, mobility (in terms of travel time to work or number of vehicles available), educational attainment, home ownership, employment status, and even location.
Halliburton	Halliburton is a US-based oilfield services corporation with international operations in more than 70 countries.

It is based in 5 Houston Center in Downtown Houston, Texas, in the United States. U.S. office locations are also in Anchorage, Alaska; Bakersfield, California; Denver, Colorado; Lafayette, Louisiana; and Oklahoma City, Oklahoma.

Iraq

Iraq , officially the Republic of Iraq JumhÅ«rÄ«yat Al-Ê¿IrÄ q, Kurdish: ÙƒÛ†Ù…ارÛŒ Ø¹ÛŽØ±Ø§Ù‚â€Ž, Komara Iraqê), is a country in Western Asia spanning most of the northwestern end of the Zagros mountain range, the eastern part of the Syrian Desert and the northern part of the Arabian Desert. Iraq shares borders with Jordan to the west, Syria to the northwest, Turkey to the north, Iran to the east, and Kuwait and Saudi Arabia to the south. Iraq has a narrow section of coastline measuring 58 km between Umm Qasr and Al Faw on the Persian Gulf.

Axis of evil

"Axis of evil" is a term coined by United States President George W. Bush in his State of the Union Address on January 29, 2002 in order to describe governments that he accused of helping terrorism and seeking weapons of mass destruction. President Bush named Iran, Iraq and North Korea in his speech. President Bush"s presidency was marked by this notion as a justification for the War on Terror.

Privatization

Privatization is the incidence or process of transferring ownership of a business, enterprise, agency or public service from the public sector (government) to the private sector (business.) In a broader sense, Privatization refers to transfer of any government function to the private sector including governmental functions like revenue collection and law enforcement.

The term "Privatization" also has been used to describe two unrelated transactions.

Freedom

Freedom is the right to act according to ones will without being held up by the power of others. From a philosophical point of view, it can be defined as the capacity to determine your own choices. It can be defined negatively as an absence of subordination, servitude and constraint.

Freedom of Information Act

The Freedom of Information Act , as amended, represents the implementation of freedom of information legislation in the United States. It was signed into law by President Lyndon B. Johnson on September 6, 1966 (Public Law 89-554, 80 Stat. 383; Amended 1996, 2002, 2007), and went into effect the following year.

Red

Red is a political adjective which associates with communism, Soviet Union, or radical left politics. Depending on the context the adjective may be perceived to bear either a pejorative or positive connotation.

In its literal meaning, the word is used in the term Red flag and Red star, the object which are in fact of Red color, but which are the symbols of communism.

Committee	A Committee (some of which are titled instead as a "Commission" larger deliberative assembly-- which when organized so that action on Committee requires a vote by all its entitled members, is called the Committee of the Whole". Committee s often serve several different functions: • Governance: in organizations considered too large for all the members to participate in decisions affecting the organization as a whole, a Committee (such as a Board of Directors or "Executive Committee) is given the power to make decisions, spend money the Board of directors can frequently enter into binding contracts and make decisions which once taken or made, can"t be taken back or undone under the law. • Coordination: individuals from different parts of an organization (for example, all senior vice presidents) might meet regularly to discuss developments in their areas, review projects that cut across organizational boundaries, talk about future options, etc. Where there is a large Committee it is common to have smaller Committee s with more specialized functions - for example, Boards of Directors of large corporations typically have an (ongoing) audit Committee finance Committee compensation Committee etc. Large academic conferences are usually organized by a co-ordinating Committee drawn from the relevant professional body.
Iraq	Iraq , officially the Republic of Iraq JumhÅ«rÄ«yat Al-Ê¿IrÄ q, Kurdish: ÙƒÛ†Ù…Ø§Ø±ÛŒ Ø¹ÛŽØ±Ø§Ù‚â€Ž, Komara Iraqê), is a country in Western Asia spanning most of the northwestern end of the Zagros mountain range, the eastern part of the Syrian Desert and the northern part of the Arabian Desert. Iraq shares borders with Jordan to the west, Syria to the northwest, Turkey to the north, Iran to the east, and Kuwait and Saudi Arabia to the south. Iraq has a narrow section of coastline measuring 58 km between Umm Qasr and Al Faw on the Persian Gulf.
Judicial activism	Judicial activism is a critical term used to describe judicial rulings that are viewed as imposing a personal biased interpretation by a given court of what a law means as opposed to what a neutral, unbiased observer would naturally interpret a law to be. The term has most often been used to describe left-wing judges, however; the Supreme Court"s activity since the confirmation of justices Alito and Roberts under George W. Bush, and the ensuing perception that the conservative court was expanding the rights of corporations at the cost of the rights of citizens, has since led to conservative judges being labeled activists. The term "Judicial activism" is frequently used in political debate without definition, which has created some confusion over its precise meaning or meanings.
Constitution	A Constitution is set of rules for government -- often codified as a written document -- that establishes principles of an autonomous political entity. In the case of countries, this term refers specifically to a national Constitution defining the fundamental political principles, and establishing the structure, procedures, powers and duties, of a government. By limiting the government"s own reach, most Constitution s guarantee certain rights to the people.

Region	Region is most commonly a geographical term that is used in various ways among the different branches of geography. In general, a Region is a medium-scale area of land or water, smaller than the whole areas of interest (which could be, for example, the world, a nation, a river basin, mountain range, and so on), and larger than a specific site. A Region may be seen as a collection of smaller units (as in "the New England states") or as one part of a larger whole (as in "the New England Region of the United States".)
Separation of powers	The Separation of powers is a model for the governance of democratic states. The model was first developed in ancient Greece and came into widespread use by the Roman Republic as part of the uncodified Constitution of the Roman Republic. Under this model, the state is divided into branches or estates, each with separate and independent powers and areas of responsibility.
Federalism	Federalism is a political philosophy in which a group of members are bound together ">covenant) with a governing representative head. The term Federalism is also used to describe a system of the government in which sovereignty is constitutionally divided between a central governing authority and constituent political units (like states or provinces.) Federalism is a system in which the power to govern is shared between national and central(state) governments, creating what is often called a federation.
Power	Power in international relations is defined in several different ways. Political scientists, historians, and practitioners of international relations (diplomats) have used the following concepts of political Power:

- Power as a goal of states or leaders;
- Power as a measure of influence or control over outcomes, events, actors and issues;
- Power as reflecting victory in conflict and the attainment of security; and,
- Power as control over resources and capabilities.

Modern discourse generally speaks in terms of state Power, indicating both economic and military Power. Those states that have significant amounts of Power within the international system are referred to as middle powers, regional powers, great powers, superpowers, or hyperpowers, although there is no commonly accepted standard for what defines a powerful state.

Entities other than states can also acquire and wield Power in international relations.

Judicial review	Judicial review is the doctrine in democratic theory under which legislative and executive action is subject to invalidation by the judiciary. Specific courts with Judicial review power must annul the acts of the state when it finds them incompatible with a higher authority, such as the terms of a written constitution. Judicial review is an example of the functioning of separation of powers in a modern governmental system (where the judiciary is one of three branches of government .)

Bill of Rights	A Bill of rights is a list or summary of rights that are considered important and essential by a nation. The purpose of these bills is to protect those rights against infringement by the government. The term "Bill of rights" originates from Britain, where it referred to a bill that was passed by Parliament in 1689.
Presidential election	A presidential election was held in Chile on 4 September 1970. A narrow plurality (36.6 percent of the total vote) was secured by Salvador Allende, the candidate of the Popular Unity coalition of leftist parties. Because he did not obtain an absolute majority, his election required a further vote by the National Congress of Chile which resulted in Allende assuming the presidency in accordance with the Chilean Constitution of 1925.
Right	A right is the legal or moral entitlement to do or refrain from doing something thing or recognition in civil society. Rights serve as rules of interaction between people, and, as such, they place constraints and obligations upon the actions of individuals or groups (for example, if one has a right to life, this means that others do not have the liberty to kill him.) Most modern conceptions of rights are universalist and egalitarian -- in other words, equal rights are granted to all people.
Habeas corpus	Habeas corpus have the body) is a legal action through which a person can seek relief from the unlawful detention of him or herself or from being harmed by the judicial system. Of English origin, the writ of Habeas corpus has historically been an important instrument for the safeguarding of individual freedom against arbitrary state action.
Mandamus	A writ of Mandamus or Mandamus is the name of one of the prerogative writs in the common law, and is "issued by a superior court to compel a lower court or a government officer to perform mandatory or purely ministerial duties correctly". Mandamus is a judicial remedy which is in the form of an order from a superior court to any government, subordinate court, corporation or public authority to do or forbear from doing some specific act which that body is obliged under law to do or refrain from doing, as the case may be, and which is in the nature of public duty and in certain cases of a statutory duty. It cannot be issued to compel an authority to do something against statutory provision.
Australia	Australia , officially the Commonwealth of Australia is a country in the southern hemisphere comprising the mainland, which is both the world"s smallest continent and the world"s largest island, the island of Tasmania, and numerous other islands in the Indian and Pacific Oceans.[N4] Australia is the only place that is simultaneously considered a continent, a country and an island. Neighbouring countries include Indonesia, East Timor and Papua New Guinea to the north, the Solomon Islands, Vanuatu and New Caledonia to the north-east and New Zealand to the southeast.

For around 40,000 years before European settlement commenced in the late 18th century, the Australia n mainland and Tasmania were inhabited by around 250 individual nations of indigenous Australia ns.

Brazil

Brazil, officially the Federative Republic of Brazil (Portuguese: República Federativa do Brasil) Â·), is a country in South America. It is the fifth largest country by geographical area, occupying nearly half of South America, the fifth most populous country, and the fourth most populous democracy in the world. Bounded by the Atlantic Ocean on the east, Brazil has a coastline of over 7,491 kilometers (4,655 mi.)

Canada

Canada has been a member of the North Atlantic Treaty Organization (NATO) since its inception in 1949.

Canada was not only a member but one of the principal initiators of the alliance. This was a marked break with Canada"s pre-war isolationism, and was the first peacetime alliance Canada had ever joined.

Czech Republic

The Czech Republic is a landlocked country in Central Europe. The country borders Poland to the northeast, Germany to the west and northwest, Austria to the south and Slovakia to the east. The capital and largest city is Prague .

Ethnicity

Ethnicity plays a prominent role in pornography. Distinct genres of pornography focus on performers of specific ethnic groups, or on the depiction of interracial sexual activity. Ethnic pornography typically employs ethnic and racial stereotypes in its depiction of performers.

France

France , officially the French Republic , is a country located in Western Europe, with several overseas islands and territories located on other continents. Metropolitan France extends from the Mediterranean Sea to the English Channel and the North Sea, and from the Rhine to the Atlantic Ocean. It is often referred to as L"Hexagone ("The Hexagon") because of the geometric shape of its territory.

Greece

Greece , officially the Hellenic Republic , is a country in southeastern Europe, situated on the southern end of the Balkan Peninsula. The country has borders with Albania, the Republic of Macedonia and Bulgaria to the north, and Turkey to the east. The Aegean Sea lies to the east and south of mainland Greece, while the Ionian Sea lies to the west.

Hungary

Hungary, officially the Republic of Hungary (Magyar Köztársaság Â·) "Hungarian Republic"), is a landlocked country in the Carpathian Basin of Central Europe, bordered by Austria, Slovakia, Ukraine, Romania, Serbia, Croatia, and Slovenia. Its capital is Budapest. Hungary is a member of OECD, NATO, EU, V4 and is a Schengen state.

Italy	Italy, in particular at the turn of the 20th century, had a strong anarcho-syndicalist movement.

- 1891: Foundation of the Socialist Revolutionary Anarchist Party
- 1912: Foundation of the Unione Sindacale Italiana trade-union (joined the International Workers Association founded in 1922)
- 1920: Publication of the newspaper Umanità Nova (New Humanity)
- 1936-1939: Sébastien Faure Century, contingent of the Durruti Column in the Spanish Civil War
- 1986: Foundation in Italy of the Federation of Anarchist Communists

Japan	Japan is an island nation in East Asia. Located in the Pacific Ocean, it lies to the east of the Sea of Japan, People"s Republic of China, North Korea, South Korea and Russia, stretching from the Sea of Okhotsk in the north to the East China Sea and Taiwan in the south. The characters which make up Japan"s name mean "sun-origin", which is why Japan is sometimes identified as the "Land of the Rising Sun".
Mexico	The United Mexican States), commonly known as Mexico [Ëˆmexiko]), is a federal constitutional republic in North America. It is bordered on the north by the United States; on the south and west by the Pacific Ocean; on the southeast by Guatemala, Belize, and the Caribbean Sea; and on the east by the Gulf of Mexico. Covering almost 2 million square kilometres, Mexico is the fifth-largest country in the Americas by total area and the 14th largest independent nation in the world.
New Zealand	New Zealand is an island country in the south-western Pacific Ocean comprising two main landmasses (commonly called the North Island and the South Island), and numerous smaller islands, most notably Stewart Island/Rakiura and the Chatham Islands. The indigenous MÄ ori named New Zealand Aotearoa, commonly translated as The Land of the Long White Cloud. The Realm of New Zealand also includes the Cook Islands and Niue (self-governing but in free association); Tokelau; and the Ross Dependency (New Zealand"s territorial claim in Antarctica.)
Peru	Peru , officially the Republic of Peru), is a country in western South America. It is bordered on the north by Ecuador and Colombia, on the east by Brazil, on the southeast by Bolivia, on the south by Chile, and on the west by the Pacific Ocean.
	Peru vian territory was home to the Norte Chico civilization, one of the oldest in the world, and to the Inca Empire, the largest state in Pre-Columbian America.
Portugal	Portugal , officially the Portuguese Republic (Portuguese: República Portuguesa), is a country on the Iberian Peninsula. Located in southwestern Europe, Portugal is the westernmost country of mainland Europe and is bordered by the Atlantic Ocean to the west and south and by Spain to the north and east. The Atlantic archipelagos of the Azores and Madeira are also part of Portugal.

Public opinion	Public opinion is the aggregate of individual attitudes or beliefs held by the adult population. Public opinion can also be defined as the complex collection of opinions of many different people and the sum of all their views. The principle approaches to the study of Public opinion may be divided into 4 categories: a) quantitative measurement of opinion distributions; b) investigation of the internal relationships among the individual opinions that make up Public opinion on an issue; c) description or analysis of the public role of Public opinion; d) study both of the communication media that disseminate the ideas on which opinions are based and of the uses that propagandists and other manipulators make of these media. Public opinion as a concept gained credence with the rise of "public" in the eighteenth century.
Spain	Spain is a country located in southwestern Europe on the Iberian Peninsula. Its mainland is bordered to the south and east by the Mediterranean Sea except for a small land boundary with Gibraltar; to the north by France, Andorra, and the Bay of Biscay; and to the northwest and west by the Atlantic Ocean and Portugal. Spanish territory also includes the Balearic Islands in the Mediterranean, the Canary Islands in the Atlantic Ocean off the African coast, and two autonomous cities in North Africa, Ceuta and Melilla, that border Morocco.
Sweden	Sweden , officially the Kingdom of Sweden), is a Nordic country on the Scandinavian Peninsula in Northern Europe. Sweden has land borders with Norway to the west and Finland to the northeast, and it is connected to Denmark by the Öresund Bridge in the south. At 450,000 km^2 (173,746 sq mi), Sweden is the third largest country in the European Union in terms of area, and it has a total population of over 9.2 million.
Public Service of Canada	The Public Service of Canada is the staff of the federal government of Canada. Its function is to support the Canadian monarch, and to handle the hiring of employees for the federal government ministries. It is represented by the Governor General, and the appointed [[list of Canadian ministries	ministry].

Led by Lorrin A. Thurston and Sanford B. Dole, the Provisional Government ruled over HawaiÊ»i until the formal establishment of a republic. Pictured above is the cabinet, (Left to Right) James A. King, Sanford B. Dole, William O. Smith and Peter C. Jones.

Capital	Flag
Capital	Honolulu
Language(s)	Hawaiian, English
Government	Not specified
Provisional Government	
- 1893-1894	Committee of Safety
Historical era	New Imperialism
- Monarchy overthrown	January 17, 1893
- Republic declared	July 4, 1894
Currency	U.S. dollar, Hawaiian dollar

The Provisional Government of HawaiÊ»i was proclaimed on January 17, 1893 by the 13 member Committee of Safety under the leadership of Lorrin A. Thurston and Sanford B. Dole. It governed the Kingdom of HawaiÊ»i after the overthrow of Queen LiliÊ»uokalani until the Republic of HawaiÊ»i was established on July 4, 1894.

Capital punishment | Capital punishment, the death penalty or execution, is the killing of a person by judicial process for retribution, general deterrence, and incapacitation. Crimes that can result in a death penalty are known as capital crimes or capital offences. The term capital originates from Latin capitalis, literally "regarding the head" .

Constitutional council | The Constitutional Council was established by the Constitution of the Fifth Republic on 4 October 1958. It is the highest constitutional authority in France. Its duty is to ensure that the principles and rules of the constitution are upheld.

Chapter 14. The Courts

Countries

This is a list of articles on the constitutions of contemporary countries, states and dependencies.

- Constitution of Abkhazia - Republic of Abkhazia
- Constitution of Afghanistan - Islamic Republic of Afghanistan
- Constitution of Akrotiri - Sovereign Base Area of Akrotiri (UK overseas territory)
- Constitution of Åland - Åland (Autonomous province of Finland)
- Constitution of Albania - Republic of Albania
- Constitution of Algeria - People"s Democratic Republic of Algeria
- Constitution of American Samoa - Territory of American Samoa (US overseas territory)
- Constitution of Andorra - Principality of Andorra
- Constitution of Angola - Republic of Angola
- Constitution of Anguilla - Anguilla (UK overseas territory)
- Constitution of Antigua and Barbuda - Antigua and Barbuda
- Constitution of Argentina - Argentine Republic
- Constitution of Armenia - Republic of Armenia
- Constitution of Aruba - Aruba (Self-governing country in the Kingdom of the Netherlands)
- Constitution of Ascension Island - Ascension Island (Dependency of the UK overseas territory of Saint Helena)
- Constitution of Australia - Commonwealth of Australia
- Constitution of Austria - Republic of Austria
- Constitution of Azerbaijan - Republic of Azerbaijan

- Constitution of The Bahamas - Commonwealth of The Bahamas
- Constitution of Bahrain - Kingdom of Bahrain
- Constitution of Bangladesh - People"s Republic of Bangladesh
- Constitution of Barbados - Barbados
- Constitution of Belarus - Republic of Belarus
- Constitution of Belgium - Kingdom of Belgium
- Constitution of Belize - Belize
- Constitution of Benin - Republic of Benin
- Constitution of Bermuda - Bermuda (UK overseas territory)
- Constitution of Bhutan - Kingdom of Bhutan
- Constitution of Bolivia - Plurinational State of Bolivia
- Constitution of Bosnia and Herzegovina - Bosnia and Herzegovina
- Constitution of Botswana - Republic of Botswana
- Constitution of Brazil - Federative Republic of Brazil
- Constitution of Brunei - Negara Brunei Darussalam
- Constitution of Bulgaria - Republic of Bulgaria
- Constitution of Burkina Faso - Burkina Faso
- Constitution of Burma - Burma (Union of Myanmar)
- Constitution of Burundi - Republic of Burundi

- Constitution of Cambodia - Kingdom of Cambodia
- Constitution of Cameroon - Republic of Cameroon
- Constitution of Canada - Canada
- Constitution of Cape Verde - Republic of Cape Verde
- Constitution of the Cayman Islands - Cayman Islands (UK overseas territory)

- Constitution of the Central African Republic - Central African Republic
- Constitution of Chad - Republic of Chad
- Constitution of Chile - Republic of Chile
- Constitution of the People"s Republic of China - People"s Republic of China
- Constitution of the Republic of China - Republic of China
- Constitution of Christmas Island - Territory of Christmas Island (Australian overseas territory)
- Constitution of the Cocos (Keeling) Islands - Territory of Cocos (Keeling) Islands (Australian overseas territory)
- Constitution of Colombia - Republic of Colombia
- Constitution of Comoros - Union of the Comoros
- Constitution of the Democratic Republic of the Congo - Democratic Republic of the Congo
- Constitution of the Republic of the Congo - Republic of the Congo
- Constitution of the Cook Islands - Cook Islands (Associated state of New Zealand)
- Constitution of Costa Rica - Republic of Costa Rica
- Constitution of Côte d"Ivoire - Republic of Côte d"Ivoire
- Constitution of Croatia - Republic of Croatia
- Constitution of Cuba - Republic of Cuba
- Constitution of Cyprus - Republic of Cyprus
- Constitution of the Czech Republic - Czech Republic

- Constitution of Denmark - Kingdom of Denmark
- Constitution of Dhekelia - Sovereign Base Areas of Dhekelia (UK overseas territory)
- Constitution of Djibouti - Republic of Djibouti
- Constitution of Dominica - Commonwealth of Dominica
- Constitution of the Dominican Republic - Dominican Republic

- Constitution of East Timor (Timor-Leste) - Democratic Republic of Timor-Leste
- Constitution of Ecuador - Republic of Ecuador
- Constitution of Egypt - Arab Republic of Egypt
- Constitution of El Salvador - Republic of El Salvador
- Constitution of Equatorial Guinea - Republic of Equatorial Guinea
- Constitution of Eritrea - State of Eritrea
- Constitution of Estonia - Republic of Estonia
- Constitution of Ethiopia - Federal Democratic Republic of Ethiopia

- Constitution of the Falkland Islands - Falkland Islands (UK overseas territory)
- Constitution of the Faroe Islands - Faroe Islands (Self-governing country in the Kingdom of Denmark)
- Constitution of Fiji - Republic of the Fiji Islands
- Constitution of Finland - Republic of Finland
- Constitution of France - French Republic
- Constitution of French Polynesia - French Polynesia

- Constitution of Gabon - Gabonese Republic
- Constitution of Gambia - Republic of The Gambia
- Constitution of Georgia - Georgia
- Constitution of Germany - Federal Republic of Germany
- Constitution of Ghana - Republic of Ghana
- Constitution of Gibraltar - Gibraltar
- Constitution of Greece - Hellenic Republic
- Constitution of Greenland - Greenland (Self-governing country in the Kingdom of Denmark)

- Constitution of Grenada - Grenada
- Constitution of Guam - Territory of Guam (US overseas territory)
- Constitution of Guatemala - Republic of Guatemala
- Constitution of Guernsey - Bailiwick of Guernsey (British Crown dependency)
- Constitution of Guinea - Republic of Guinea
- Constitution of Guinea-Bissau - Republic of Guinea-Bissau
- Constitution of Guyana - Co-operative Republic of Guyana

- Constitution of Iceland - Republic of Iceland
- Constitution of India - Republic of India
- Constitution of Indonesia - Republic of Indonesia
- Constitution of Iran - Islamic Republic of Iran
- Constitution of Iraq - Republic of Iraq
- Constitution of Ireland - Ireland

Constitutional court	A Constitutional court is a high court that deals primarily with constitutional law. Its main authority is to rule on whether or not laws that are challenged are in fact unconstitutional, i.e. whether or not they conflict with constitutionally established rights and freedoms
Federal district	Federal district s are a type of administrative division of a federation, under the direct control of the federal government. District of Columbia (Washington D.C.)

The seat of the U.S. federal government in Washington is a Federal district known as the District of Columbia. In addition, the U.S. government has several other kinds of " Federal district s" which are not specifically related to a capital city:

- The federal court system divides each state principal, the District of Columbia, and Puerto Rico, into one or more federal judicial districts. A United States district court and a bankruptcy court are located in each. There are also regional federal judicial circuits, each consisting of a group of states (except for the District of Columbia Circuit, which consists only of the Federal district ; Puerto Rico and the United States territorial courts are also assigned to circuits. Each circuit has a United States court of appeals.
- The U.S. central bank, the Federal Reserve, consists of twelve banks located around the country; each of these banks serves a Federal Reserve district.

Argentine Capital District (Buenos Aires City)

The term Distrito Federal, meaning Federal district in both the Spanish and Portuguese languages, is used to refer to:

- Argentine Capital District, known as "Autonomous City of Buenos Aires" since 1996.
- Brazilian Federal district
- Mexican Federal district
- Venezuelan Capital District

In Malaysia, the term Federal Territory is used for the three territories governed directly by the federal government, namely Kuala Lumpur (national capital), Putrajaya (federal government administrative centre) and Labuan Island (international offshore financial centre.)

Andaman Islands, India

In India, the term Union Territory is used for the six territories governed indirectly by the federal national government with its own Chief minister and governor of Delhi, others namely include - Andaman and Nicobar Islands, Chandigarh, Dadra and Nagar Haveli, Daman and Diu, Lakshadweep and Pondicherry.

Vietnam	Vietnam " href="/wiki/Battle_of_B%E1%BA%A1ch_%C4%90%E1%BA%B1ng_River_(938)">battle of Bá°ịch Ã á°±ng River. Successive dynasties flourished along with geographic and political expansion deeper into Southeast Asia, until it was colonized by the French in the mid-19th century. Efforts to resist the French eventually led to their expulsion from the country in the mid-20th century, leaving a nation divided politically into two countries.

Vietnam War

The Vietnam War was a military conflict that occurred in Vietnam, Laos and Cambodia from 1959 to 30 April 1975. The war was fought between the communist North Vietnam, supported by its communist allies, and the government of South Vietnam, supported by the United States and other member nations of the Southeast Asia Treaty Organization (SEATO.)

The following outline is provided as an overview of and topical guide to the Vietnam War:

Listed by starting date:

- Operation 34A - (1964)
- Operation Starlite - August 18-24 1965
- Operation Hump- November 5 1965
- Operation Crimp - January 7, 1966
- Operation Birmingham - April 1966
- Operation Hastings - Late May 1966
- Operation Prairie - August 1966
- Operation Deckhouse Five - January 6, 1967
- Operation Cedar Falls - January 8, 1967
- Operation Junction City - February 21, 1967
- Operation Francis Marion - April 6 - April 30, 1967
- Operation Union - April 21-May 16, 1967
- Operations Malheur I and Malheur II - 11 May - July 1, 1967
- Operation Baker - May 11, 1967
- Operation Scotland - See Battle of Khe Sanh
- Operation Pegasus - August 8, 1968
- Operation Dewey Canyon - January 22, 1969
- Operation Twinkletoes - 1969
- Operation Apache Snow - May 10 - May 20, 1969
- Operation Chicago Peak - April 1970
- Operation Texas Star - April - September, 1970
- Operation Ivory Coast - November 21, 1970
- Operation Jefferson Glenn - 1970-1971
- Operation Lam Son 719 - February 8, 1971
- Ho Chi Minh Campaign January 24 - April 30, 1975
- Operation Frequent Wind - April, 1975

- Battle of Ap Bac - January 2, 1963
- Battle of Kien Long - April 11 - April 15, 1964
- Battle of Thanh Hóa - July 31, 1964
- Battle of Binh Gia - December 28, 1964 - January 1, 1965
- Battle of Dong Xoai - June 10, 1965
- Battle near Minh Thanh - October 25 - October 27, 1965
- Battle of Ia Drang - November 14 - November 16, 1965
- Battle of Cu Nghi - January 28 - January 31, 1966
- Battle of Kim Son Valley - February 16 - February 28, 1966
- Battle of A Shau - March 9 - March 10, 1966
- Battle of Xa Cam My - April 11 - April 12, 1966
- First Battle of Dong Ha - Late May - June, 1966
- Battle on Minh Thanh Road - July 9, 1966
- Battle of Ä á»©c CÆ¡ - August 9, 1966
- Battle of Long Táº§n - August 18- August 19, 1966
- Viet Cong attack on Tan Son Nhut airbase - December 4, 1966
- Battle of LZ Bird - December 27, 1966

- Battle of Tra Binh Dong - February 14 - February 15, 1967
- Battle of Hills 881 and 861 - April 24-May 9, 1967
- Nine Days in May - May 18 - May 28, 1967
- Battle of Vinh Huy - May 30 - June 2, 1967
- Battle of Con Thien - July 2 - July 3, 1967
- Battle of Dong Son - September 4, 1967
- Battle of Ong Thang - October 17, 1967
- First Battle of Loc Ninh - October 29 - November, 1967
- Battle of Dak To - November 3-November 22, 1967
- Battle in the Mekong Delta - December 4, 1967
- Battle of Tam Quan - December 6 - December 20, 1967
- Battle of Thom Tham Khe - December 27 - December 28, 1967
- Phoenix Program - 1967 - 1972
- Battle of Khe Sanh - January 21 - April 8, 1968
- Tet Offensive - January 30 - February 25, 1968
- Battle of Bien Hoa - January 31 - July 1, 1968
- Battle of Kham Duc - May 10 - May 12, 1968
- First Battle of Saigon - January 31, - February 3, 1968
- Battle of Hue - January 31, - February 25, 1968
- Tet 1969 - February 1969
- Battle of Hamburger Hill - May 10 - May 20, 1969
- Firebase Ripcord - March 12 - July 23, 1970
- Cambodian Incursion - April 29 - July 22, 1970
- Battle of Snoul - January 5 - May 30, 1971
- Easter Offensive - March 30 - October 22, 1972
- First Battle of Quang Tri - March 30 - May 1, 1972
- Battle of Loc Ninh - April 4 - April 7, 1972
- Battle of An Loc - April 20 - July 20, 1972
- Second Battle of Quang Tri - June 28 - September 16, 1972
- Battle of Phuoc Long - December 13, 1974 - January 6, 1975
- Battle of Buon Me Thuot - March 10 - March 12, 1975
- Battle of Xuan Loc - April 9 - April 20, 1975

- Operation Farm Gate
- Operation Chopper (1962)
- Operation Ranch Hand (1962-1971)
- Operation Pierce Arrow (1964)
- Operation Barrell Roll (1964-1972)
- Operation Pony Express (1965-1970)
- Operation Flaming Dart (1965)
- Operation Rolling Thunder (1965-1968)
- Operation Steel Tiger (1965-1968)
- Operation Arc Light (1965-1973)
- Operation Tiger Hound (1965-1968)
- Operation Shed Light (1966-1972)
- Operation Carolina Moon (1966)
- Operation Wahiawa (1966)
- Operation Bolo (1967)
- Operation Popeye (1967-1972
- Operation Niagara (1968)
- Operation Igloo White (1968-1973

- Operation Giant Lance (1969)
- Operation Commando Hunt (1968-1972)
- Operation Menu (1969-1970)
- Operation Patio (1970)
- Operation Freedom Deal (1970-1973)
- Operation Linebacker (1972)
- Operation Enhance Plus (1972)
- Operation Linebacker II (1972)
- Operation Homecoming (1973)
- Operation Baby Lift (1975)
- Operation Eagle Pull (1975)
- Operation Frequent Wind (1975)

- National Order of Vietnam
- Vietnam Military Merit Medal
- Vietnam Distinguished Service Order
- Vietnam Meritorious Service Medal
- Vietnam Special Service Medal
- Vietnam Gallantry Cross
- Vietnam Air Gallantry Cross
- Vietnam Navy Gallantry Cross
- Vietnam Armed Forces Honor Medal
- Vietnam Civil Actions Medal
- Vietnam Staff Service Medal
- Vietnam Technical Service Medal
- Vietnam Wound Medal
- Vietnam Campaign Medal
- Presidential Unit Citation (Vietnam)
- Vietnam Gallantry Cross Unit Citation
- Vietnam Civil Actions Unit Citation

- Golden Star Medal
- Ho Chi Minh Order
- Defeat American Aggression Badge
- Vietnam Liberation Order
- Resolution for Victory Order

- Medal of Honor rare
- Distinguished Service Cross rare
- Navy Cross uncommon
- Air Force Cross uncommon
- Silver Star uncommon
- Purple Heart frequent
- Bronze Star frequent
- Presidential Unit Citation rare
- Vietnam Service Medal very common
- National Defense Service Medal very common
- Commendation Medal common

- "Fatigue Press" at Fort Hood,
- "Last Harass" at Fort Gordon, Georgia
- "Pawn"s Pawn" at Fort Leonard Wood, Missouri

- "Ultimate Weapon" at Fort Dix, New Jersey
- "Attitude Check" at Camp Pendleton, California
- "Green Machine" at Fort Greely, Alaska
- "Napalm" at Fort Campbell, Tennessee
- "Arctic Arsenal" at Fort Greely, Alaska
- "Black Voice" at Fort McClellan, Alabama
- "Fragging Action" at Fort Dix
- "Fort Polk Puke" at Fort Polk, Louisiana
- "Custer"s Last Stand" at Fort Riley, Kansas
- "Whack!" from the Women"s Army Corps School
- "Where Are We?" at Fort Huachuca, Arizona
- "Voice of the Lumpen" (affiliated with the Black Panther Party) in Frankfurt
- "Can You Bear McNair?" at McNair Barracks, Berlin
- "Seasick" at Subic Bay
- "The Man Can"t Win If You Grin" in Okinawa
- "Korea Free Press"
- "Semper Fi" in Japan
- "Stars and Bars" in England
- "Separated From Life" in England
- "Duck Power" in San Diego
- "Harass the Brass" at Canute Air Force Base, Illinois
- "All Hands Abandon Ship", Newport, Rhode Island
- "Now Hear This", Long Beach
- "Potemkin" on the USS Forestall
- "Star Spangled Bummer" at Wright-Patterson Air Force Base in Ohio
- "Fat Albert"s Death Ship" in Charlestown
- "Pig Boat Blues", USS Agerholm
- "Special Weapons", Kirtland AFB, New Mexico
- "I Will Fear No Evil", Kirtland AFB, New Mexico
- "Blows Against the Empire", Kirtland AFB, New Mexico

source: "The American War" - see references below

- Bao Dai
- Duong Van Minh
- Madame Ngo Dinh Nhu
- Ngo Dinh Diem
- Ngo Dinh Nhu
- Nguyen Cao Ky
- Nguyen Khanh
- Nguyen Van Thieu

- Creighton W. Abrams
- Dean Acheson
- Spiro Agnew
- Ellsworth Bunker
- McGeorge Bundy
- William Bundy
- William Calley
- Clark Clifford
- William Colby
- A. Peter Dewey
- John Foster Dulles
- Dwight D. Eisenhower
- Daniel Ellsberg
- J. William Fulbright
- Barry Goldwater
- David Hackworth
- Alexander Haig
- Paul D. Harkins
- Seymour Hersh
- Hubert Humphrey
- Lyndon Johnson
- John F. Kennedy
- John Kerry
- Henry Kissinger
- Melvin Laird
- Edward Lansdale
- Henry Cabot Lodge, Jr.
- Mike Mansfield
- Graham Martin
- Robert McNamara
- George McGovern
- Richard Nixon
- Pete Peterson
- Charika Pugh
- Dean Rusk

- Maxwell D. Taylor
- Hugh C. Thompson, Jr
- John Paul Vann
- Gary Varsel
- William Westmoreland

- Ho Chi Minh
- Le Duan
- Tran Van Tra
- Le Duc Tho
- Pham Van Dong
- General Giap
- Poewll Ward

- Lon Nol
- Pol Pot
- Norodom Sihanouk
- Sirik Matak
- Sosthene Fernandez

- David H. Hackworth. 1989 About Face
- A.J. Langguth. 2000. Our Vietnam: the War 1954-1975.
- Mann, Robert. 2002. Grand Delusion, A: America"s Descent Into Vietnam.
- Windrow, Martin. 2005. The Last Valley: Dien Bien Phu and the French Defeat in Vietnam.
- Bernard Fall. 1967. Hell in a Very Small Place: the Siege of Dien Bien Phu.
- Harvey Pekar. 2003. American Splendor: Unsung Hero
- Prados, John. 2000. The Blood Road: The Ho Chi Minh Trail and the Vietnam War.
- Prados, John. 1999. Valley of Decision: The Siege of Khe Sanh.
- Shultz, Robert H. Jr. 2000. The Secret War Against Hanoi: The Untold Story of Spies, Saboteurs, and Covert Warriors in North Vietnam.
- Plaster, John L. 1998. SOG: The Secret Wars of America"s Commandos in Vietnam.
- Murphy, Edward F. 1995. Dak To: America"s Sky Soldiers in South Vietnam"s Central Highlands.
- Nolan, Keith W. 1996. The Battle for Saigon: Tet 1968.
- Nolan, Keith W. 1996. Sappers in the Wire: The Life and Death of Firebase Mary Ann.
- Nolan, Keith W. 1992. Operation Buffalo: USMC Fight for the DMZ.
- Nolan, Keith W. 2003. Ripcord : Screaming Eagles Under Siege, Vietnam 1970.
- Robert S. McNamara. 1996. In Retrospect: The Tragedy and Lessons of Vietnam.
- Larry Berman. 2002. No Peace, No Honor: Nixon, Kissinger, and Betrayal in Vietnam.
- Bergerud, Eric M. 1994. Red Thunder, Tropic Lightning: The World of a Combat Division in Vietnam.
- Bernard Edelman. 2002. Dear America: Letters Home from Vietnam.
- Darrel D. Whitcomb. 1999. The Rescue of Bat 21.
- Oberdorfer, Don. 1971. Tet: the Story of a Battle and its Historic Aftermath.
- LTG Harold G. Moore and Joseph L. Galloway. 1992. We Were Soldiers Once ... And Young.
- Duiker, William J. 2002. Ho Chi Minh: A Life.
- John Laurence. 2002. The Cat from Hue: A Vietnam War Story.
- Emerson, Gloria. 1976. Winners and Losers: Battles, Retreats, Gains, Losses and Ruins from a Long War.
- Philip Caputo. 1977. A Rumor of War.

- Al Santoli. 1981. Everything We Had: an Oral History of the Vietnam War by 33 American Soldiers Who Fought It.
- Robert C. Mason. 1983. Chickenhawk.
- Michael Herr. 1977. Dispatches.
- Joseph T. Ward. 1991. Dear Mom: a Sniper"s Vietnam.
- Hemphill, Robert. 1998. Platoon: Bravo Company.
- Noam Chomsky. 1967. The Responsibility of Intellectuals.
- Moore, Robin. 1965 The Green Berets (ISBN 0-312-98492-8)

- Robert Olen Butler. 1992.

New Deal	The New Deal is a programme of active labour market policies introduced in the United Kingdom by the Labour government in 1998, initially funded by a one off Â£5bn windfall tax on privatised utility companies. The stated purpose is to reduce unemployment by providing training, subsidised employment and voluntary work to the unemployed. Spending on the New Deal was Â£1.3 billion in 2001.
Politics	Politics are an integral part of the Unification Church"s concerns and activities, although the church itself largely remains aloof from Politics The degree of involvement of the movement, as well as some of its specific stances, have also been part of the reason for the movement"s controversial status over the years. The belief in the establishment of a literal Kingdom of Heaven on earth and Rev. Moon"s teaching that religion alone is not enough to bring this provides a motivation for political involvement.
Norm	In the general sense of meaning, a Norm is something to help depict a phenomenon or system by means of averaging or bordering e.g. people are normally heterosexual, or good people live without sin. Comparison, classification and measurement all require some normative factor, e.g. altitude normal to sea level.
	Norms are sentences or sentence meanings with practical, i. e. action-oriented (rather than descriptive, explanatory, or expressive) import, the most common of which are commands, permissions, and prohibitions.
Property right	A Property right is the exclusive authority to determine how a resource is used, whether that resource is owned by government or by individuals. All economic goods have a property rights attribute. This attribute has three broad components

1. The right to use the good
2. The right to earn income from the good
3. The right to transfer the good to others

The concept of property rights as used by economists and legal scholars are related but distinct. The distinction is largely seen in the economists" focus on the ability of an individual or collective to control the use of the good. |
| Centralized government | A Centralized government is the form of government in which power is concentrated in a central authority to which local governments are subject. Centralization occurs both geographically and politically. |
| | A Centralized government is characterized in which the local governments are designated by the central Government of the country, like the local administrative authorities. |

Due process

Due process is the principle that the government must respect all of the legal rights that are owed to a person according to the law of the land. As developed through a large body of case law in the United States, this principle gives individuals a varying ability to enforce their rights against alleged violations by governments and their agents (that is, state actors), but normally not against other private citizens.

Due process has also been frequently interpreted as placing limitations on laws and legal proceedings, in order for judges instead of legislators to define and guarantee fundamental fairness, justice, and liberty.

Laissez-faire

Laissez-faire) is a term used to describe a policy of allowing events to take their own course. The term is a French phrase literally meaning "let do". It is a doctrine that states that government generally should not intervene in the marketplace.

Chief justice

Chief Justice Reynato PunoCourt of Appeals Â· SandiganbayanCourt of Tax Appeals Â· Ombudsman

Elections Commission on ElectionsChairman: Jose MeloElections: 2010 | 2004 | 1998 | 1992 | 1986 | AllReferenda: 1987 | 1984 | 1981

Foreign relationsGovernment WebsiteHuman rights

Other countries Â· AtlasPolitics portal

The Philippine Constitutional Commission of 1986 was the commission of the tasked to draft the Constitution of the Philippines in 1986.

- Regular Session: June 2 - October 15, 1986

- Corazon C. Aquino (UNIDO)

- Salvador H. Laurel (UNIDO)

- Cecilia Muñoz-Palma

- Ambrosio B. Padilla

- Napoleon G. Rama

- Jose D. Calderon
- Ahmad Domcao Alonto

1. Resigned

.

Citizenship

Citizenship is an act of being a citizen of one community.

Citizenship status, under social contract theory, carries with it both rights and responsibilities. "Active Citizenship" is the philosophy that citizens should work towards the betterment of their community through economic participation, public service, volunteer work, and other such efforts to improve life for all citizens.

Minimum wage

A Minimum wage is the lowest hourly, daily or monthly wage that employers may legally pay to employees or workers. Equivalently, it is the lowest wage at which workers may sell their labor. Although Minimum wage laws are in effect in a great many jurisdictions, there are differences of opinion about the benefits and drawbacks of a Minimum wage.

Original intent

Original intent is a theory in law concerning constitutional and statutory interpretation. It is frequently--and usually spuriously--used as a synonym for originalism generally; while Original intent is indeed one theory in the originalist family, it has some extremely salient differences which has led originalists from more predominant schools of thought such as original meaning to castigate Original intent as much as legal realists do.

Original intent maintains that in interpreting a text, a court should determine what the authors of the text were trying to achieve, and to give effect to what they intended the statute to accomplish, the actual text of the legislation notwithstanding.

Communism

Communism is a socioeconomic structure and political ideology that promotes the establishment of an egalitarian, classless, stateless society based on common ownership and control of the means of production and property in general. In political science, however, the term "Communism", usually spelled with the capital letter C is often used to refer to the Communist states, a form of government in which the state operates under a one-party system and declares allegiance to Marxism-Leninism or a derivative thereof, even if the party does not actually claim that it has already reached Communism.

Forerunners of communist ideas existed in antiquity and particularly in the 18th and early 19th century France, with thinkers such as Jean-Jacques Rousseau and the more radical Gracchus Babeuf.

Joseph

Joseph or Josephus Scottus (died between 791 and 804), called the Deacon, was an Irish scholar, diplomat, poet, and ecclesiastic, a minor figure in the Carolingian Renaissance. He has been cited as an early example of "the scholar in public life".

His early life is obscure, but he studied first under Colcu, probably at Clonmacnoise, and then under Alcuin at York, probably in the 770s.

Civil liberties

Civil liberties are freedoms that protect an individual from the government of the nation in which they reside. Civil liberties set limits for government so that it cannot abuse its power and interfere unduly with the lives of its citizens.

Common Civil liberties include the rights of people, freedom of religion, and freedom of speech, and additionally, the right to due process, to a fair trial, to own property, and to privacy.

Chapter 15. Freedom: The Struggle for Civil Liberties

First Amendment	The First Amendment to the United States Constitution is the part of the United States Bill of Rights that expressly prohibits the United States Congress from making laws "respecting an establishment of religion" or that prohibit the free exercise of religion, infringe the freedom of speech, infringe the freedom of the press, limit the right to peaceably assemble, or limit the right to petition the government for a redress of grievances. Although the First Amendment only explicitly applies to the Congress, the Supreme Court has interpreted it as applying to the executive and judicial branches. Additionally, in the 20th century, the Supreme Court held that the Due Process Clause of the Fourteenth Amendment applies the limitations of the First Amendment to each state, including any local government within a state.
Bill of Rights	A Bill of rights is a list or summary of rights that are considered important and essential by a nation. The purpose of these bills is to protect those rights against infringement by the government. The term "Bill of rights" originates from Britain, where it referred to a bill that was passed by Parliament in 1689.
Constitution	A Constitution is set of rules for government -- often codified as a written document -- that establishes principles of an autonomous political entity. In the case of countries, this term refers specifically to a national Constitution defining the fundamental political principles, and establishing the structure, procedures, powers and duties, of a government. By limiting the government"s own reach, most Constitution s guarantee certain rights to the people.
Ex post facto law	An Ex post facto law or retroactive law, is a law that retroactively changes the legal consequences of acts committed or the legal status of facts and relationships that existed prior to the enactment of the law. In reference to criminal law, it may criminalize actions that were legal when committed; or it may aggravate a crime by bringing it into a more severe category than it was in at the time it was committed; or it may change or increase the punishment prescribed for a crime, such as by adding new penalties or extending terms; or it may alter the rules of evidence in order to make conviction for a crime more likely than it would have been at the time of the action for which a defendant is prosecuted. Conversely, a form of Ex post facto law commonly known as an amnesty law may decriminalize certain acts or alleviate possible punishments retroactively.
Habeas corpus	Habeas corpus have the body) is a legal action through which a person can seek relief from the unlawful detention of him or herself or from being harmed by the judicial system. Of English origin, the writ of Habeas corpus has historically been an important instrument for the safeguarding of individual freedom against arbitrary state action.
Right	A right is the legal or moral entitlement to do or refrain from doing something thing or recognition in civil society. Rights serve as rules of interaction between people, and, as such, they place constraints and obligations upon the actions of individuals or groups (for example, if one has a right to life, this means that others do not have the liberty to kill him.) Most modern conceptions of rights are universalist and egalitarian -- in other words, equal rights are granted to all people.

Chapter 15. Freedom: The Struggle for Civil Liberties

Civil liberties	Civil liberties are freedoms that protect an individual from the government of the nation in which they reside. Civil liberties set limits for government so that it cannot abuse its power and interfere unduly with the lives of its citizens. Common Civil liberties include the rights of people, freedom of religion, and freedom of speech, and additionally, the right to due process, to a fair trial, to own property, and to privacy.
Contract	Agreement is said to be reached when an offer capable of immediate acceptance is met with a "mirror image" acceptance (ie, an unqualified acceptance.) The parties must have the necessary capacity to Contract and the Contract must not be either trifling, indeterminate, impossible or illegal. Contract law is based on the principle expressed in the Latin phrase pacta sunt servanda .
New Deal	The New Deal is a programme of active labour market policies introduced in the United Kingdom by the Labour government in 1998, initially funded by a one off Â£5bn windfall tax on privatised utility companies. The stated purpose is to reduce unemployment by providing training, subsidised employment and voluntary work to the unemployed. Spending on the New Deal was Â£1.3 billion in 2001.
Property right	A Property right is the exclusive authority to determine how a resource is used, whether that resource is owned by government or by individuals. All economic goods have a property rights attribute. This attribute has three broad components 1. The right to use the good 2. The right to earn income from the good 3. The right to transfer the good to others The concept of property rights as used by economists and legal scholars are related but distinct. The distinction is largely seen in the economists" focus on the ability of an individual or collective to control the use of the good.
Nationalization	Nationalization, also spelled nationalisation, is the act of taking an industry or assets into the public ownership of a national government or state. Nationalization usually refers to private assets, but may also mean assets owned by lower levels of government, such as municipalities, being state operated or owned by the state. The opposite of Nationalization is usually privatization or de-nationalisation, but may also be municipalization.
Citizenship	Citizenship is an act of being a citizen of one community. Citizenship status, under social contract theory, carries with it both rights and responsibilities. "Active Citizenship" is the philosophy that citizens should work towards the betterment of their community through economic participation, public service, volunteer work, and other such efforts to improve life for all citizens.

Chapter 15. Freedom: The Struggle for Civil Liberties

Due process	Due process is the principle that the government must respect all of the legal rights that are owed to a person according to the law of the land. As developed through a large body of case law in the United States, this principle gives individuals a varying ability to enforce their rights against alleged violations by governments and their agents (that is, state actors), but normally not against other private citizens. Due process has also been frequently interpreted as placing limitations on laws and legal proceedings, in order for judges instead of legislators to define and guarantee fundamental fairness, justice, and liberty.
Strict scrutiny	Strict scrutiny is the most stringent standard of judicial review used by United States courts reviewing federal law. Along with the lower standards of rational basis review and intermediate scrutiny, Strict scrutiny is part of a hierarchy of standards courts employ to weigh an asserted government interest against a constitutional right or principle that conflicts with the manner in which the interest is being pursued. Strict scrutiny is applied based on the constitutional conflict at issue, regardless of whether a law or action of the U.S. federal government, a state government, or a local municipality is at issue.
The Bill of Rights	The Bill of Rights is an act of the Parliament of England, whose title is An Act Declaring the Rights and Liberties of the Subject and Settling the Succession of the Crown. It is often called the English Bill of Rights The Bill of Rights was passed by Parliament in December 1689 and was a re-statement in statutory form of the Declaration of Right, presented by the Convention Parliament to William and Mary in February 1689, inviting them to become joint sovereigns of England. It enumerates certain rights to which subjects and permanent residents of a constitutional monarchy were thought to be entitled in the late 17th century, asserting subjects" right to petition the monarch, as well as to bear arms in defence.
Ku Klux Klan	Ku Klux Klan , informally known as The Klan, is the name of several past and present hate group organizations in the United States whose avowed purpose was to protect the rights of and further the interests of white Americans by violence and intimidation. The first such organizations originated in the Southern states and eventually grew to national scope. They developed iconic white costumes consisting of robes, masks, and conical hats.
Power	Power in international relations is defined in several different ways. Political scientists, historians, and practitioners of international relations (diplomats) have used the following concepts of political Power: • Power as a goal of states or leaders; • Power as a measure of influence or control over outcomes, events, actors and issues; • Power as reflecting victory in conflict and the attainment of security; and, • Power as control over resources and capabilities.

Modern discourse generally speaks in terms of state Power, indicating both economic and military Power. Those states that have significant amounts of Power within the international system are referred to as middle powers, regional powers, great powers, superpowers, or hyperpowers, although there is no commonly accepted standard for what defines a powerful state.

Entities other than states can also acquire and wield Power in international relations.

Committee

A Committee (some of which are titled instead as a "Commission" larger deliberative assembly-- which when organized so that action on Committee requires a vote by all its entitled members, is called the Committee of the Whole". Committee s often serve several different functions:

- Governance: in organizations considered too large for all the members to participate in decisions affecting the organization as a whole, a Committee (such as a Board of Directors or "Executive Committee) is given the power to make decisions, spend money the Board of directors can frequently enter into binding contracts and make decisions which once taken or made, can"t be taken back or undone under the law.

- Coordination: individuals from different parts of an organization (for example, all senior vice presidents) might meet regularly to discuss developments in their areas, review projects that cut across organizational boundaries, talk about future options, etc. Where there is a large Committee it is common to have smaller Committee s with more specialized functions - for example, Boards of Directors of large corporations typically have an (ongoing) audit Committee finance Committee compensation Committee etc. Large academic conferences are usually organized by a co-ordinating Committee drawn from the relevant professional body.

Flag

The flag of former South Vietnam was designed by Emperor Thành Thái in 1890 and was used by Emperor Báº£o Ä áºįi in 1948. It was the flag of the former State of Vietnam from 1949 to 1955 and later of the Republic of Vietnam from 1955 until April 30, 1975 when the south unconditionally surrendered to the north, where it was officially joined in a unified Vietnam a year later. The flag consists of a yellow field and three horizontal red stripes to and can be explained as either symbolising the unifying blood running through northern, central, and southern Vietnam, or as representing the symbol for "south" (as in, south from China and also "nam" meaning south), in Daoist trigrams.

Joseph

Joseph or Josephus Scottus (died between 791 and 804), called the Deacon, was an Irish scholar, diplomat, poet, and ecclesiastic, a minor figure in the Carolingian Renaissance. He has been cited as an early example of "the scholar in public life".

His early life is obscure, but he studied first under Colcu, probably at Clonmacnoise, and then under Alcuin at York, probably in the 770s.

Chapter 15. Freedom: The Struggle for Civil Liberties

National Security	National security refers to the requirement to maintain the survival of the nation-state through the use of economic, military and political power and the exercise of diplomacy. Measures taken to ensure National security include: • using diplomacy to rally allies and isolate threats • marshalling economic power to facilitate or compel cooperation • maintaining effective armed forces • implementing civil defense and emergency preparedness measures (including anti-terrorism legislation) • ensuring the resilience and redundancy of critical infrastructure • using intelligence services to detect and defeat or avoid threats and espionage, and to protect classified information • using counterintelligence services or secret police to protect the nation from internal threats The relatively new concept of National security was first introduced in the United States after World War II, and has to some degree replaced other concepts that describe the struggle of states to overcome various external and internal threats. The concept of National security became an official guiding principle of foreign policy in the United States when the National security Act of 1947 was signed on July 26, 1947 by U.S. President Harry S. Truman. The majority of the provisions of the Act took effect on 18 September 1947, the day after the Senate confirmed James V. Forrestal as the first Secretary of Defense.
Security Agency	A Security agency is an organization which conducts intelligence activities for the internal security of a nation, state or organization. They are the domestic cousins of foreign intelligence agencies.
Public Service of Canada	The Public Service of Canada is the staff of the federal government of Canada. Its function is to support the Canadian monarch, and to handle the hiring of employees for the federal government ministries. It is represented by the Governor General, and the appointed [[list of Canadian ministries	ministry].
Pentagon Papers	The Pentagon Papers, officially titled United States-Vietnam Relations, 1945-1967: A Study Prepared by the Department of Defense, were a top-secret United States Department of Defense history of the United States" political-military involvement in Vietnam from 1945 to 1967. Commissioned by United States Secretary of Defense Robert S. McNamara in 1967, the study was completed in 1968. The papers first surfaced on the front page on the New York Times in 1971.

Prior restraint	Prior restraint is a legal term referring to a government"s actions that prevent communications from reaching the public. Its main use is to keep materials from being published. Censorship that requires a person to seek governmental permission in the form of a license or imprimatur before publishing anything constitutes Prior restraint every time permission is denied.
Vietnam	Vietnam " href="/wiki/Battle_of_B%E1%BA%A1ch_%C4%90%E1%BA%B1ng_River_(938)">battle of Báºịch Ä áº±ng River. Successive dynasties flourished along with geographic and political expansion deeper into Southeast Asia, until it was colonized by the French in the mid-19th century. Efforts to resist the French eventually led to their expulsion from the country in the mid-20th century, leaving a nation divided politically into two countries.
Vietnam War	The Vietnam War was a military conflict that occurred in Vietnam, Laos and Cambodia from 1959 to 30 April 1975. The war was fought between the communist North Vietnam, supported by its communist allies, and the government of South Vietnam, supported by the United States and other member nations of the Southeast Asia Treaty Organization (SEATO.) The following outline is provided as an overview of and topical guide to the Vietnam War:

Listed by starting date:

- Operation 34A - (1964)
- Operation Starlite - August 18-24 1965
- Operation Hump- November 5 1965
- Operation Crimp - January 7, 1966
- Operation Birmingham - April 1966
- Operation Hastings - Late May 1966
- Operation Prairie - August 1966
- Operation Deckhouse Five - January 6, 1967
- Operation Cedar Falls - January 8, 1967
- Operation Junction City - February 21, 1967
- Operation Francis Marion - April 6 - April 30, 1967
- Operation Union - April 21-May 16, 1967
- Operations Malheur I and Malheur II - 11 May - July 1, 1967
- Operation Baker - May 11, 1967
- Operation Scotland - See Battle of Khe Sanh
- Operation Pegasus - August 8, 1968
- Operation Dewey Canyon - January 22, 1969
- Operation Twinkletoes - 1969
- Operation Apache Snow - May 10 - May 20, 1969
- Operation Chicago Peak - April 1970
- Operation Texas Star - April - September, 1970
- Operation Ivory Coast - November 21, 1970
- Operation Jefferson Glenn - 1970-1971
- Operation Lam Son 719 - February 8, 1971
- Ho Chi Minh Campaign January 24 - April 30, 1975
- Operation Frequent Wind - April, 1975

- Battle of Ap Bac - January 2, 1963
- Battle of Kien Long - April 11 - April 15, 1964
- Battle of Thanh Hóa - July 31, 1964
- Battle of Binh Gia - December 28, 1964 - January 1, 1965
- Battle of Dong Xoai - June 10, 1965
- Battle near Minh Thanh - October 25 - October 27, 1965
- Battle of Ia Drang - November 14 - November 16, 1965
- Battle of Cu Nghi - January 28 - January 31, 1966
- Battle of Kim Son Valley - February 16 - February 28, 1966
- Battle of A Shau - March 9 - March 10, 1966
- Battle of Xa Cam My - April 11 - April 12, 1966
- First Battle of Dong Ha - Late May - June, 1966
- Battle on Minh Thanh Road - July 9, 1966
- Battle of Ä á»©c CÆ¡ - August 9, 1966
- Battle of Long Tá°§n - August 18- August 19, 1966
- Viet Cong attack on Tan Son Nhut airbase - December 4, 1966
- Battle of LZ Bird - December 27, 1966

- Battle of Tra Binh Dong - February 14 - February 15, 1967
- Battle of Hills 881 and 861 - April 24-May 9, 1967
- Nine Days in May - May 18 - May 28, 1967
- Battle of Vinh Huy - May 30 - June 2, 1967
- Battle of Con Thien - July 2 - July 3, 1967
- Battle of Dong Son - September 4, 1967
- Battle of Ong Thang - October 17, 1967
- First Battle of Loc Ninh - October 29 - November, 1967
- Battle of Dak To - November 3-November 22, 1967
- Battle in the Mekong Delta - December 4, 1967
- Battle of Tam Quan - December 6 - December 20, 1967
- Battle of Thom Tham Khe - December 27 - December 28, 1967
- Phoenix Program - 1967 - 1972
- Battle of Khe Sanh - January 21 - April 8, 1968
- Tet Offensive - January 30 - February 25, 1968
- Battle of Bien Hoa - January 31 - July 1, 1968
- Battle of Kham Duc - May 10 - May 12, 1968
- First Battle of Saigon - January 31, - February 3, 1968
- Battle of Hue - January 31, - February 25, 1968
- Tet 1969 - February 1969
- Battle of Hamburger Hill - May 10 - May 20, 1969
- Firebase Ripcord - March 12 - July 23, 1970
- Cambodian Incursion - April 29 - July 22, 1970
- Battle of Snoul - January 5 - May 30, 1971
- Easter Offensive - March 30 - October 22, 1972
- First Battle of Quang Tri - March 30 - May 1, 1972
- Battle of Loc Ninh - April 4 - April 7, 1972
- Battle of An Loc - April 20 - July 20, 1972
- Second Battle of Quang Tri - June 28 - September 16, 1972
- Battle of Phuoc Long - December 13, 1974 - January 6, 1975
- Battle of Buon Me Thuot - March 10 - March 12, 1975
- Battle of Xuan Loc - April 9 - April 20, 1975

- Operation Farm Gate
- Operation Chopper (1962)
- Operation Ranch Hand (1962-1971)
- Operation Pierce Arrow (1964)
- Operation Barrell Roll (1964-1972)
- Operation Pony Express (1965-1970)
- Operation Flaming Dart (1965)
- Operation Rolling Thunder (1965-1968)
- Operation Steel Tiger (1965-1968)
- Operation Arc Light (1965-1973)
- Operation Tiger Hound (1965-1968)
- Operation Shed Light (1966-1972)
- Operation Carolina Moon (1966)
- Operation Wahiawa (1966)
- Operation Bolo (1967)
- Operation Popeye (1967-1972)
- Operation Niagara (1968)
- Operation Igloo White (1968-1973

- Operation Giant Lance (1969)
- Operation Commando Hunt (1968-1972)
- Operation Menu (1969-1970)
- Operation Patio (1970)
- Operation Freedom Deal (1970-1973)
- Operation Linebacker (1972)
- Operation Enhance Plus (1972)
- Operation Linebacker II (1972)
- Operation Homecoming (1973)
- Operation Baby Lift (1975)
- Operation Eagle Pull (1975)
- Operation Frequent Wind (1975)

- National Order of Vietnam
- Vietnam Military Merit Medal
- Vietnam Distinguished Service Order
- Vietnam Meritorious Service Medal
- Vietnam Special Service Medal
- Vietnam Gallantry Cross
- Vietnam Air Gallantry Cross
- Vietnam Navy Gallantry Cross
- Vietnam Armed Forces Honor Medal
- Vietnam Civil Actions Medal
- Vietnam Staff Service Medal
- Vietnam Technical Service Medal
- Vietnam Wound Medal
- Vietnam Campaign Medal
- Presidential Unit Citation (Vietnam)
- Vietnam Gallantry Cross Unit Citation
- Vietnam Civil Actions Unit Citation

- Golden Star Medal
- Ho Chi Minh Order
- Defeat American Aggression Badge
- Vietnam Liberation Order
- Resolution for Victory Order

- Medal of Honor rare
- Distinguished Service Cross rare
- Navy Cross uncommon
- Air Force Cross uncommon
- Silver Star uncommon
- Purple Heart frequent
- Bronze Star frequent
- Presidential Unit Citation rare
- Vietnam Service Medal very common
- National Defense Service Medal very common
- Commendation Medal common

- "Fatigue Press" at Fort Hood,
- "Last Harass" at Fort Gordon, Georgia
- "Pawn"s Pawn" at Fort Leonard Wood, Missouri

- "Ultimate Weapon" at Fort Dix, New Jersey
- "Attitude Check" at Camp Pendleton, California
- "Green Machine" at Fort Greely, Alaska
- "Napalm" at Fort Campbell, Tennessee
- "Arctic Arsenal" at Fort Greely, Alaska
- "Black Voice" at Fort McClellan, Alabama
- "Fragging Action" at Fort Dix
- "Fort Polk Puke" at Fort Polk, Louisiana
- "Custer"s Last Stand" at Fort Riley, Kansas
- "Whack!" from the Women"s Army Corps School
- "Where Are We?" at Fort Huachuca, Arizona
- "Voice of the Lumpen" (affiliated with the Black Panther Party) in Frankfurt
- "Can You Bear McNair?" at McNair Barracks, Berlin
- "Seasick" at Subic Bay
- "The Man Can"t Win If You Grin" in Okinawa
- "Korea Free Press"
- "Semper Fi" in Japan
- "Stars and Bars" in England
- "Separated From Life" in England
- "Duck Power" in San Diego
- "Harass the Brass" at Canute Air Force Base, Illinois
- "All Hands Abandon Ship", Newport, Rhode Island
- "Now Hear This", Long Beach
- "Potemkin" on the USS Forestall
- "Star Spangled Bummer" at Wright-Patterson Air Force Base in Ohio
- "Fat Albert"s Death Ship" in Charlestown
- "Pig Boat Blues", USS Agerholm
- "Special Weapons", Kirtland AFB, New Mexico
- "I Will Fear No Evil", Kirtland AFB, New Mexico
- "Blows Against the Empire", Kirtland AFB, New Mexico

source: "The American War" - see references below

- Bao Dai
- Duong Van Minh
- Madame Ngo Dinh Nhu
- Ngo Dinh Diem
- Ngo Dinh Nhu
- Nguyen Cao Ky
- Nguyen Khanh
- Nguyen Van Thieu

- Creighton W. Abrams
- Dean Acheson
- Spiro Agnew
- Ellsworth Bunker
- McGeorge Bundy
- William Bundy
- William Calley
- Clark Clifford
- William Colby
- A. Peter Dewey
- John Foster Dulles
- Dwight D. Eisenhower
- Daniel Ellsberg
- J. William Fulbright
- Barry Goldwater
- David Hackworth
- Alexander Haig
- Paul D. Harkins
- Seymour Hersh
- Hubert Humphrey
- Lyndon Johnson
- John F. Kennedy
- John Kerry
- Henry Kissinger
- Melvin Laird
- Edward Lansdale
- Henry Cabot Lodge, Jr.
- Mike Mansfield
- Graham Martin
- Robert McNamara
- George McGovern
- Richard Nixon
- Pete Peterson
- Charika Pugh
- Dean Rusk

- Maxwell D. Taylor
- Hugh C. Thompson, Jr
- John Paul Vann
- Gary Varsel
- William Westmoreland

- Ho Chi Minh
- Le Duan
- Tran Van Tra
- Le Duc Tho
- Pham Van Dong
- General Giap
- Poewll Ward

- Lon Nol
- Pol Pot
- Norodom Sihanouk
- Sirik Matak
- Sosthene Fernandez

- David H. Hackworth. 1989 About Face
- A.J. Langguth. 2000. Our Vietnam: the War 1954-1975.
- Mann, Robert. 2002. Grand Delusion, A: America"s Descent Into Vietnam.
- Windrow, Martin. 2005. The Last Valley: Dien Bien Phu and the French Defeat in Vietnam.
- Bernard Fall. 1967. Hell in a Very Small Place: the Siege of Dien Bien Phu.
- Harvey Pekar. 2003. American Splendor: Unsung Hero
- Prados, John. 2000. The Blood Road: The Ho Chi Minh Trail and the Vietnam War.
- Prados, John. 1999. Valley of Decision: The Siege of Khe Sanh.
- Shultz, Robert H. Jr. 2000. The Secret War Against Hanoi: The Untold Story of Spies, Saboteurs, and Covert Warriors in North Vietnam.
- Plaster, John L. 1998. SOG: The Secret Wars of America"s Commandos in Vietnam.
- Murphy, Edward F. 1995. Dak To: America"s Sky Soldiers in South Vietnam"s Central Highlands.
- Nolan, Keith W. 1996. The Battle for Saigon: Tet 1968.
- Nolan, Keith W. 1996. Sappers in the Wire: The Life and Death of Firebase Mary Ann.
- Nolan, Keith W. 1992. Operation Buffalo: USMC Fight for the DMZ.
- Nolan, Keith W. 2003. Ripcord : Screaming Eagles Under Siege, Vietnam 1970.
- Robert S. McNamara. 1996. In Retrospect: The Tragedy and Lessons of Vietnam.
- Larry Berman. 2002. No Peace, No Honor: Nixon, Kissinger, and Betrayal in Vietnam.
- Bergerud, Eric M. 1994. Red Thunder, Tropic Lightning: The World of a Combat Division in Vietnam.
- Bernard Edelman. 2002. Dear America: Letters Home from Vietnam.
- Darrel D. Whitcomb. 1999. The Rescue of Bat 21.
- Oberdorfer, Don. 1971. Tet: the Story of a Battle and its Historic Aftermath.
- LTG Harold G. Moore and Joseph L. Galloway. 1992. We Were Soldiers Once ... And Young.
- Duiker, William J. 2002. Ho Chi Minh: A Life.
- John Laurence. 2002. The Cat from Hue: A Vietnam War Story.
- Emerson, Gloria. 1976. Winners and Losers: Battles, Retreats, Gains, Losses and Ruins from a Long War.
- Philip Caputo. 1977. A Rumor of War.

- Al Santoli. 1981. Everything We Had: an Oral History of the Vietnam War by 33 American Soldiers Who Fought It.
- Robert C. Mason. 1983. Chickenhawk.
- Michael Herr. 1977. Dispatches.
- Joseph T. Ward. 1991. Dear Mom: a Sniper"s Vietnam.
- Hemphill, Robert. 1998. Platoon: Bravo Company.
- Noam Chomsky. 1967. The Responsibility of Intellectuals.
- Moore, Robin. 1965 The Green Berets (ISBN 0-312-98492-8)

- Robert Olen Butler. 1992.

American Civil Liberties Union	The American Civil Liberties Union consists of two separate non-profit organizations: the American Civil Liberties Union Foundation, a 501(c)(3) organization which focuses on litigation and communication efforts, and the American Civil Liberties Union, a 501(c)(4) organization which focuses on legislative lobbying. The American Civil Liberties Union"s stated mission is "to defend and preserve the individual rights and liberties guaranteed to every person in this country by the Constitution and laws of the United States." It works through litigation, legislation, and community education. Founded in 1920 by Crystal Eastman, Roger Baldwin and Walter Nelles, the American Civil Liberties Union was the successor organization to the earlier National Civil Liberties Bureau founded during World War I. The American Civil Liberties Union reported over 500,000 members at the end of 2005.
News media	The News media refers to the section of the mass media that focuses on presenting current news to the public. These include print media (newspapers, magazines); broadcast media (radio stations, television stations, television networks), and increasingly Internet-based media (World Wide Web pages, weblogs.)
	The term news trade refers to the concept of the News media as a business separate from, but integrally connected to, the profession of journalism.
Declaration of Independence	A Declaration of independence is an assertion of the independence of an aspiring state or states. Such places are usually declared from part or all of the territory of another nation or failed nation, or are breakaway territories from within the larger state. Not all declarations of independence were successful and resulted in independence for these regions.
Freedom	Freedom is the right to act according to ones will without being held up by the power of others. From a philosophical point of view, it can be defined as the capacity to determine your own choices. It can be defined negatively as an absence of subordination, servitude and constraint.
Church and state	The relationship between church and state during the medieval period went through a number of developments, roughly from the end of the Roman Empire through to the beginning of the Reformation. The events of the struggles for power between kings and popes shaped the western world. Antichristus, a woodcut by Lucas Cranach the Elder of the pope using the temporal power to grant authority to a generously contributing ruler
	For centuries, monarchs ruled by the idea of divine right, which said the king ruled both Crown and Church, a theory known as caesaropapism.
Boosterism	Boosterism is the act of "boosting," or promoting, one"s town, city with the goal of improving public perception of it. Boosting can be as simple as "talking up" the entity at a party or as elaborate as establishing a visitors" bureau. It is somewhat associated with American small towns.
Pledge of Allegiance	The Pledge of Allegiance to the United States flag is an oath of loyalty to the republic of the United States of America. It is often recited at public events. Congressional sessions open with a recitation of the Pledge.

Penalty	In the Latter Day Saint movement, a Penalty is an oath made by participants of the original Nauvoo Endowment instituted by Joseph Smith, Jr. in 1843 and further developed by Brigham Young after Smith"s death. Mormon antagonists refer to the Penalty as a blood oath, because it required the participant to swear never to reveal certain key symbols of the Endowment ceremony, including the Penalty itself, while symbolically enacting ways in which a person may be executed.
Presidential election	A presidential election was held in Chile on 4 September 1970. A narrow plurality (36.6 percent of the total vote) was secured by Salvador Allende, the candidate of the Popular Unity coalition of leftist parties. Because he did not obtain an absolute majority, his election required a further vote by the National Congress of Chile which resulted in Allende assuming the presidency in accordance with the Chilean Constitution of 1925.

Led by Lorrin A. Thurston and Sanford B. Dole, the Provisional Government ruled over HawaiÊ»i until the formal establishment of a republic. Pictured above is the cabinet, (Left to Right) James A. King, Sanford B. Dole, William O. Smith and Peter C. Jones.

Capital	Flag

Capital	Honolulu
Language(s)	Hawaiian, English
Government	Not specified
Provisional Government	
- 1893-1894	Committee of Safety
Historical era	New Imperialism
- Monarchy overthrown	January 17, 1893
- Republic declared	July 4, 1894
Currency	U.S. dollar, Hawaiian dollar

	The Provisional Government of HawaiÊ»i was proclaimed on January 17, 1893 by the 13 member Committee of Safety under the leadership of Lorrin A. Thurston and Sanford B. Dole. It governed the Kingdom of HawaiÊ»i after the overthrow of Queen LiliÊ»uokalani until the Republic of HawaiÊ»i was established on July 4, 1894.
Capital punishment	Capital punishment, the death penalty or execution, is the killing of a person by judicial process for retribution, general deterrence, and incapacitation. Crimes that can result in a death penalty are known as capital crimes or capital offences. The term capital originates from Latin capitalis, literally "regarding the head" .
Public opinion	Public opinion is the aggregate of individual attitudes or beliefs held by the adult population. Public opinion can also be defined as the complex collection of opinions of many different people and the sum of all their views. The principle approaches to the study of Public opinion may be divided into 4 categories:

a) quantitative measurement of opinion distributions;

b) investigation of the internal relationships among the individual opinions that make up Public opinion on an issue;

c) description or analysis of the public role of Public opinion;

d) study both of the communication media that disseminate the ideas on which opinions are based and of the uses that propagandists and other manipulators make of these media.

Public opinion as a concept gained credence with the rise of "public" in the eighteenth century.

European Union	The European Union is an economic and political union of 27 member states, located primarily in Europe. Committed to regional integration, the European Union was established by the Treaty of Maastricht on 1 November 1993 upon the foundations of the pre-existing European Economic Community. Encompassing a population of 500 million the European Union generates an estimated 30% share (US$18.4 trillion in 2008) of the nominal gross world product.
India	India, officially the Republic of India , is a country in South Asia. It is the seventh-largest country by geographical area, the second-most populous country, and the most populous democracy in the world. Bounded by the Indian Ocean on the south, the Arabian Sea on the west, and the Bay of Bengal on the east, India has a coastline of 7,517 kilometres .
Japan	Japan is an island nation in East Asia. Located in the Pacific Ocean, it lies to the east of the Sea of Japan, People"s Republic of China, North Korea, South Korea and Russia, stretching from the Sea of Okhotsk in the north to the East China Sea and Taiwan in the south. The characters which make up Japan"s name mean "sun-origin", which is why Japan is sometimes identified as the "Land of the Rising Sun".
Saudi Arabia	Saudi Arabia , is an Arab country and the largest country of the Arabian Peninsula. It is bordered by Jordan on the northwest, Iraq on the north and northeast, Kuwait, Qatar, Bahrain, and the United Arab Emirates on the east, Oman on the southeast, and Yemen on the south. The Persian Gulf lies to the northeast and the Red Sea to its west.
Turkey	Turkey , known officially as the Republic of Turkey Â·)), is a Eurasian country that stretches across the Anatolian peninsula in western Asia and Thrace in the Balkan region of southeastern Europe. Turkey is bordered by eight countries: Bulgaria to the northwest; Greece to the west; Georgia to the northeast; Armenia, Azerbaijan (the exclave of Nakhichevan) and Iran to the east; and Iraq and Syria to the southeast. The Mediterranean Sea and Cyprus are to the south; the Aegean Sea and Archipelago are to the west; and the Black Sea is to the north.

Countries

This is a list of articles on the constitutions of contemporary countries, states and dependencies.

- Constitution of Abkhazia - Republic of Abkhazia
- Constitution of Afghanistan - Islamic Republic of Afghanistan
- Constitution of Akrotiri - Sovereign Base Area of Akrotiri (UK overseas territory)
- Constitution of Åland - Åland (Autonomous province of Finland)
- Constitution of Albania - Republic of Albania
- Constitution of Algeria - People"s Democratic Republic of Algeria
- Constitution of American Samoa - Territory of American Samoa (US overseas territory)
- Constitution of Andorra - Principality of Andorra
- Constitution of Angola - Republic of Angola
- Constitution of Anguilla - Anguilla (UK overseas territory)
- Constitution of Antigua and Barbuda - Antigua and Barbuda
- Constitution of Argentina - Argentine Republic
- Constitution of Armenia - Republic of Armenia
- Constitution of Aruba - Aruba (Self-governing country in the Kingdom of the Netherlands)
- Constitution of Ascension Island - Ascension Island (Dependency of the UK overseas territory of Saint Helena)
- Constitution of Australia - Commonwealth of Australia
- Constitution of Austria - Republic of Austria
- Constitution of Azerbaijan - Republic of Azerbaijan

- Constitution of The Bahamas - Commonwealth of The Bahamas
- Constitution of Bahrain - Kingdom of Bahrain
- Constitution of Bangladesh - People"s Republic of Bangladesh
- Constitution of Barbados - Barbados
- Constitution of Belarus - Republic of Belarus
- Constitution of Belgium - Kingdom of Belgium
- Constitution of Belize - Belize
- Constitution of Benin - Republic of Benin
- Constitution of Bermuda - Bermuda (UK overseas territory)
- Constitution of Bhutan - Kingdom of Bhutan
- Constitution of Bolivia - Plurinational State of Bolivia
- Constitution of Bosnia and Herzegovina - Bosnia and Herzegovina
- Constitution of Botswana - Republic of Botswana
- Constitution of Brazil - Federative Republic of Brazil
- Constitution of Brunei - Negara Brunei Darussalam
- Constitution of Bulgaria - Republic of Bulgaria
- Constitution of Burkina Faso - Burkina Faso
- Constitution of Burma - Burma (Union of Myanmar)
- Constitution of Burundi - Republic of Burundi

- Constitution of Cambodia - Kingdom of Cambodia
- Constitution of Cameroon - Republic of Cameroon
- Constitution of Canada - Canada
- Constitution of Cape Verde - Republic of Cape Verde
- Constitution of the Cayman Islands - Cayman Islands (UK overseas territory)

- Constitution of the Central African Republic - Central African Republic
- Constitution of Chad - Republic of Chad
- Constitution of Chile - Republic of Chile
- Constitution of the People"s Republic of China - People"s Republic of China
- Constitution of the Republic of China - Republic of China
- Constitution of Christmas Island - Territory of Christmas Island (Australian overseas territory)
- Constitution of the Cocos (Keeling) Islands - Territory of Cocos (Keeling) Islands (Australian overseas territory)
- Constitution of Colombia - Republic of Colombia
- Constitution of Comoros - Union of the Comoros
- Constitution of the Democratic Republic of the Congo - Democratic Republic of the Congo
- Constitution of the Republic of the Congo - Republic of the Congo
- Constitution of the Cook Islands - Cook Islands (Associated state of New Zealand)
- Constitution of Costa Rica - Republic of Costa Rica
- Constitution of Côte d"Ivoire - Republic of Côte d"Ivoire
- Constitution of Croatia - Republic of Croatia
- Constitution of Cuba - Republic of Cuba
- Constitution of Cyprus - Republic of Cyprus
- Constitution of the Czech Republic - Czech Republic

- Constitution of Denmark - Kingdom of Denmark
- Constitution of Dhekelia - Sovereign Base Areas of Dhekelia (UK overseas territory)
- Constitution of Djibouti - Republic of Djibouti
- Constitution of Dominica - Commonwealth of Dominica
- Constitution of the Dominican Republic - Dominican Republic

- Constitution of East Timor (Timor-Leste) - Democratic Republic of Timor-Leste
- Constitution of Ecuador - Republic of Ecuador
- Constitution of Egypt - Arab Republic of Egypt
- Constitution of El Salvador - Republic of El Salvador
- Constitution of Equatorial Guinea - Republic of Equatorial Guinea
- Constitution of Eritrea - State of Eritrea
- Constitution of Estonia - Republic of Estonia
- Constitution of Ethiopia - Federal Democratic Republic of Ethiopia

- Constitution of the Falkland Islands - Falkland Islands (UK overseas territory)
- Constitution of the Faroe Islands - Faroe Islands (Self-governing country in the Kingdom of Denmark)
- Constitution of Fiji - Republic of the Fiji Islands
- Constitution of Finland - Republic of Finland
- Constitution of France - French Republic
- Constitution of French Polynesia - French Polynesia

- Constitution of Gabon - Gabonese Republic
- Constitution of Gambia - Republic of The Gambia
- Constitution of Georgia - Georgia
- Constitution of Germany - Federal Republic of Germany
- Constitution of Ghana - Republic of Ghana
- Constitution of Gibraltar - Gibraltar
- Constitution of Greece - Hellenic Republic
- Constitution of Greenland - Greenland (Self-governing country in the Kingdom of Denmark)

- Constitution of Grenada - Grenada
- Constitution of Guam - Territory of Guam (US overseas territory)
- Constitution of Guatemala - Republic of Guatemala
- Constitution of Guernsey - Bailiwick of Guernsey (British Crown dependency)
- Constitution of Guinea - Republic of Guinea
- Constitution of Guinea-Bissau - Republic of Guinea-Bissau
- Constitution of Guyana - Co-operative Republic of Guyana

- Constitution of Iceland - Republic of Iceland
- Constitution of India - Republic of India
- Constitution of Indonesia - Republic of Indonesia
- Constitution of Iran - Islamic Republic of Iran
- Constitution of Iraq - Republic of Iraq
- Constitution of Ireland - Ireland

Iran	Iran , officially the Islamic Republic of Iran and formerly known internationally as Persia until 1935, is a country in Central Eurasia, located on the northeastern shore of the Persian Gulf, northwestern shore of the Gulf of Oman, and the southern shore of the Caspian Sea. Both "Persia" and "Iran" are used interchangeably in cultural context; however, Iran is the name used officially in political context. The name Iran is a cognate of Aryan, and means "Land of the Aryans".
Axis of evil	"Axis of evil" is a term coined by United States President George W. Bush in his State of the Union Address on January 29, 2002 in order to describe governments that he accused of helping terrorism and seeking weapons of mass destruction. President Bush named Iran, Iraq and North Korea in his speech. President Bush"s presidency was marked by this notion as a justification for the War on Terror.
Communism	Communism is a socioeconomic structure and political ideology that promotes the establishment of an egalitarian, classless, stateless society based on common ownership and control of the means of production and property in general. In political science, however, the term "Communism", usually spelled with the capital letter C is often used to refer to the Communist states, a form of government in which the state operates under a one-party system and declares allegiance to Marxism-Leninism or a derivative thereof, even if the party does not actually claim that it has already reached Communism.
	Forerunners of communist ideas existed in antiquity and particularly in the 18th and early 19th century France, with thinkers such as Jean-Jacques Rousseau and the more radical Gracchus Babeuf.
Enemy combatant	Enemy combatant is a term historically referring to members of the armed forces of the state with which another state is at war. Prior to 2008, the definition was: "Any person in an armed conflict who could be properly detained under the laws and customs of war)
	In the United States the use of the phrase "Enemy combatant" may also mean an alleged member of al Qaeda or the Taliban being held in detention by the U.S. government as part of the war on terror.
Anti-Americanism	Dictionaries tend to define Anti-Americanism, often anti-American sentiment, as a widespread opposition or hostility to the people, government or policies of the United States. In practice, a broad range of attitudes and actions critical of or opposed to the United States have been labeled Anti-Americanism. Thus, the nature and applicability of the term is often disputed.
Intelligence	Intelligence refers to discrete information with currency and relevance, and the abstraction, evaluation, and understanding of such information for its accuracy and value.

Geneva Convention	The Geneva Convention s consist of four treaties and three additional protocols that set the standards in international law for humanitarian treatment of the victims of war. The singular term Geneva Convention refers to the agreements of 1949, negotiated in the aftermath of World War II, updating the terms of the first three treaties and adding a fourth treaty. The language is extensive, with articles defining the basic rights of those captured during a military conflict, establishing protections for the wounded, and addressing protections for civilians in and around a war zone.

Right	A right is the legal or moral entitlement to do or refrain from doing something thing or recognition in civil society. Rights serve as rules of interaction between people, and, as such, they place constraints and obligations upon the actions of individuals or groups (for example, if one has a right to life, this means that others do not have the liberty to kill him.) Most modern conceptions of rights are universalist and egalitarian -- in other words, equal rights are granted to all people.
Suffrage	Suffrage is the civil right to vote, or the exercise of that right. In that context, it is also called political franchise or simply the franchise. Suffrage is very valuable to the extent that there are opportunities to vote .
Citizenship	Citizenship is an act of being a citizen of one community. Citizenship status, under social contract theory, carries with it both rights and responsibilities. "Active Citizenship" is the philosophy that citizens should work towards the betterment of their community through economic participation, public service, volunteer work, and other such efforts to improve life for all citizens.
Constitution	A Constitution is set of rules for government -- often codified as a written document -- that establishes principles of an autonomous political entity. In the case of countries, this term refers specifically to a national Constitution defining the fundamental political principles, and establishing the structure, procedures, powers and duties, of a government. By limiting the government"s own reach, most Constitution s guarantee certain rights to the people.
Strict scrutiny	Strict scrutiny is the most stringent standard of judicial review used by United States courts reviewing federal law. Along with the lower standards of rational basis review and intermediate scrutiny, Strict scrutiny is part of a hierarchy of standards courts employ to weigh an asserted government interest against a constitutional right or principle that conflicts with the manner in which the interest is being pursued. Strict scrutiny is applied based on the constitutional conflict at issue, regardless of whether a law or action of the U.S. federal government, a state government, or a local municipality is at issue.
Democratic party	Democratic Party was a political party in Gambia. The party was founded during the pre-independence period in the colony of Bathurst (currently the national capital Banjul.) Ahead of the 1962 election, the Democratic Party merged with the Muslim Congress Party to form the Democratic Congress Alliance.
Public opinion	Public opinion is the aggregate of individual attitudes or beliefs held by the adult population. Public opinion can also be defined as the complex collection of opinions of many different people and the sum of all their views. The principle approaches to the study of Public opinion may be divided into 4 categories:

a) quantitative measurement of opinion distributions;

b) investigation of the internal relationships among the individual opinions that make up Public opinion on an issue;

c) description or analysis of the public role of Public opinion;

d) study both of the communication media that disseminate the ideas on which opinions are based and of the uses that propagandists and other manipulators make of these media.

Public opinion as a concept gained credence with the rise of "public" in the eighteenth century.

Pro-life	Pro-life is a term representing a variety of perspectives and activist movements in medical ethics. It is most commonly used, especially in the media and popular discourse, to refer to opposition to abortion. More generally, the term describes a political and ethical view which maintains that human fetuses and embryos are persons and therefore have a right to live.
Coalition	A Coalition is an alliance among individuals or groups, during which they cooperate in joint action, each in his own self-interest, joining forces together for a common cause. This alliance may be temporary or a matter of convenience. A Coalition thus differs from a more formal covenant.
Leadership	Leadership has been described as the "process of social influence in which one person can enlist the aid and support of others in the accomplishment of a common task". A definition more inclusive of followers comes from Alan Keith of Genentech who said "Leadership is ultimately about creating a way for people to contribute to making something extraordinary happen." Leadership is one of the most salient aspects of the organizational context. However, defining Leadership has been challenging.
Civil liberties	Civil liberties are freedoms that protect an individual from the government of the nation in which they reside. Civil liberties set limits for government so that it cannot abuse its power and interfere unduly with the lives of its citizens. Common Civil liberties include the rights of people, freedom of religion, and freedom of speech, and additionally, the right to due process, to a fair trial, to own property, and to privacy.

Chapter 17. Domestic Policy

Constitution	A Constitution is set of rules for government -- often codified as a written document -- that establishes principles of an autonomous political entity. In the case of countries, this term refers specifically to a national Constitution defining the fundamental political principles, and establishing the structure, procedures, powers and duties, of a government. By limiting the government"s own reach, most Constitution s guarantee certain rights to the people.
Federal budget	In economics, a Federal budget is a plan for the Federal government"s revenues and spending for the coming year.
Fiscal policy	In economics, Fiscal policy is the use of government spending and revenue collection to influence the economy.
	Fiscal policy can be contrasted with the other main type of economic policy, monetary policy, which attempts to stabilize the economy by controlling interest rates and the supply of money. The two main instruments of Fiscal policy are government spending and taxation.
Government spending	Government spending or government expenditure is classified by economists into three main types. Government purchases of goods and services for current use are classed as government consumption. Government purchases of goods and services intended to create future benefits, such as infrastructure investment or research spending, are classed as government investment.
Presidential election	A presidential election was held in Chile on 4 September 1970. A narrow plurality (36.6 percent of the total vote) was secured by Salvador Allende, the candidate of the Popular Unity coalition of leftist parties. Because he did not obtain an absolute majority, his election required a further vote by the National Congress of Chile which resulted in Allende assuming the presidency in accordance with the Chilean Constitution of 1925.
Welfare state	There are two main interpretations of the idea of a Welfare state
	• A model in which the state assumes primary responsibility for the welfare of its citizens. This responsibility in theory ought to be comprehensive, because all aspects of welfare are considered and universally applied to citizens as a "right". Welfare state can also mean the creation of a "social safety net" of minimum standards of varying forms of welfare. Here is found some confusion between a Welfare state and a "welfare society" in common debate about the definition of the term.
	• The provision of welfare in society. In many " Welfare state s", especially in continental Europe, welfare is not actually provided by the state, but by a combination of independent, voluntary, mutualist and government services. The functional provider of benefits and services may be a central or state government, a state-sponsored company or agency, a private corporation, a charity or another form of non-profit organization. However, this phenomenon has been more appropriately termed a "welfare society," and the term "welfare system" has been used to describe the range of Welfare state and welfare society mixes that are found.

The English term Welfare state is believed by Asa Briggs to have been coined by Archbishop William Temple during the Second World War, contrasting wartime Britain with the "warfare state" of Nazi Germany. Friedrich Hayek contends that the term derived from the older German word Wohlfahrtsstaat, which itself was used by nineteenth century historians to describe a variant of the ideal of Polizeistaat . It was fully developed by the German academic Sozialpolitiker--"socialists of the chair"--from 1870 and first implemented through Bismarck"s "state socialism". Bismarck"s policies have also been seen as the creation of a Welfare state

Outsourcing

Outsourcing is subcontracting a process, such as product design or manufacturing, to a third-party company. The decision to outsource is often made in the interest of lowering cost or making better use of time and energy costs, redirecting or conserving energy directed at the competencies of a particular business, or to make more efficient use of land, labor, capital, (information) technology and resources. Outsourcing became part of the business lexicon during the 1980s.

Balance

Balance is sometimes used in reference to political content in the mass media. This usage began in Britain in the early part of the 20th century when the conservative Tories were unpopular and receiving little coverage through the BBC. In order to provide an intellectual rationalization for an increased level of Conservative content, Lord John Reith, the BBC"s founding General Manager and later Chairman, promoted a concept called Balance.

In practise Balance means ensuring that statements by those challenging the establishment are balanced with statements of those whom they are criticising, though not necessarily the other way round.

Balance of payments

In economics, the Balance of payments, (or Balance of payments) measures the payments that flow between any individual country and all other countries. It is used to summarize all international economic transactions for that country during a specific time period, usually a year. The Balance of payments is determined by the country"s exports and imports of goods, services, and financial capital, as well as financial transfers.

Monetary policy

Monetary policy is the process by which the government, central bank (ii) availability of money, and (iii) cost of money or rate of interest, in order to attain a set of objectives oriented towards the growth and stability of the economy. Monetary theory provides insight into how to craft optimal Monetary policy.

Monetary policy is referred to as either being an expansionary policy where an expansionary policy increases the total supply of money in the economy, and a contractionary policy decreases the total money supply.

Committee	A Committee (some of which are titled instead as a "Commission" larger deliberative assembly-- which when organized so that action on Committee requires a vote by all its entitled members, is called the Committee of the Whole". Committee s often serve several different functions:

- Governance: in organizations considered too large for all the members to participate in decisions affecting the organization as a whole, a Committee (such as a Board of Directors or "Executive Committee) is given the power to make decisions, spend money the Board of directors can frequently enter into binding contracts and make decisions which once taken or made, can"t be taken back or undone under the law.

- Coordination: individuals from different parts of an organization (for example, all senior vice presidents) might meet regularly to discuss developments in their areas, review projects that cut across organizational boundaries, talk about future options, etc. Where there is a large Committee it is common to have smaller Committee s with more specialized functions - for example, Boards of Directors of large corporations typically have an (ongoing) audit Committee finance Committee compensation Committee etc. Large academic conferences are usually organized by a co-ordinating Committee drawn from the relevant professional body.

Power	Power in international relations is defined in several different ways. Political scientists, historians, and practitioners of international relations (diplomats) have used the following concepts of political Power:

- Power as a goal of states or leaders;
- Power as a measure of influence or control over outcomes, events, actors and issues;
- Power as reflecting victory in conflict and the attainment of security; and,
- Power as control over resources and capabilities.

Modern discourse generally speaks in terms of state Power, indicating both economic and military Power. Those states that have significant amounts of Power within the international system are referred to as middle powers, regional powers, great powers, superpowers, or hyperpowers, although there is no commonly accepted standard for what defines a powerful state.

Entities other than states can also acquire and wield Power in international relations.

Demographic	Demographic s or Demographic data refers to selected population characteristics as used in government, marketing or opinion research, or the Demographic profiles used in such research. Note the distinction from the term "demography" Commonly-used Demographic s include race, age, income, disabilities, mobility (in terms of travel time to work or number of vehicles available), educational attainment, home ownership, employment status, and even location.

Medicare	Medicare is a social insurance program administered by the United States government, providing health insurance coverage to people who are aged 65 and over, or who meet other special criteria. Medicare operates as a single-payer health care system. The Social Security Act of 1965 was passed by Congress in late-spring of 1965 and signed into law on July 30, 1965, by President Lyndon B. Johnson as amendments to Social Security legislation.
War economy	War economy is the term used to describe the contingencies undertaken by the modern state to mobilise its economy for war production. Philippe Le Billon describes a War economy as a "system of producing, mobilising and allocating resources to sustain the violence". The War economy can form an economic system termed the "military-industrial complex".

Led by Lorrin A. Thurston and Sanford B. Dole, the Provisional Government ruled over HawaiÊ»i until the formal establishment of a republic. Pictured above is the cabinet, (Left to Right) James A. King, Sanford B. Dole, William O. Smith and Peter C. Jones.

Capital | Flag

Capital	Honolulu
Language(s)	Hawaiian, English
Government	Not specified
Provisional Government	
- 1893-1894	Committee of Safety
Historical era	New Imperialism
- Monarchy overthrown	January 17, 1893
- Republic declared	July 4, 1894
Currency	U.S. dollar, Hawaiian dollar

The Provisional Government of HawaiÊ»i was proclaimed on January 17, 1893 by the 13 member Committee of Safety under the leadership of Lorrin A. Thurston and Sanford B. Dole. It governed the Kingdom of HawaiÊ»i after the overthrow of Queen LiliÊ»uokalani until the Republic of HawaiÊ»i was established on July 4, 1894.

Social Security	Social Security, in Australia, refers to a system of social welfare payments provided by Commonwealth Government of Australia. These payments are administered by a Government body named Centrelink. In Australia, most benefits are subject to a means test.
Democratic party	Democratic Party was a political party in Gambia. The party was founded during the pre-independence period in the colony of Bathurst (currently the national capital Banjul.) Ahead of the 1962 election, the Democratic Party merged with the Muslim Congress Party to form the Democratic Congress Alliance.
Environmental Protection Agency	The Environmental Protection Agency (Irish: An Ghníomhaireacht um Chaomhnú Comhshaoil) has responsibilities for a wide range of licensing, enforcement, monitoring and assessment activities associated with environmental protection.

Equal Opportunity	Equal opportunity is a term which has differing definitions and there is no consensus as to the precise meaning. Some use it as a descriptive term for an approach intended to provide a certain social environment in which people are not excluded from the activities of society, such as education, employment, or health care, on the basis of immutable traits. Equal opportunity practices include measures taken by organizations to ensure fairness in the employment process.
Federal Trade Commission	The Federal Trade Commission is an independent agency of the United States government, established in 1914 by the Federal Trade Commission Act. Its principal mission is the promotion of "consumer protection" and the elimination and prevention of what regulators perceive to be harmfully "anti-competitive" business practices, such as coercive monopoly. The Federal Trade Commission Act was one of President Wilson"s major acts against trusts.
New Deal	The New Deal is a programme of active labour market policies introduced in the United Kingdom by the Labour government in 1998, initially funded by a one off Â£5bn windfall tax on privatised utility companies. The stated purpose is to reduce unemployment by providing training, subsidised employment and voluntary work to the unemployed. Spending on the New Deal was Â£1.3 billion in 2001.
Deregulation	Deregulation is the removal or simplification of government rules and regulations that constrain the operation of market forces. Deregulation does not mean elimination of laws against fraud, but eliminating or reducing government control of how business is done, thereby moving toward a more free market. The stated rationale for "Deregulation" is often that fewer and simpler regulations will lead to a raised level of competitiveness, therefore higher productivity, more efficiency and lower prices overall.
Kyoto Protocol	The Kyoto Protocol is a protocol to the United Nations Framework Convention on Climate Change (UNFCCC or FCCC), an international environmental treaty with the goal of achieving "stabilization of greenhouse gas concentrations in the atmosphere at a level that would prevent dangerous anthropogenic interference with the climate system." The Kyoto Protocol establishes legally binding commitment for the reduction of four greenhouse gases (carbon dioxide, methane, nitrous oxide, sulphur hexafluoride), and two groups of gases (hydrofluorocarbons and perfluorocarbons) produced by "annex I" (industrialized) nations, as well as general commitments for all member countries. As of January 2009, 183 parties have ratified the protocol, which was initially adopted for use on 11 December 1997 in Kyoto, Japan and which entered into force on 16 February 2005. Under Kyoto, industrialized countries agreed to reduce their collective green house gas emissions by 5.2% from the level in 1990.

| Social insurance | Social insurance is any government-sponsored program with the following four characteristics: |

- the benefits, eligibility requirements and other aspects of the program are defined by statute;
- explicit provision is made to account for the income and expenses (often through a trust fund);
- it is funded by taxes or premiums paid by (or on behalf of) participants (although additional sources of funding may be provided as well); and
- the program serves a defined population, and participation is either compulsory or the program is heavily enough subsidized that most eligible individuals choose to participate.

Social insurance has also been defined as a program where risks are transferred to and pooled by an organization, often governmental, that is legally required to provide certain benefits.

In the U.S., programs that meet these definitions include Social Security, Medicare, the PBGC program, the railroad retirement program and state-sponsored unemployment insurance programs. The Canada Pension Plan (CPP) is also a Social insurance program.

Typical similarities between Social insurance programs and private insurance programs include:

- Wide pooling of risks;
- Specific definitions of the benefits provided;
- Specific definitions of eligibility rules and the amount of coverage provided;
- Specific premium, contribution or tax rates required to meet the expected costs of the system.

Typical differences between private insurance programs and Social insurance programs include:

- Equity versus Adequacy: Private insurance programs are generally designed with greater emphasis on equity between individual purchasers of coverage, while Social insurance programs generally place a greater emphasis on the social adequacy of benefits for all participants.
- Voluntary versus Mandatory Participation: Participation in private insurance programs is often voluntary, and where the purchase of insurance is mandatory, individuals usually have a choice of insurers. Participation in Social insurance programs is generally mandatory, and where participation is voluntary, the cost is heavily enough subsidized to ensure essentially universal participation.
- Contractual versus Statutory Rights: The right to benefits in a private insurance program is contractual, based on an insurance contract. The insurer generally does not have a unilateral right to change or terminate coverage before the end of the contract period (except in such cases as non-payment of premiums.) Social insurance programs are not generally based on a contract, but rather on a statute, and the right to benefits is thus statutory rather than contractual. The provisions of the program can be changed if the statute is modified.
- Funding: Individually purchased private insurance generally must be fully funded. Full funding is a desirable goal for private pension plans as well, but is often not achieved. Social insurance programs are often not fully funded, and some argue that full funding is not economically desirable.

Prescription	In law, Prescription is the method of sovereignty transfer of a territory through international law analogous to the common law doctrine of adverse possession for private real-estate. Prescription involves the open encroachment by the new sovereign upon the territory in question for a prolonged period of time, acting as the sovereign, without protest or other contest by the original sovereign. This doctrine legalizes de jure the de facto transfer of sovereignty caused in part by the original sovereign"s extended negligence and/or neglect of the area in question.
Public opinion	Public opinion is the aggregate of individual attitudes or beliefs held by the adult population. Public opinion can also be defined as the complex collection of opinions of many different people and the sum of all their views. The principle approaches to the study of Public opinion may be divided into 4 categories:

a) quantitative measurement of opinion distributions;

b) investigation of the internal relationships among the individual opinions that make up Public opinion on an issue;

c) description or analysis of the public role of Public opinion;

d) study both of the communication media that disseminate the ideas on which opinions are based and of the uses that propagandists and other manipulators make of these media.

Public opinion as a concept gained credence with the rise of "public" in the eighteenth century.

Anti-Americanism	Dictionaries tend to define Anti-Americanism, often anti-American sentiment, as a widespread opposition or hostility to the people, government or policies of the United States. In practice, a broad range of attitudes and actions critical of or opposed to the United States have been labeled Anti-Americanism. Thus, the nature and applicability of the term is often disputed.
Australia	Australia , officially the Commonwealth of Australia is a country in the southern hemisphere comprising the mainland, which is both the world"s smallest continent and the world"s largest island, the island of Tasmania, and numerous other islands in the Indian and Pacific Oceans.[N4] Australia is the only place that is simultaneously considered a continent, a country and an island. Neighbouring countries include Indonesia, East Timor and Papua New Guinea to the north, the Solomon Islands, Vanuatu and New Caledonia to the north-east and New Zealand to the southeast. For around 40,000 years before European settlement commenced in the late 18th century, the Australia n mainland and Tasmania were inhabited by around 250 individual nations of indigenous Australia ns.
Austria	Austria), officially the Republic of Austria , is a landlocked country of roughly 8.3 million people in Central Europe. It borders both Germany and the Czech Republic to the north, Slovakia and Hungary to the east, Slovenia and Italy to the south, and Switzerland and Liechtenstein to the west. The territory of Austria covers 83,872 square kilometres (32,383 sq mi), and is influenced by a temperate and alpine climate.
Finland	Finland , officially the Republic of Finland), is a Nordic country situated in the Fennoscandian region of northern Europe. It borders Sweden on the west, Russia on the east, and Norway on the north, while Estonia lies to its south across the Gulf of Finland. The capital city is Helsinki.
Japan	Japan is an island nation in East Asia. Located in the Pacific Ocean, it lies to the east of the Sea of Japan, People"s Republic of China, North Korea, South Korea and Russia, stretching from the Sea of Okhotsk in the north to the East China Sea and Taiwan in the south. The characters which make up Japan"s name mean "sun-origin", which is why Japan is sometimes identified as the "Land of the Rising Sun".
Netherlands	The Netherlands is known under various terms both in English and other languages. These are used to describe the different overlapping geographical, linguistic and political areas of the Netherlands. This is often a source of confusion for people from other parts of the world.

Norway	Norway , Noreg (Nynorsk)) or Norga (North Sami), officially the Kingdom of Norway, is a country in Northern Europe occupying the western portion of the Scandinavian Peninsula, as well as Jan Mayen and the Arctic archipelago of Svalbard under the Spitsbergen Treaty. The majority of the country shares a border to the east with Sweden; its northernmost region is bordered by Finland to the south and Russia to the east. The United Kingdom and Faroe Islands lie to its west across the North Sea, Iceland and Greenland lies to its west across the Norwegian Sea, and Denmark lies south of its southern tip across the Skagerrak Strait.
Boosterism	Boosterism is the act of "boosting," or promoting, one"s town, city with the goal of improving public perception of it. Boosting can be as simple as "talking up" the entity at a party or as elaborate as establishing a visitors" bureau. It is somewhat associated with American small towns.
Sweden	Sweden , officially the Kingdom of Sweden), is a Nordic country on the Scandinavian Peninsula in Northern Europe. Sweden has land borders with Norway to the west and Finland to the northeast, and it is connected to Denmark by the Öresund Bridge in the south. At 450,000 km^2 (173,746 sq mi), Sweden is the third largest country in the European Union in terms of area, and it has a total population of over 9.2 million.
Capital punishment	Capital punishment, the death penalty or execution, is the killing of a person by judicial process for retribution, general deterrence, and incapacitation. Crimes that can result in a death penalty are known as capital crimes or capital offences. The term capital originates from Latin capitalis, literally "regarding the head" .
Civil service	The term Civil service has two distinct meanings: • Branch of governmental service in which individuals are hired on the basis of merit which is proven by the use of competitive examinations. • Body of employees in any government agency, except the military. A civil servant or public servant is a civilian public sector employee working for a government department or agency. The term explicitly excludes the armed services, although civilian officials will work at "Defence Ministry" headquarters. The term always includes the (sovereign) state"s employees; whether regional, or sub-state, or even municipal employees are called "civil servants" varies from country to country. In the United Kingdom, for instance, only Crown employees are civil servants, county or city employees are not.
Canada	Canada has been a member of the North Atlantic Treaty Organization (NATO) since its inception in 1949. Canada was not only a member but one of the principal initiators of the alliance. This was a marked break with Canada"s pre-war isolationism, and was the first peacetime alliance Canada had ever joined.

Universal health care	Universal health care is health care coverage for all eligible residents of a political region and often covers medical, dental and mental health care. These programs vary in their structure and funding mechanisms. Typically, most costs are met via a single-payer health care system or national health insurance, or else by compulsory regulated pluralist insurance (public, private or mutual) meeting certain regulated standards.
Federalism	Federalism is a political philosophy in which a group of members are bound together ">covenant) with a governing representative head. The term Federalism is also used to describe a system of the government in which sovereignty is constitutionally divided between a central governing authority and constituent political units (like states or provinces.) Federalism is a system in which the power to govern is shared between national and central(state) governments, creating what is often called a federation.
Ethnicity	Ethnicity plays a prominent role in pornography. Distinct genres of pornography focus on performers of specific ethnic groups, or on the depiction of interracial sexual activity. Ethnic pornography typically employs ethnic and racial stereotypes in its depiction of performers.

Medicare	Medicare is a social insurance program administered by the United States government, providing health insurance coverage to people who are aged 65 and over, or who meet other special criteria. Medicare operates as a single-payer health care system. The Social Security Act of 1965 was passed by Congress in late-spring of 1965 and signed into law on July 30, 1965, by President Lyndon B. Johnson as amendments to Social Security legislation.
Political culture	Political culture can be defined as "The orientation of the citizens of a nation toward politics, and their perceptions of political legitimacy and the traditions of political practice," and the feelings expressed by individuals in the position of the elected offices that allow for the nurture of a political society. • Dennis Kavanagh defines Political culture as "A shorthand expression to denote the set of values within which the political system operates". • Lucian Pye describes it as "the sum of the fundamental values, sentiments and knowledge that give form and substance to political process". Political culture is how we think government should be carried out. It is different from ideology because people can disagree on ideology, but still have a common Political culture.
Social Security	Social Security, in Australia, refers to a system of social welfare payments provided by Commonwealth Government of Australia. These payments are administered by a Government body named Centrelink. In Australia, most benefits are subject to a means test.
Welfare state	There are two main interpretations of the idea of a Welfare state • A model in which the state assumes primary responsibility for the welfare of its citizens. This responsibility in theory ought to be comprehensive, because all aspects of welfare are considered and universally applied to citizens as a "right". Welfare state can also mean the creation of a "social safety net" of minimum standards of varying forms of welfare. Here is found some confusion between a Welfare state and a "welfare society" in common debate about the definition of the term. • The provision of welfare in society. In many " Welfare state s", especially in continental Europe, welfare is not actually provided by the state, but by a combination of independent, voluntary, mutualist and government services. The functional provider of benefits and services may be a central or state government, a state-sponsored company or agency, a private corporation, a charity or another form of non-profit organization. However, this phenomenon has been more appropriately termed a "welfare society," and the term "welfare system" has been used to describe the range of Welfare state and welfare society mixes that are found.

The English term Welfare state is believed by Asa Briggs to have been coined by Archbishop William Temple during the Second World War, contrasting wartime Britain with the "warfare state" of Nazi Germany. Friedrich Hayek contends that the term derived from the older German word Wohlfahrtsstaat, which itself was used by nineteenth century historians to describe a variant of the ideal of Polizeistaat . It was fully developed by the German academic Sozialpolitiker--"socialists of the chair"--from 1870 and first implemented through Bismarck"s "state socialism". Bismarck"s policies have also been seen as the creation of a Welfare state

Anti-Americanism

Dictionaries tend to define Anti-Americanism, often anti-American sentiment, as a widespread opposition or hostility to the people, government or policies of the United States. In practice, a broad range of attitudes and actions critical of or opposed to the United States have been labeled Anti-Americanism. Thus, the nature and applicability of the term is often disputed.

Public Service of Canada

The Public Service of Canada is the staff of the federal government of Canada. Its function is to support the Canadian monarch, and to handle the hiring of employees for the federal government ministries. It is represented by the Governor General, and the appointed [[list of Canadian ministries | ministry].

Public opinion

Public opinion is the aggregate of individual attitudes or beliefs held by the adult population. Public opinion can also be defined as the complex collection of opinions of many different people and the sum of all their views. The principle approaches to the study of Public opinion may be divided into 4 categories:

> a) quantitative measurement of opinion distributions;
> b) investigation of the internal relationships among the individual opinions that make up Public opinion on an issue;
> c) description or analysis of the public role of Public opinion;
> d) study both of the communication media that disseminate the ideas on which opinions are based and of the uses that propagandists and other manipulators make of these media.

Public opinion as a concept gained credence with the rise of "public" in the eighteenth century.

Civil liberties

Civil liberties are freedoms that protect an individual from the government of the nation in which they reside. Civil liberties set limits for government so that it cannot abuse its power and interfere unduly with the lives of its citizens.

Common Civil liberties include the rights of people, freedom of religion, and freedom of speech, and additionally, the right to due process, to a fair trial, to own property, and to privacy.

Chapter 18. Foreign Policy and National Defense

Axis of evil	"Axis of evil" is a term coined by United States President George W. Bush in his State of the Union Address on January 29, 2002 in order to describe governments that he accused of helping terrorism and seeking weapons of mass destruction. President Bush named Iran, Iraq and North Korea in his speech. President Bush"s presidency was marked by this notion as a justification for the War on Terror.
Iran	Iran , officially the Islamic Republic of Iran and formerly known internationally as Persia until 1935, is a country in Central Eurasia, located on the northeastern shore of the Persian Gulf, northwestern shore of the Gulf of Oman, and the southern shore of the Caspian Sea. Both "Persia" and "Iran" are used interchangeably in cultural context; however, Iran is the name used officially in political context. The name Iran is a cognate of Aryan, and means "Land of the Aryans".
Iraq	Iraq , officially the Republic of Iraq JumhÅ«rÄ«yat Al-Ê¿IrÄ q, Kurdish: ÙƒÛ†Ù…Ø§Ø±ÛŒ Ø¹ÛŽØ±Ø§Ù‚â€Ž, Komara Iraqê), is a country in Western Asia spanning most of the northwestern end of the Zagros mountain range, the eastern part of the Syrian Desert and the northern part of the Arabian Desert. Iraq shares borders with Jordan to the west, Syria to the northwest, Turkey to the north, Iran to the east, and Kuwait and Saudi Arabia to the south. Iraq has a narrow section of coastline measuring 58 km between Umm Qasr and Al Faw on the Persian Gulf.
National Security	National security refers to the requirement to maintain the survival of the nation-state through the use of economic, military and political power and the exercise of diplomacy. Measures taken to ensure National security include: <ul><li>using diplomacy to rally allies and isolate threats</li><li>marshalling economic power to facilitate or compel cooperation</li><li>maintaining effective armed forces</li><li>implementing civil defense and emergency preparedness measures (including anti-terrorism legislation)</li><li>ensuring the resilience and redundancy of critical infrastructure</li><li>using intelligence services to detect and defeat or avoid threats and espionage, and to protect classified information</li><li>using counterintelligence services or secret police to protect the nation from internal threats</li></ul> The relatively new concept of National security was first introduced in the United States after World War II, and has to some degree replaced other concepts that describe the struggle of states to overcome various external and internal threats. The concept of National security became an official guiding principle of foreign policy in the United States when the National security Act of 1947 was signed on July 26, 1947 by U.S. President Harry S. Truman.

The majority of the provisions of the Act took effect on 18 September 1947, the day after the Senate confirmed James V. Forrestal as the first Secretary of Defense.

Foreign policy

A country"s Foreign policy is a set of goals outlining how the country will interact with other countries economically, politically, socially and militarily, and to a lesser extent, how the country will interact with non-state actors. The aforementioned interaction is evaluated and monitored in attempts to maximize benefits of multilateral international cooperation. Foreign policies are designed to help protect a country"s national interests, national security, ideological goals, and economic prosperity.

Italy

Italy, in particular at the turn of the 20th century, had a strong anarcho-syndicalist movement.

- 1891: Foundation of the Socialist Revolutionary Anarchist Party
- 1912: Foundation of the Unione Sindacale Italiana trade-union (joined the International Workers Association founded in 1922)
- 1920: Publication of the newspaper Umanità Nova (New Humanity)
- 1936-1939: Sébastien Faure Century, contingent of the Durruti Column in the Spanish Civil War
- 1986: Foundation in Italy of the Federation of Anarchist Communists

Spain

Spain is a country located in southwestern Europe on the Iberian Peninsula. Its mainland is bordered to the south and east by the Mediterranean Sea except for a small land boundary with Gibraltar; to the north by France, Andorra, and the Bay of Biscay; and to the northwest and west by the Atlantic Ocean and Portugal. Spanish territory also includes the Balearic Islands in the Mediterranean, the Canary Islands in the Atlantic Ocean off the African coast, and two autonomous cities in North Africa, Ceuta and Melilla, that border Morocco.

Unilateralism

Unilateralism is any doctrine or agenda that supports one-sided action. Such action may be in disregard for other parties, or as an expression of a commitment toward a direction which other parties may find agreeable. Unilateralism is a neologism, (used in all countries) coined to be an antonym for multilateralism --the doctrine which asserts the benefits of participation from as many parties as possible.

National interest

The National interest, often referred to by the French term raison d"État, is a country"s goals and ambitions whether economic, military, or cultural. The notion is an important one in international relations where pursuit of the National interest is the foundation of the realist school.

The National interest of a state is multi faceted.

Free Trade

Free trade is a type of trade policy that allows traders to act and transact without interference from government. Thus, the policy permits trading partners mutual gains from trade, with goods and services produced according to the theory of comparative advantage.

Under a Free trade policy, prices are a reflection of true supply and demand, and are the sole determinant of resource allocation.

| North Atlantic Treaty | The North Atlantic Treaty is the treaty that brought North Atlantic Treaty O into existence, signed in Washington, DC on April 4, 1949. The original twelve nations that signed it and thus became the founding members of North Atlantic Treaty O were: Map of North Atlantic Treaty O countries chronological membership.

Later the following nations joined:

When Germany was reunified in 1990, the country as a whole became a member of North Atlantic Treaty O.

During the April 2008 summit in Bucharest, Croatia and Albania were officially invited to join North Atlantic Treaty O. They both signed the treaty and officially joined North Atlantic Treaty O on April 1st, 2009 |

North Atlantic Treaty Organization

During the early years of the Cold War, the United States Air Force deployed thousands of personnel and hundreds of combat aircraft to France to counter the buildup of Soviet forces in Eastern Europe.

The Cold War that developed in Europe during 1948 and escalated into the attempted seizure of West Berlin, convinced the western nations to form a common defense organization. Discussions led to a multinational defense agreement that evolved into the North Atlantic Treaty Organization .

Superpower

A Superpower is a state with a leading position in the international system and the ability to influence events and its own interests and project power on a worldwide scale to protect those interests; it is traditionally considered to be one step higher than a great power. Alice Lyman Miller (Professor of National Security Affairs at the Naval Postgraduate School), defines a Superpower as "a country that has the capacity to project dominating power and influence anywhere in the world, and sometimes, in more than one region of the globe at a time, and so may plausibly attain the status of global hegemon." It was a term first applied in 1944 to the United States, the Soviet Union, and the British Empire. Following World War II, as the British Empire transformed itself into the Commonwealth and its territories became independent, the Soviet Union and the United States generally came to be regarded as the only two Superpower s, and confronted each other in the Cold War.

World Trade Organization	The World Trade Organization is an international organization designed by its founders to supervise and liberalize international trade. The organization officially commenced on January 1, 1995 under the Marrakesh Agreement, replacing the General agreements on Tariffs and Trade (GATT), wich commenced in 1947. The World Trade Organization deals with regulation of trade between participating countries; it provides a framework for negotiating and formalising trade agreements, and a dispute resolution process aimed at enforcing participants" adherence to World Trade Organization agreements which are signed by representatives of member governments and ratified by their parliaments.
Foundation	A Foundation in the United States is a type of charitable organization. However, the Internal Revenue Code distinguishes between private foundations (usually funded by an individual, family, or corporation) and public charities (community foundations and other nonprofit groups that raise money from the general public.) Private foundations have more restrictions and fewer tax benefits than public charities like community foundations.
Status	A person"s Status is a set of social conditions or relationships created and vested in an individual by an act of law rather than by the consensual acts of the parties, and it is in rem, i.e. these conditions must be recognised by the world. It is the qualities of universality and permanence that distinguish Status from consensual relationships such as employment and agency. Hence, a person"s Status and its attributes are set by the law of the domicile if born in a common law state, or by the law of nationality if born in a civil law state and this Status and its attendant capacities should be recognised wherever the person may later travel.
Individualism	Individualism is the moral stance, political philosophy, ideology, or social outlook that stresses independence and self-reliance. Individualists promote the exercise of one"s goals and desires, while opposing most external interference upon one"s choices, whether by society, or any other group or institution. Individualism is opposed to collectivism, which stress that communal, community, group, societal, or national goals should take priority over individual goals.
National Guard	The National Guard was the name given at the time of the French Revolution to the militias formed in each city, in imitation of the National Guard created in Paris. It was a military force separate from the regular army. Initially under the command of the Marquis de la Fayette, then briefly under the Marquis de Mandat, it was strongly identified until the summer of 1792 with the middle class and its support for constitutional monarchy.
France	France , officially the French Republic , is a country located in Western Europe, with several overseas islands and territories located on other continents. Metropolitan France extends from the Mediterranean Sea to the English Channel and the North Sea, and from the Rhine to the Atlantic Ocean. It is often referred to as L"Hexagone ("The Hexagon") because of the geometric shape of its territory.

Germany	Germany), officially the Federal Republic of Germany), is a country in Central Europe. It is bordered to the north by the North Sea, Denmark, and the Baltic Sea; to the east by Poland and the Czech Republic; to the south by Austria and Switzerland; and to the west by France, Luxembourg, Belgium, and the Netherlands. The territory of Germany covers 357,021 square kilometers and is influenced by a temperate seasonal climate.
Israel	Israel officially the State of Israel , Medinat Yisra"el; Arabic: Ø˜ ÙŽÙ^Ù'Ù„ÙŽØ©Ù Ø¥Ù Ø³Ù'رÙŽØ§Ø¦Ù ÙŠÙ„ÙŽâ‚Ž, Dawlat IsrÄ "Ä«l), is a country in Western Asia located on the eastern shore of the Mediterranean Sea. It borders Lebanon in the north, Syria in the northeast, Jordan in the east, and Egypt on the southwest, and contains geographically diverse features within its relatively small area. Also adjacent are the West Bank to the east and Gaza Strip to the southwest.
Joseph	Joseph or Josephus Scottus (died between 791 and 804), called the Deacon, was an Irish scholar, diplomat, poet, and ecclesiastic, a minor figure in the Carolingian Renaissance. He has been cited as an early example of "the scholar in public life".
	His early life is obscure, but he studied first under Colcu, probably at Clonmacnoise, and then under Alcuin at York, probably in the 770s.
Russia	Russia is a federation that consists of 83 subjects. These subjects are of equal federal rights in the sense that they have equal representation--two delegates each--in the Federation Council . However, they do differ in the degree of autonomy they enjoy.
Soft power	Soft power is the ability to obtain what you want through co-option and attraction. It is in contradistinction to "hard power", which is the use of coercion and payment. It is similar in substance but not identical to a combination of the second dimension(agenda setting) and the third dimensions (or the radical dimension) of power as expounded by Steven Lukes in Power a Radical View.
Empire	Empire is a text written by Marxist philosophers Antonio Negri and Michael Hardt. The book, written in the mid 90s, was published in 2000 and quickly sold beyond its expectations as an academic work. In general, the book theorizes an ongoing transition from a "modern" phenomenon of imperialism, centered around individual nation-states, to an emergent postmodern construct created amongst ruling powers which the authors call Empire, with different forms of warfare:
	If, according to Hardt and Negri"s Empire, the rise of Empire is the end of national conflict, the "enemy" now, whoever he is, can no longer be ideological or national.

International Monetary Fund	The International Monetary Fund is an international organization that oversees the global financial system by following the macroeconomic policies of its member countries, in particular those with an impact on exchange rates and the balance of payments. It is an organization formed to stabilize international exchange rates and facilitate development. It also offers highly leveraged loans mainly to poorer countries.
Intelligence	Intelligence refers to discrete information with currency and relevance, and the abstraction, evaluation, and understanding of such information for its accuracy and value.
Hamas	Hamas is a Palestinian Islamic socio-political organization which includes a paramilitary force, the Izz ad-Din al-Qassam Brigades. Since June 2007, after winning a large majority in the Palestinian Parliament and defeating rival Palestinian party Fatah in a series of violent clashes, Hamas has governed the Gaza portion of the Palestinian Territories. The European Union, the United States, and three other countries have classified Hamas as a terrorist organization.
Soviet	A Soviet originally was a workers" local council in late Imperial Russia. According to the official historiography of the Soviet Union, the first Soviet was organized during the 1905 Russian Revolution in Ivanovo (Ivanovo region) in May 1905. However in his memoirs Volin claims that he witnessed the creation of the St Petersburg Soviet in Saint Petersburg in January 1905.
Union of Soviet Socialist Republics	The Union of Soviet Socialist Republics, occasionally called the United Soviet Socialist Republic, was a constitutionally socialist state that existed in Eurasia from 1922 to 1991. The name is a translation of the Russian: Â·), tr. Soyuz Sovetskikh Sotsialisticheskikh Respublik, abbreviated Ð¡Ð¡Ð¡Ð , SSSR. The common short name is Soviet Union, from Ð¡Ð¾Ð²ÐµÑ,Ñ ÐºÐ¸Ð¹ Ð¡Ð¾ÑŽÐ·, Sovetskiy Soyuz.

Countries

This is a list of articles on the constitutions of contemporary countries, states and dependencies.

- Constitution of Abkhazia - Republic of Abkhazia
- Constitution of Afghanistan - Islamic Republic of Afghanistan
- Constitution of Akrotiri - Sovereign Base Area of Akrotiri (UK overseas territory)
- Constitution of Åland - Åland (Autonomous province of Finland)
- Constitution of Albania - Republic of Albania
- Constitution of Algeria - People"s Democratic Republic of Algeria
- Constitution of American Samoa - Territory of American Samoa (US overseas territory)
- Constitution of Andorra - Principality of Andorra
- Constitution of Angola - Republic of Angola
- Constitution of Anguilla - Anguilla (UK overseas territory)
- Constitution of Antigua and Barbuda - Antigua and Barbuda
- Constitution of Argentina - Argentine Republic
- Constitution of Armenia - Republic of Armenia
- Constitution of Aruba - Aruba (Self-governing country in the Kingdom of the Netherlands)
- Constitution of Ascension Island - Ascension Island (Dependency of the UK overseas territory of Saint Helena)
- Constitution of Australia - Commonwealth of Australia
- Constitution of Austria - Republic of Austria
- Constitution of Azerbaijan - Republic of Azerbaijan

- Constitution of The Bahamas - Commonwealth of The Bahamas
- Constitution of Bahrain - Kingdom of Bahrain
- Constitution of Bangladesh - People"s Republic of Bangladesh
- Constitution of Barbados - Barbados
- Constitution of Belarus - Republic of Belarus
- Constitution of Belgium - Kingdom of Belgium
- Constitution of Belize - Belize
- Constitution of Benin - Republic of Benin
- Constitution of Bermuda - Bermuda (UK overseas territory)
- Constitution of Bhutan - Kingdom of Bhutan
- Constitution of Bolivia - Plurinational State of Bolivia
- Constitution of Bosnia and Herzegovina - Bosnia and Herzegovina
- Constitution of Botswana - Republic of Botswana
- Constitution of Brazil - Federative Republic of Brazil
- Constitution of Brunei - Negara Brunei Darussalam
- Constitution of Bulgaria - Republic of Bulgaria
- Constitution of Burkina Faso - Burkina Faso
- Constitution of Burma - Burma (Union of Myanmar)
- Constitution of Burundi - Republic of Burundi

- Constitution of Cambodia - Kingdom of Cambodia
- Constitution of Cameroon - Republic of Cameroon
- Constitution of Canada - Canada
- Constitution of Cape Verde - Republic of Cape Verde
- Constitution of the Cayman Islands - Cayman Islands (UK overseas territory)

- Constitution of the Central African Republic - Central African Republic
- Constitution of Chad - Republic of Chad
- Constitution of Chile - Republic of Chile
- Constitution of the People"s Republic of China - People"s Republic of China
- Constitution of the Republic of China - Republic of China
- Constitution of Christmas Island - Territory of Christmas Island (Australian overseas territory)
- Constitution of the Cocos (Keeling) Islands - Territory of Cocos (Keeling) Islands (Australian overseas territory)
- Constitution of Colombia - Republic of Colombia
- Constitution of Comoros - Union of the Comoros
- Constitution of the Democratic Republic of the Congo - Democratic Republic of the Congo
- Constitution of the Republic of the Congo - Republic of the Congo
- Constitution of the Cook Islands - Cook Islands (Associated state of New Zealand)
- Constitution of Costa Rica - Republic of Costa Rica
- Constitution of Côte d"Ivoire - Republic of Côte d"Ivoire
- Constitution of Croatia - Republic of Croatia
- Constitution of Cuba - Republic of Cuba
- Constitution of Cyprus - Republic of Cyprus
- Constitution of the Czech Republic - Czech Republic

- Constitution of Denmark - Kingdom of Denmark
- Constitution of Dhekelia - Sovereign Base Areas of Dhekelia (UK overseas territory)
- Constitution of Djibouti - Republic of Djibouti
- Constitution of Dominica - Commonwealth of Dominica
- Constitution of the Dominican Republic - Dominican Republic

- Constitution of East Timor (Timor-Leste) - Democratic Republic of Timor-Leste
- Constitution of Ecuador - Republic of Ecuador
- Constitution of Egypt - Arab Republic of Egypt
- Constitution of El Salvador - Republic of El Salvador
- Constitution of Equatorial Guinea - Republic of Equatorial Guinea
- Constitution of Eritrea - State of Eritrea
- Constitution of Estonia - Republic of Estonia
- Constitution of Ethiopia - Federal Democratic Republic of Ethiopia

- Constitution of the Falkland Islands - Falkland Islands (UK overseas territory)
- Constitution of the Faroe Islands - Faroe Islands (Self-governing country in the Kingdom of Denmark)
- Constitution of Fiji - Republic of the Fiji Islands
- Constitution of Finland - Republic of Finland
- Constitution of France - French Republic
- Constitution of French Polynesia - French Polynesia

- Constitution of Gabon - Gabonese Republic
- Constitution of Gambia - Republic of The Gambia
- Constitution of Georgia - Georgia
- Constitution of Germany - Federal Republic of Germany
- Constitution of Ghana - Republic of Ghana
- Constitution of Gibraltar - Gibraltar
- Constitution of Greece - Hellenic Republic
- Constitution of Greenland - Greenland (Self-governing country in the Kingdom of Denmark)

European Union	The European Union is an economic and political union of 27 member states, located primarily in Europe. Committed to regional integration, the European Union was established by the Treaty of Maastricht on 1 November 1993 upon the foundations of the pre-existing European Economic Community. Encompassing a population of 500 million the European Union generates an estimated 30% share (US$18.4 trillion in 2008) of the nominal gross world product.
Globalization	Globalization or (globalisation) is the process by which the people of the world are unified into a single society and function together. Globalization is often used to refer to economic Globalization: the integration of national economies into the international economy through trade, foreign direct investment, capital flows, migration, and the spread of technology. This process is usually recognized as being driven by a combination of economic, technological, sociocultural, political and biological factors.
India	India, officially the Republic of India , is a country in South Asia. It is the seventh-largest country by geographical area, the second-most populous country, and the most populous democracy in the world. Bounded by the Indian Ocean on the south, the Arabian Sea on the west, and the Bay of Bengal on the east, India has a coastline of 7,517 kilometres .
Pakistan	Pakistan), officially the Islamic Republic of Pakistan, is a country located in South Asia. It has a 1,046 kilometre coastline along the Arabian Sea and Gulf of Oman in the south, and is bordered by Afghanistan and Iran in the west, the Republic of India in the east and the People"s Republic of China in the far northeast. Tajikistan also lies adjacent to Pakistan but is separated by the narrow Wakhan Corridor.
Constitution	A Constitution is set of rules for government -- often codified as a written document -- that establishes principles of an autonomous political entity. In the case of countries, this term refers specifically to a national Constitution defining the fundamental political principles, and establishing the structure, procedures, powers and duties, of a government. By limiting the government"s own reach, most Constitution s guarantee certain rights to the people.
General Agreement on Tariffs and Trade	The General Agreement on Tariffs and Trade was the outcome of the failure of negotiating governments to create the International Trade Organization (ITO.) GATT was formed in 1947 and lasted until 1994, when it was replaced by the World Trade Organization in 1995. The Bretton Woods Conference had introduced the idea for an organization to regulate trade as part of a larger plan for economic recovery after World War II. As governments negotiated the ITO, 15 negotiating states began parallel negotiations for the GATT as a way to attain early tariff reductions.
Mexico	The United Mexican States), commonly known as Mexico [Ĕˆmexiko]), is a federal constitutional republic in North America. It is bordered on the north by the United States; on the south and west by the Pacific Ocean; on the southeast by Guatemala, Belize, and the Caribbean Sea; and on the east by the Gulf of Mexico. Covering almost 2 million square kilometres, Mexico is the fifth-largest country in the Americas by total area and the 14th largest independent nation in the world.

Boosterism	Boosterism is the act of "boosting," or promoting, one"s town, city with the goal of improving public perception of it. Boosting can be as simple as "talking up" the entity at a party or as elaborate as establishing a visitors" bureau. It is somewhat associated with American small towns.
Property right	A Property right is the exclusive authority to determine how a resource is used, whether that resource is owned by government or by individuals. All economic goods have a property rights attribute. This attribute has three broad components 1. The right to use the good 2. The right to earn income from the good 3. The right to transfer the good to others The concept of property rights as used by economists and legal scholars are related but distinct. The distinction is largely seen in the economists" focus on the ability of an individual or collective to control the use of the good.
Canada	Canada has been a member of the North Atlantic Treaty Organization (NATO) since its inception in 1949. Canada was not only a member but one of the principal initiators of the alliance. This was a marked break with Canada"s pre-war isolationism, and was the first peacetime alliance Canada had ever joined.
Leadership	Leadership has been described as the "process of social influence in which one person can enlist the aid and support of others in the accomplishment of a common task". A definition more inclusive of followers comes from Alan Keith of Genentech who said "Leadership is ultimately about creating a way for people to contribute to making something extraordinary happen." Leadership is one of the most salient aspects of the organizational context. However, defining Leadership has been challenging.
Kyoto Protocol	The Kyoto Protocol is a protocol to the United Nations Framework Convention on Climate Change (UNFCCC or FCCC), an international environmental treaty with the goal of achieving "stabilization of greenhouse gas concentrations in the atmosphere at a level that would prevent dangerous anthropogenic interference with the climate system." The Kyoto Protocol establishes legally binding commitment for the reduction of four greenhouse gases (carbon dioxide, methane, nitrous oxide, sulphur hexafluoride), and two groups of gases (hydrofluorocarbons and perfluorocarbons) produced by "annex I" (industrialized) nations, as well as general commitments for all member countries. As of January 2009, 183 parties have ratified the protocol, which was initially adopted for use on 11 December 1997 in Kyoto, Japan and which entered into force on 16 February 2005. Under Kyoto, industrialized countries agreed to reduce their collective green house gas emissions by 5.2% from the level in 1990.

Civil service	The term Civil service has two distinct meanings: • Branch of governmental service in which individuals are hired on the basis of merit which is proven by the use of competitive examinations. • Body of employees in any government agency, except the military. A civil servant or public servant is a civilian public sector employee working for a government department or agency. The term explicitly excludes the armed services, although civilian officials will work at "Defence Ministry" headquarters. The term always includes the (sovereign) state"s employees; whether regional, or sub-state, or even municipal employees are called "civil servants" varies from country to country. In the United Kingdom, for instance, only Crown employees are civil servants, county or city employees are not.
National Security Council	The White House National Security Council in the United States is the principal forum used by the President for considering national security and foreign policy matters with his senior national security advisors and Cabinet officials and is part of the Executive Office of the President of the United States. Since its inception under President Harry S. Truman, the function of the Council has been to advise and assist the President on national security and foreign policies. The Council also serves as the President"s principal arm for coordinating these policies among various government agencies.
Security Agency	A Security agency is an organization which conducts intelligence activities for the internal security of a nation, state or organization. They are the domestic cousins of foreign intelligence agencies.
Ban	A Ban is, generally, any decree that prohibits something. Bans are frequently decreed by Roachy with devestating consequences. He is the world"s premier access-restriction technician.
Panama	Panama, officially the Republic of Panama , is the southernmost country of both Central America and, in turn, North America. Situated on the isthmus connecting North and South America, it is bordered by Costa Rica to the northwest, Colombia to the southeast, the Caribbean Sea to the north and the Pacific Ocean to the south. The capital is Panama City.
Power	Power in international relations is defined in several different ways. Political scientists, historians, and practitioners of international relations (diplomats) have used the following concepts of political Power: • Power as a goal of states or leaders; • Power as a measure of influence or control over outcomes, events, actors and issues; • Power as reflecting victory in conflict and the attainment of security; and, • Power as control over resources and capabilities.

Modern discourse generally speaks in terms of state Power, indicating both economic and military Power. Those states that have significant amounts of Power within the international system are referred to as middle powers, regional powers, great powers, superpowers, or hyperpowers, although there is no commonly accepted standard for what defines a powerful state.

Entities other than states can also acquire and wield Power in international relations.

CPSIA information can be obtained at www.ICGtesting.com
Printed in the USA
LVOW10s2329060114

368377LV00003B/32/P